ON
LIBERTY
AND
LIBERALISM

John Stuart Mill and Helen Taylor

ON
LIBERTY
AND
LIBERALISM

THE CASE OF
JOHN STUART MILL

by Gertrude Himmelfarb

ALFRED · A · KNOPF

NEW YORK   1974

This is a Borzoi Book
Published by Alfred A. Knopf, Inc.

Copyright © 1974 by Gertrude Himmelfarb

Library of Congress Cataloging in Publication Data:

Himmelfarb, Gertrude, date.   On liberty and
liberalism: the case of John Stuart Mill.
   Includes bibliographical references.
   1. Mill, John Stuart, 1806–1873. 2. Liberty.
3. Liberalism. I. Title.
B1608.L5H55   192   73-20777
ISBN 0-394-49028-2

MANUFACTURED IN THE UNITED STATES OF AMERICA
FIRST EDITION

77427

To my mother
and
the memory of my father

CONTENTS

Contents

ON
LIBERTY
AND
LIBERALISM

INTRODUCTION

T̲H̲E̲ ̲T̲I̲T̲L̲E̲ ̲O̲F̲ ̲T̲H̲I̲S̲ ̲B̲O̲O̲K̲ is deliberately ambiguous. It refers to John Stuart Mill's *On Liberty*, but also to the idea of liberty as reflected in the whole body of Mill's writings. "The Case of John Stuart Mill" is an allusion to the conflict between John Stuart Mill, author of *On Liberty*, and the "other" John Stuart Mill, the bulk of whose work, it is argued here, represents a quite different mode of liberal thought. And "liberalism" itself partakes of the same ambivalence, having sometimes the quality Mill gave it in *On Liberty*, sometimes that which it had for the other Mill. And not only for the other Mill but also for other liberals before and after Mill. The ambiguities and ambivalences that are to be found in him are those that have beset much of modern political thought and that continue to plague us today. In this sense we are all interested parties in the case of John Stuart Mill.

The focus on *On Liberty* requires little justification. Most commentators feel obliged to apologize for repeating what has so often been said before, what was said, in large part, over a century ago when the essay first appeared; and having apologized, they then go on to restate the thesis of the book and to recapitulate the familiar arguments about it. Even academics do not normally behave in so tiresome a fashion. That distinguished scholars, men of letters, and even men of affairs should return time and again to *On Liberty*, to inquire into its meaning and import, to question, qualify, or reaffirm its principle, suggests that the reading of this book is more than an academic exercise.

The more apologetic of these commentators cite practical evidence of its "relevance": the debate on the legalization of homosexuality in England which turned into a debate on the meaning and validity of *On Liberty*; First Amendment cases in the United States which ritualistically invoke the authority of Mill; questions raised on both sides of the Atlantic about censorship, pornography, obscenity, birth control, the use of drugs; discussions about "alternative life-styles" recalling Mill's pleas for "experiments of living." But it is not these practical contemporary problems which establish the contemporary relevance of *On Liberty*. It is the philosophical issues posed by Mill that have created, so to speak, these practical problems—that have made problematic the moral and legal status of homosexuality or obscenity, of this or that mode of life. Less dramatically but no less effectively (perhaps more effectively because less dramatically), Mill represents in the Anglo-American world what Nietzsche does in the Continental tradition: the apogee of "modernity." It is no wonder *On Liberty* is so perennially relevant, so enduringly contemporary.

This is not to say that the doctrine of *On Liberty* prevails today in the form Mill originally gave to it, nor even that most men are agreed upon the meaning of that doctrine. Even in those parts of the world where it is, to a fair degree, accepted in practice and theory, it presents serious problems both for the polity and its philosophy. To the sympathetic reader of *On Liberty*, this may suggest that Mill's conception of liberty, while not completely realizable in practice or entirely satisfactory in theory, is nevertheless a valid and functional ideal, serving as a standard against which regimes and policies may be measured, a means of recalling us to first principles. As in Plato's parable of the cave, it may be thought of as the light which permits us to see the shadows in the cave, permits us to see truth and reality the only way we can see them, as shadows, but also knowing them to be such. A less sympathetic reader may respond quite differently, finding fault with an ideal that is so difficult of attainment, a doctrine that is philosophically as well as practically so dubious; the doctrine may appear to him to be a badly distorted shadow of the truth, a perversion of reality. Both readers, however, would probably agree that, for good or bad, liberty is the central issue of our time. And both would probably also agree that nowhere is that issue better posed than in *On Liberty*.

What is generally ignored, by both the partisans and the critics of *On Liberty*, is that Mill himself did not always subscribe to the idea of liberty presented in that work. When Lord Devlin, disputing the findings of the Wolfenden Committee on homosexuality, argued that society had a right and duty to legislate on matters of morality, the distinguished jurist H. L. A. Hart pointed out that his arguments had been anticipated almost a century earlier by James Fitzjames Stephen in his famous polemic against Mill, *Liberty, Equality, Fraternity*. Hart himself then came to the support of the Wolfenden Committee by defending *On Liberty* against Stephen's criticisms.[1] But Lord Devlin, as much as Professor Hart, might have based his own case entirely on Mill—not, to be sure, the Mill of *On Liberty* but another Mill, the author of other writings less famous than *On Liberty* but no less cogent.

At this stage in the controversy over *On Liberty*, after all that has been said by Mill's contemporaries and by com-

---

1. Patrick Devlin, *The Enforcement of Morals* (Oxford, 1968); H. L. A. Hart, *Law, Liberty, and Morality* (New York, 1963); James Fitzjames Stephen, *Liberty, Equality, Fraternity*, ed. R. J. White (Cambridge, Eng., 1967). See below, pp. 316 ff.

mentators since, it may be worthwhile to return the discussion to Mill himself—to both Mills, the critic as well as the expounder of *On Liberty*. The strategy recommends itself as something other than an intellectual exercise, a means of relieving the tedium of the familiar debate; although if it does only this, if it helps in some small measure to recover the freshness and vitality of the issues, this alone would justify it. But there is more at stake in the case of Mill *versus* Mill. If, as is suggested here, Mill was indeed his own best critic, the argument of *On Liberty* appears in a new light. For then we must assume (what perhaps we should assume of all serious thinkers) that the author was fully conscious of every aspect and implication of his work, of the thesis in its largest generality and fullest particularity, in all its strength and with all its weaknesses. Any notable difficulty, inconsistency, evasion, or extravagance we may find in the work, Mill must have been aware of as well. On this assumption, that Mill wrote with knowledge aforethought, sensible of all the arguments that could be brought to bear against him because he himself had once used those arguments against others, the commentator has a double burden of responsibility: to give full measure to those arguments and at the same time to take seriously the doctrine advanced in spite of them.

To make out such a case, however—the case of Mill *versus* Mill—one must be able to show not only that Mill himself had anticipated the main criticisms, but also that he was conscious of those criticisms at the time he wrote *On Liberty*. Without the second condition, the first would be reduced to a historical accident or biographical curiosity. If Mill had simply forgotten what he had once known, the situation would be psychologically intriguing but intellectually of no consequence. It becomes consequential only if we can be certain that while writing *On Liberty* Mill was conscious of his earlier arguments. Fortunately the evidence of consciousness is indisputable.

Mill wrote the first draft of *On Liberty* in 1854.[2] This was expanded and revised, with the assistance of his wife, in the following years. After his wife's death, he had it published in exactly the form in which it then stood, and all subsequent editions were unchanged by so much as a word. At the same time that he was working on *On Liberty* he was also writing the first draft of his *Autobiography* (covering the period up to his marriage in 1851); and this too was subjected to a similar process of cooperative revision. The *Autobiography*, which he intended as an intellectual autobiography, a record of his "mental progress,"[3] obliged him to review his early opinions and reread his early essays. The manuscript of the early draft of this work, with its numerous additions, deletions, and revisions, is extremely revealing, for it shows how carefully Mill attended to all the nuances and shades of belief which distinguished the several stages of his intellectual history, how deliberately he summarized each of his writings so as to present it fairly in its own terms and at the same time put it in the perspective of his later opinions. And all this was done under the watchful eye of his wife, who kept him alert to every shift of emphasis and opinion.

As if this were not enough, Mill was also, during the period when he was writing and rewriting *On Liberty*, preparing his early essays for republication. Although he had had the idea of collecting these essays as far back as 1839, two decades elapsed before they actually appeared. During the same trip to Italy, in the winter of 1855, when he suggested to his wife that the first version of the essay on liberty be expanded and published as a separate volume, he also revived the idea of republishing his earlier essays. If it were not done while they were alive, he reasoned, others would do it after their death: "Now if *we* do it, we can exclude

2. This draft has unfortunately not survived.

3. *The Autobiography of John Stuart Mill*, ed. John Jacob Coss (Columbia Univ. Press edn.; New York, 1924), pp. 129, 133, 155, 161. Unless otherwise specified, all references are to this edition. (See note in the Bibliography.)

what we should not choose to republish, and nobody would think of reprinting what the writer had purposely rejected."[4] There is no record of his wife's reply, but one can assume that it was in the negative. For in spite of Mill's entreaties, neither these essays nor any of his other writings of this period were published until after her death. Within months of her death, however, they were all published: *On Liberty* in February 1859, and the essays in two volumes, under the title of *Dissertations and Discussions*, in April. (Two further volumes under the same title were published subsequently.)

While his wife may have been dilatory in the matter of publication, she was zealous enough in the discharge of her editorial functions. She shared with Mill the task of selecting and revising the essays, as she also helped revise *On Liberty* and the *Autobiography*; and the revision of all these works belong to the same period, 1855 through 1858. Moreover, the selection of the essays was more deliberate and the revision more extensive than Mill suggested either in the preface to the *Dissertations* or in his *Autobiography*. Omitted from the published volumes were several major early essays, some of considerable intellectual as well as biographical interest, apparently because they diverged so much from his later views as to make them unacceptable, while other essays were subjected to meticulous editing to bring them into closer correspondence with his later opinions.

Something of the same editorial process can be followed in the several editions of the *Principles of Political Economy*. First published in 1848, a second edition appeared the following year, a third extensively revised in 1852, and a fourth, slightly revised, in 1857. The evident care with which these revisions were made leaves no doubt that Mill was fully aware of the bearing of everything he had

---

4. *The Later Letters of John Stuart Mill, 1849–1873*, ed. Francis E. Mineka and Dwight N. Lindley (vols. XIV–XVII of *Collected Works*; Toronto, 1972), I, 348 (Feb. 25, 1855).

thought and written in the past upon the important work on which he was currently engaged, *On Liberty*.

These biographical and bibliographical details are introduced here to establish what might not otherwise be evident: that the case of Mill *versus* Mill is not a tour de force but a quite literal reconstruction of Mill's thinking at the time he was writing his most important and influential work. *On Liberty* is not an isolated text standing alone and apart from the rest of his *oeuvre*, to be read and judged in isolation. It is, on the contrary, most intimately related to everything else Mill had written. If at times it contradicts his other writings, these contradictions must be taken with the utmost seriousness—not as contradictions which the commentator, with the superior wisdom of hindsight, has ferreted out, but rather as those which Mill, in the fullness of his own wisdom, deliberately permitted to stand. The commentator can, in fact, add little to what Mill himself has already said or implied; and if he calls in evidence Mill's other works, he does so not in the spirit of the biographer charting the intellectual development of Mill's thought (itself a worthy but quite different enterprise), but rather in the spirit of the textual critic working with a variorum edition of Mill's complete works.

To add to the gravity of the case, one may also note that Mill wrote *On Liberty* in the full expectation that it would be as important and influential as it has since become. In his *Autobiography* he gave it a genesis worthy of a classic— indeed the same genesis that Gibbon, almost a century earlier, had given to his classic. Like Gibbon, who had said that the idea for the *Decline and Fall of the Roman Empire* had come to him while he was sitting among the ruins of the Capitol, so Mill claimed to have thought of writing a book on liberty while "mounting the steps of the Capitol."[5] His memory may be faulty in detail; the letter to his wife in

5. *Autobiography*, p. 170. See below, p. 249.

which he first proposed such a volume was written the day after he arrived in Rome, before he had yet visited the Capitol. But there is no doubt of the importance he attached to it from the beginning. "So many things might be brought into it and nothing seems more to be needed," he wrote.[6] A month later, he was even more enthusiastic: "The more I think of the plan of a volume on Liberty, the more likely it seems to me that it will be read and will make a sensation. The title itself with any known name to it would sell an edition. We must cram into it as much as possible of what we wish not to leave unsaid."[7]

The actual composition of the volume also reflects the importance Mill attached to it. None of his writings, his *Autobiography* assures us, was so carefully composed or corrected as this. "After it had been written as usual twice over, we kept it by us, bringing it out from time to time, and going through it *de novo*, reading, weighing, and criticizing every sentence."[8]

Since *On Liberty* has attained the classical status he anticipated, we are warranted in taking it as seriously as Mill himself did—"reading, weighing, and criticizing every sentence," if that should prove useful. By the same token, we should be prepared to read, weigh, and criticize every sentence of *On Liberty* in the light of everything else he had written on the subject, every sentence of which he too was then reading, weighing, and criticizing. If Mill did as much, we can hardly do less.

THE FIRST PART of this book is an analysis of *On Liberty* in the light of Mill's other writings. Each of the chapters corresponds to a chapter of *On Liberty*. Within each chapter the argument presented in *On Liberty* is confronted

6. *Later Letters*, I, 294 (Jan. 15, 1855).
7. *Ibid.*, p. 332 (Feb. 17, 1855).
8. *Autobiography*, p. 170.

with Mill's views on the same subject expressed on other occasions. For the most part, the other works cited predate or coincide with *On Liberty*, since only these can be presumed to have a direct bearing upon the writing of *On Liberty*. Occasionally a later work by Mill may be quoted if it is especially pertinent—partly to offset the impression one might otherwise have that the "other" Mill is an "early" Mill. As far as possible, isolated or random quotations have been avoided so as not to distort Mill's meaning. Instead his arguments have been presented at some length and with a clear indication of the context in which they originally appeared.

In this first section, there is little intrusion of views other than Mill's. This is not to belittle the work of the multitude of critics, biographers, historians, and philosophers who have, in Mill's time and since, analyzed and criticized *On Liberty*. Indeed, the history of Mill criticism would make a fascinating study in the history of ideas. But that is another subject. In this context, the judgments of others would be a distraction. Besides, Mill himself spoke so adequately on these issues that anything more might be superfluous.

The second section is an attempt to account for the extraordinary disparity between the Mill of *On Liberty* and the "other" Mill, to account, in effect, for the particular thesis of *On Liberty*. Some plausible explanations—the repressive nature of the Victorian ethic, for example—turn out to be less helpful than one might think in understanding either the disparity or the thesis itself. Other explanations, less likely at first sight, prove to be more illuminating. If these are rather surprising, this itself may befit so strange a situation. It is with great reluctance that I have myself come to them, and I am acutely sensible of how odd they may seem to others.

One of these explanations, the case of women as it affected the case of liberty, may seem too trivial to account for so momentous an event as *On Liberty*. Or would have seemed so until recently; today we can appreciate, as Mill's generation could not, the potency of the idea of women's liberation, the way it can shape an entire ideology and have ramifications, both personal and intellectual, that go far beyond its immediate intent. In any event, the fact is that Mill's essays on women present striking parallels to the argument of *On Liberty*. And this fact is all the more impressive because these are the only writings by Mill which do have a real affinity with *On Liberty*, indeed, which do not actually conflict with it.

Another explanation, the role of Mill's wife in the conception and composition of *On Liberty*, is one that, for obvious reasons, makes me at least as uncomfortable as it will make some readers. Yet the evidence for their "joint production," as Mill described it, seems to me massive and incontrovertible—and not only because Mill repeatedly claimed it to be so, but because his claim is borne out by a comparison of this work with some of her writings.

But whatever the genesis and history of *On Liberty*, whatever personal or social circumstances may have impinged upon it, it is, finally, the doctrine of *On Liberty* that is at issue. And it is the working out of this doctrine over the past century that is the subject of the final section of this book. By a kind of cultural lag the practical implications of Mill's idea of liberty did not make themselves felt until long after the idea itself had become thoroughly familiar, so familiar that we have almost lost sight of its origin. Only now are we experiencing its full impact. And we are experiencing it, as ideas always are experienced, in all the complexity and confusion of reality. The idea of liberty has been carried out in ways Mill did not anticipate; it has combined with other facts of life to create peculiar and paradoxical situations. But it is essentially his idea that is at the heart of these complications and paradoxes.

In what is called the "free world" today, Mill's doctrine of liberty is preeminent. It has usurped the place once occupied by the ideas of God, nature, reason, and justice. In an age which prides itself on its liberation from all absolutes, which has succeeded in making the very word "absolute" sound archaic, the one idea that has very nearly the status of an absolute is liberty.[9] Even when we violate it in practice, we do so not out of respect for another idea but in default of any other—out of "necessity" or "practicality," as we say. In a notably changeful world, liberty remains the only value commanding general assent.

Mill once described *On Liberty* as a "philosophic textbook of a single truth."[10] Like all successful textbooks, it no longer has to be read to make itself felt. We imbibe its "truth" by osmosis, so to speak, from the culture at large. But it is there to be read. And it remains, even today, the most sustained and respectable argument for a creed that is more often accepted on faith than examined critically.

If upon critical examination, the doctrine of *On Liberty* proves not altogether satisfactory, the corrective to it may be found in the "other" Mill, the *contra* Mill of the first part of this book. The other Mill belongs to an older liberal tradition, the tradition of Montesquieu, Burke, the Founding Fathers, and Tocqueville. It is a tradition that is eminently modern and yet resonant of classical thought. It is also a genuinely liberal tradition, although its liberalism is very different from that of *On Liberty*. It does not belittle the importance of liberty; on the contrary, one of

9. One of the most serious recent attempts to reinstate an older principle is *A Theory of Justice* by John Rawls (Cambridge, Mass., 1971). But even here, the primacy of justice, which is the initial proposition of the book—"justice is the first virtue of social institutions" (p. 3)—turns out to be predicated on the "priority of liberty": "the precedence of the principle of equal liberty over the second principle of justice" (p. 244). Many of the complications and difficulties of Rawls's argument derive from this insistence upon the priority of liberty: "the claims of liberty are to be satisfied first"; "liberty can be restricted only for the sake of liberty itself" (*ibid.*).

10. *Autobiography*, p. 177. See below, p. 3.

its purposes is to make liberty more secure by buttressing it with other principles essential to a good life and a good society. If it denies the absoluteness of liberty, it does so to ensure the integrity and viability of liberty. It is a temperate, humane, and capacious liberalism, a philosophy that can accommodate liberty together with such other values as justice, virtue, community, tradition, prudence, and moderation.

The case of Mill *versus* Mill presents us with alternatives that are as real in our time as they were in Mill's. If the verdict of modernity has been so far largely in favor of the Mill of *On Liberty*, that judgment may yet be reversed. As we are confronted with the practical consequences of a doctrine whose measure we have not yet fully taken, we may find ourselves more and more drawn to the other Mill, whose vision of a proper moral and social order encompassed liberty—and much else.

For many years *On Liberty* has fascinated and disturbed me. It has always seemed to me to be a momentous document and yet a tantalizing one, its thesis far bolder and more problematic than its deceptively simple, common-sensical manner makes it appear. It was largely my inability to come to terms with it that persuaded me, fifteen or so years ago, to scrap hundreds of pages of what had been intended as an intellectual biography of Mill. A more modest enterprise a few years later, the introduction to a volume of Mill's essays, permitted me to begin to place *On Liberty* in the context of his other writings. More recently the editing and writing of an introduction to a new edition of *On Liberty* obliged me to reconsider that work more carefully.[11] But it is only now

11. John Stuart Mill, *Essays on Politics and Culture*, ed. Gertrude Himmelfarb (New York, 1962); the revised version of the introduction in Himmelfarb, *Victorian Minds* (New York, 1968); *On Liberty* (Penguin edn.; London, 1974).

that I have allowed myself the luxury of devoting an entire book to *On Liberty* that I have been able to work out in detail the logic of that work and to confront it with the rest of Mill's writings, to try to understand it in itself and in relation to the alternative mode of liberalism represented by those other writings.

Over the course of these years, while working on other subjects but intermittently on this as well, I have incurred more intellectual debts that I can conveniently recount. I should particularly like to thank Ann and Martin Diamond, whose more rigorous philosophical stance has been a useful corrective to my own historical cast of mind; Diana and Lionel Trilling, who are an unfailing source of intellectual stimulation; my brother, Milton Himmelfarb, whose work in a very different field of thought has served me as a model and inspiration; and my husband, Irving Kristol, whose sympathy and criticism have been invaluable. My research assistants, Ellen Jacobs and Janet Wasserman, have been conscientious beyond the call of duty, as have been the librarians of the Graduate School of the City University of New York. I am also grateful to the National Endowment for the Humanities and to the American Council of Learned Societies for their encouragement and generous support.

PART ONE

Mill versus *Mill*

"ONE VERY SIMPLE PRINCIPLE"

IN HIS AUTOBIOGRAPHY Mill described *On Liberty* as "a kind of philosophic text-book of a single truth."[1] In *On Liberty* he characterized that single truth as "one very simple principle":

> *The object of this Essay is to assert one very simple principle, as entitled to govern absolutely the dealings of society with the individual in the way of compulsion and control, whether the means used be physical force in the form of legal penalties, or the moral coercion of public opinion. That principle is, that the sole end for which mankind are warranted, individually or collectively, in interfering with the liberty of action of any of their number is self-protection.*[2]

The substance of this principle has raised so many issues and been so hotly debated that it has distracted attention from what may be the more significant part of this passage: the presumption that the entire "dealings of society with the individual in the way of compulsion and control"—social

1. *Autobiography*, p. 177.
2. *On Liberty* (Everyman edn.; London, 1940), pp. 72–73.

3

and moral as well as legal compulsion and control—can be fully comprehended, "absolutely" governed, by "one very simple principle." Quite apart from the content of that principle, the idea of formulating a principle of that nature —single, simple, and absolute—is itself remarkable.

It is all the more remarkable in view of Mill's intellectual history. For Mill had had intimate experience with attempts to base an entire philosophy upon a single principle, and he had dramatically rejected those attempts—rejected not only the particular principle at issue but the simplistic view of human nature and social affairs implied in the assertion of such a principle.

Mill's first encounter with this mode of thought was Benthamism, which prided itself on its ability to reduce the entire range of human behavior, individual as well as social behavior, to the single principle of happiness, a calculus of pleasure and pain. The traumatic effects upon Mill of that philosophy, the "crisis" he went through when he lost his faith in it, are recounted in his *Autobiography*. And the entire episode must have been fresh in his mind when he wrote this crucial passage of *On Liberty*, since he was working on the *Autobiography* at the same time.

His crisis was "mental" in both senses of that word, intellectual and emotional. He later reflected that it must have been very much like the experience of the Methodist smitten for the first time by a "conviction of sin."[3] The situation was even more poignant than this analogy suggests because in Mill's case it was no ordinary parishioner who was smitten. If Bentham was the father of the church, James Mill was the first apostle and John Mill the chief novitiate. The oldest son and a child prodigy, John had been reared for the express purpose of disseminating the true faith. His crisis, therefore, involved not only a loss of faith but also a loss of vocation. It was only after he had discovered that the

3. *Autobiography*, p. 94.

greatest-happiness principle was not a sufficient *raison d'être* for himself that he began to suspect that happiness, as the Benthamite understood it, was not a sufficient *raison* for human beings in general. In the autumn of 1826, at the age of twenty, he put to himself the fateful question that was to challenge the basic tenet of utilitarianism:

> *"Suppose that all your objects in life were realized; that all the changes in institutions and opinions which you are looking forward to, could be completely effected at this very instant; would this be a great joy and happiness to you?"* And an irrepressible self-consciousness distinctly answered "No!" At this my heart sank within me: the whole foundation on which my life was constructed fell down. All my happiness was to have been found in the continual pursuit of this end. The end had ceased to charm, and how could there ever again be any interest in the means? I seemed to have nothing left to live for.[4]

In its most acute phase, Mill's depression lasted for about six months, his misery aggravated by the fact that he could not confess it even to his closest friends, still less to his father, since they were all implicated in his grief. When he was on the verge of black despair, a ray of light broke through. He happened to be reading Marmontel's *Mémoires* and came upon the passage in which Marmontel's father died and his young son was seized with an inspiration. As Mill told it, the boy suddenly felt, and managed to make his family feel, that "he would be everything to them—would supply the place of all that they had lost." Moved to tears by this account, Mill found that his own burden was instantly lightened. "The oppression of the thought that all feeling was dead within

4. *Ibid.*

me, was gone. I was no longer hopeless: I was not a stock or a stone."[5]

The psychological implications of the Marmontel episode —the death of the father and his replacement by the son— are obvious enough, and, in view of the momentousness of this crisis, can hardly be minimized.[6] But more important in the present context are its philosophical and political implications. For when Mill discovered that the object of his education failed him so disastrously in his private life, he was obliged to rethink the public aspects of that philosophy. If

5. *Ibid.*, p. 99.

6. The psychological implications become even more obvious when one reads the actual account in Marmontel's *Mémoires* which had so galvanizing an effect on Mill. The young Marmontel, then eighteen (Mill was only two years older when he read this), returned home from school after learning of his father's death and greeted his mourning family: "Mother, my brothers and sisters, we are suffering the greatest affliction; do not let us be overwhelmed. My children, you have lost a father and you have found one; I will be one to you; I am and wish to be; I accept all its duties; you are orphans no longer." That night, while vainly seeking sleep in his father's bed (the only one available), he kept seeing his father's image and sought his approval. "Say at least," he besought him, "that you are satisfied with me!" (*Memoirs of Marmontel*, trans. Brigit Patmore [London, 1930], pp. 36–37.)

Apart from the classical Oedipal situation, one can see other reasons for Mill's being so deeply moved by this episode. The tension he himself felt in relation to his father arose from a philosophy that was intellectually unsatisfactory and emotionally stultifying; in Marmontel's case, the father was trying to force his son into an uncongenial livelihood and to thwart his intellectual ambitions. Upon his father's death, the young Marmontel was free to indulge his interests and live the life he pleased. In Mill's case the fantasy of his father's death was only a partial liberation; for ten years he had to equivocate and compromise, so that he finally came of age, so to speak, not at eighteen, as Marmontel had, but at thirty.

A conspicuous difference between the two was in their relations with their mothers. Marmontel's mother was far warmer, emotionally closer to the boy, than his father was; it was also she who was more sympathetic to his intellectual interests. Mill's sense of his mother was quite the reverse (see chap. VIII, below). Perhaps it was this difference in their situations, the image of a mother who had the qualities he thought so grievously lacking in his own, that contributed to the emotional power of this episode.

he, so carefully nurtured in the doctrine of utilitarianism and so entirely committed to it, found that it rendered life "hopeless," meaningless, he could hardly expect it to satisfy others lacking his education and commitment.

The crisis prompted Mill to reconsider the basic values of utilitarianism, to seek salvation in a different order of experience. Instead of being totally preoccupied, as the Benthamite was, with the "external culture"—the self-conscious, analytic, purely rational mode of thought and behavior—Mill decided that attention should be directed to the "internal culture of the individual," the cultivation of feeling, the development of the poetic and artistic sensibilities. And instead of making happiness the direct and self-conscious end of all activities, he now thought happiness attainable only if it were not pursued self-consciously, only if a variety of ends—art, feeling, the improvement of mankind, or any other object of desire—were cultivated for their own sakes, as ends in themselves. The political implications of this new orientation were obvious. It meant that the "ordering of outward circumstances" did not have the "almost exclusive importance" the Benthamite attached to it, that there was much that did not come within the purview of the reformer or legislator, that no one set of "model institutions" would do for all people.[7]

In his *Autobiography*, Mill explained that he did not at this time seek a new "system of political philosophy" in place of the old; instead he was content to have "no system," to have only the "conviction that the true system was something much more complex and many-sided than I had previously had any idea of." It was in this spirit that he exposed himself to a variety of thinkers—Wordsworth, Coleridge, Saint-Simon, Carlyle—not all of them reconcilable with each other, let alone with the remnant of Benthamism which he still thought to be salvageable, but each contributing some

7. *Autobiography*, pp. 100, 113.

important truths or parts of the truth. Where Bentham and others mistook their "half-truths" for the whole truth, he was content to apply to himself the motto of Goethe: "Many-sidedness."[8]

It was soon after he had lost faith in utilitarianism as a philosophy that his faith in it as a principle of government was undermined—and for the same reason, its single-mindedness. Here disbelief took an even more agonizingly personal turn by focusing upon his father rather than Bentham. The occasion for this political reevaluation was the attack launched by Macaulay in 1829 upon James Mill's "Essay on Government." The debate that followed was an event of great public importance. With rebuttals and counterrebuttals, the dispute spread over three issues of the *Edinburgh Review*, the organ of the Whigs, and the *Westminster Review*, the new journal of the Philosophic Radicals. For the better part of a year it remained a *cause célèbre* in London literary and political circles. (Macaulay's thrusts were so telling that out of compassion, after James Mill's death, he generously refrained from including these articles in the first edition of his collected essays and reluctantly reprinted them later only after they had appeared in a pirated American edition.) In his *Autobiography* John Mill remarked that Macaulay had given him "much to think about."[9] And so he had. For it was Macaulay's attack upon James Mill's deductive method that eventually provoked the son to write *A System of Logic*, in which he devised a method that was neither empirical in Macaulay's sense nor deductive in his father's.

If Macaulay had been only half right in the matter of logic, he had been entirely right, Mill conceded, on another point. This was the charge, as Mill recalled it in the *Autobiography*, that James Mill's premises were too narrow, that his whole political system had been built on the assumption

8. *Ibid.,* pp. 113–14.
9. *Ibid.,* p. 110.

that "the only thing" on which good government depends is an identity of interests between the governed and the governing body and that this could be secured by the "mere" conditions of election.[10] Mill did not mention Macaulay's additional charge (although it was a point he himself was to make in other connections) that James Mill's theory of human behavior was similarly based upon the assumption that there was "a single general rule" regarding human motives.[11] Nor did he mention the cruel and memorable passage in which Macaulay had likened James Mill's system to the "pill of the advertising quack which is to cure all human beings, in all climates, of all diseases."[12]

A letter written by John Mill at the very time the controversy was at its height suggests the extent of his agreement with Macaulay on this question of single-mindedness. The letter was in criticism of French philosophers, particularly Comte, but its strictures apply as well to Bentham and James Mill:

> *They deduce politics like mathematics from a set of axioms and definitions, forgetting that in mathematics there is no danger of partial views: a proposition is either true or it is not, and if it is true, we may safely apply it to every case which the proposition comprehends in its terms: but in politics and social science, this is so far from being the case, that error seldom arises from our assuming premises which are not true, but generally from our overlooking other truths which limit and modify the effect of the former. It appears to me therefore that most French philosophers are chargeable with the fault which Cousin imputes to Condillac, of insisting upon only seeing one thing when there are*

10. *Ibid.*, p. 111.
11. *The Works of Lord Macaulay*, ed. Lady Trevelyan (London, 1875), V, 268.
12. *Ibid.*, p. 270.

many, or seeing a thing only on one side, only in one point of view when there are many others equally essential to a just estimate of it. . . . It is this fault which alone enables him [Comte] to give his ideas that compact and systematic form by which they are rendered in appearance something like a science positive. *To begin with the very first and fundamental principle of the whole system, that government and the social union exist for the purpose of concentrating and directing all the forces of society to some one end. . . . What a foundation for a system of political science this is! Government exists for all purposes whatever that are for man's good: and the highest and most important of these purposes is the improvement of man himself as a moral and intelligent being, which is an end not included in M. Comte's category at all. The united forces of society never were, nor can be, directed to one single end, nor is there, so far as I can perceive, any reason for desiring that they should. Men do not come into the world to fulfil one single end, and there is no single end which if fulfilled even in the most complete manner would make them happy.*[13]

It is a remarkable letter, not only for what it says about Comte—his obsession with a "single end"—but even more for what it implies about Benthamism, and still more for what it tells us about Mill. Were it not for the proper nouns, one might well read this as yet another installment in Macaulay's critique of the utilitarians.

After Bentham's death Mill was emboldened—although only anonymously—to make some of the same points in an essay published as an appendix to Bulwer Lytton's *England and the English.* (The essay was not reprinted in the *Dis-*

13. *The Earlier Letters of John Stuart Mill, 1812–1848,* ed. Francis E. Mineka (vols. XII–XIII of *Collected Works;* Toronto, 1963), I, 36 (JSM to Gustave d'Eichthal, Oct. 8, 1829).

sertations but was mentioned and acknowledged to be his in the *Autobiography*.) The words "only," "solely," "sole" appear again and again as Mill harped upon the fundamental characteristic of Bentham's philosophy, the attempt to reduce the most complicated phenomena to a single, simple principle.[14] Mill's most famous essay on Bentham written five years later, as well as the companion piece on Coleridge, repeated and elaborated upon the same theme. The predominant image here was of a "half-man hunting half-truths," a "one-eyed" and "one-sided" thinker who had the "rooted habit of surveying a complex object (though ever so carefully) in only one of its aspects."[15]

If Mill could make so much of Bentham's and Comte's disposition to look for a single principle behind the most complex affairs, we may perhaps be justified in finding a similar significance in the "one very simple principle" that was the heart of *On Liberty*, a principle intended to govern "absolutely" the whole area of "the dealings of society with the individual." The singleness and simplicity of that principle are the very substance of Mill's doctrine of liberty, exactly as the single principle of happiness, or utility, was the heart of the utilitarian doctrine. No one knew better than Mill himself that the strength of Benthamism, its entire claim to validity, lay in the fact that the whole system was presumed to derive from the single, simple principle of utility, so that once that principle was granted the rest followed ineluctably, with the irresistible logic of a geometric theorem. No one saw more clearly than Mill the connection

14. *Essays on Ethics, Religion and Society*, ed. J. M. Robson (vol. X of *Collected Works*; Toronto, 1969), pp. 5 ff.

15. *Ibid.*, pp. 89, 93-94, 109, 112. "Half-man" was deleted from the version reprinted in *Dissertations and Discussions* (London, 1859). Toward the end of his life, Mill had occasion to make much the same point. Criticizing Mrs. Fawcett for being "a little doctrinaire," he defined that term: "to see a principle in its full force, and not to see the opposing principles by which it must be qualified." (*Later Letters*, IV, 1850 [JSM to George C. Robertson, Nov. 6, 1871].)

between Bentham's method as an analytic philosopher and his function as a social critic. In the guise of reducing all human behavior to its simplest essentials, Bentham prepared the way for the most radical reforms. In the name of utility, he was able to sweep before him all the complicated, confused, contradictory institutions in society which had been fostered by tradition, history, and experience and to put in their place a new set of institutions based simply and solely on a calculus of happiness.

In his essays Mill had conceded the negative, destructive power of Bentham's method, but had denied its positive, constructive power—had denied, moreover, the wisdom of destroying everything in order to create everything anew. Yet in *On Liberty* he adopted the same method to accomplish the same end. The principle he then appealed to was liberty rather than utility. But that principle was every bit as single-minded and simplistic as Bentham's.[16]

16. Both in his *Logic* and in his *Utilitarianism,* Mill defined himself as a utilitarian. But it was a far more complicated and qualified kind of utilitarianism than the Benthamite variety. In the *Logic,* for example, he spoke of the need to refer all moral judgments to "some one principle," an "ultimate," "general" principle which would serve as a test of conduct and a standard of consistency. And he declared his own adherence to utility as that general principle, utility defined as "the happiness of mankind, or rather, of all sentient beings." But he then went on to qualify that principle until it became anything but the single, simple principle Bentham had in mind.

> I do not mean to assert that the promotion of happiness should be itself the end of all actions, or even of all rules of action. It is the justification, and ought to be the controller, of all ends, but is not itself the sole end. There are many virtuous actions, and even virtuous modes of action . . . by which happiness in the particular instance is sacrificed, more pain being produced than pleasure. . . . The cultivation of an ideal nobleness of will and conduct should be to individual human beings an end, to which the specific pursuit either of their own happiness or of that of others . . . should, in any case of conflict, give way. But I hold that the very question, what constitutes this elevation of character, is itself to be decided by a reference to happiness as the standard. The character itself should be, to the individual, a paramount end, simply because the existence of this ideal nobleness of char-

The content of Mill's principle is as notable as its simplicity. The principle has by now become so familiar, either in the form Mill gave it or in the more amorphous form in which our culture has assimilated it, that we forget how radical it was—indeed how radical it still is. It has become so much a habit of thought that we tend to accept it as unproblematic, as self-evidently true. That "the individual is sovereign," that his liberty is "absolute" except where it might injure another, is a proposition hardly anyone would dispute. The exception, to be sure, provides opportunity for dispute. But it is the exception, or rather particular cases of that exception, that are disputed. And in disputing the particular exceptions, the principle itself is implicitly, often explicitly, affirmed.

Just how radical, how absolute, that principle is may appear from a closer reading of the crucial passage. Even if we were skeptical of Mill's claim to have read, weighed, and criticized every sentence of *On Liberty* as often as he said he had, we cannot doubt that this particular passage was composed with the utmost deliberation. It contains the heart of his doctrine. In a sense, everything else in the book is by way of explanation, amplification, or qualification of this paragraph:

---

acter, or of a near approach to it, in any abundance, would go further than all things else towards making human life happy, both in the comparatively humble sense of pleasure and freedom from pain, and in the higher meaning of rendering life, not what it now is almost universally, puerile and insignificant, but such as human beings with highly developed faculties can care to have. [*A System of Logic* (London, 1949), pp. 621-22 (bk. VI, chap. XII, sect. 7).]

In this passage and similar ones in *Utilitarianism*, the concept of happiness was essentially tautological, all other "virtuous actions" and ends (including "ideal nobleness of character" which for any individual might be a "paramount end") being assumed to be conducive to happiness in some "higher" sense, even though in specific instances such virtuous actions would and should require the sacrifice of happiness. It is no wonder that utilitarians have found so much to criticize in this very elastic notion of utility.

The object of this Essay is to assert one very simple principle, as entitled to govern absolutely the dealings of society with the individual in the way of compulsion and control, whether the means used be physical force in the form of legal penalties, or the moral coercion of public opinion. That principle is, that the sole end for which mankind are warranted, individually or collectively, in interfering with the liberty of action of any of their number, is self-protection. That the only purpose for which power can be rightfully exercised over any member of a civilised community, against his will, is to prevent harm to others. His own good, either physical or moral, is not a sufficient warrant. He cannot rightfully be compelled to do or forbear because it will be better for him to do so, because it will make him happier, because, in the opinions of others, to do so would be wise, or even right. These are good reasons for remonstrating with him, or reasoning with him, or persuading him, or entreating him, but not for compelling him, or visiting him with any evil in case he do otherwise. To justify that, the conduct from which it is desired to deter him must be calculated to produce evil to some one else. The only part of the conduct of any one, for which he is amenable to society, is that which concerns others. In the part which merely concerns himself, his independence, is, of right, absolute. Over himself, over his own body and mind, the individual is sovereign.[17]

The language is simple, as befits so simple a principle. The words are commonplace and matter-of-fact, not those of a professional philosopher (compare this passage with any from Bentham or Kant or Marx), but of a plain-spoken, reasonable man addressing other plain and reasonable men. There is nothing abstruse or difficult here. Yet its very

17. *On Liberty*, pp. 72–73.

simplicity is a token of its boldness. The key words bear out the single-mindedness of the doctrine: "one," "sole," "only," "absolute." The entire argument hinges upon them; they appear in almost every sentence. There is "one" principle, the "sole" end, the "only" purpose, and the "only" part of conduct; the principle governs "absolutely," and the independence of the individual is "absolute."

Another constellation of words centers upon the concept of individuality: the "individual" is sovereign over "himself," over his "own" good and his "own" body and mind. And it is only for "self"-protection that another or others can interfere with his liberty. Moreover the words attached to the individual are honorific while those describing society are generally pejorative. The individual has "liberty" of action and "will"; it is his own "good" that is his own concern, his "independence" that is absolute. Society, on the other hand, acts by way of "compulsion," "control," "force," and "coercion." Even in the one circumstance when society can rightfully act, it does so by "interfering" with the individual's liberty and only to prevent "harm" to others. It cannot further the individual's "good," cannot presume to make him "better" or "happier," cannot do what it might think "wise" or "right." In short, the individual is endowed with all the positive qualities, society with all the negative ones. And this is not an accident of words; Mill's point is precisely that society be enjoined from pursuing positive ends, that its only function is to "prevent harm."

The antithesis between the individual and society, as Mill described it, has in it another linguistic assumption: that society is as much an entity, as real and distinct, as the individual. But if the individual is as absolute as he is made out to be, then what is the society that is presumed to stand so willfully and dangerously opposed to him? Is not society merely the sum of individuals—in which case, would it not be more accurate to speak of the individual *versus* another individual or other individuals? Sometimes Mill did speak of "another" or "others"—more often, in fact, in this passage than in the rest of the book. In general, however, he tended to hypostasize the others, to make them into a collective abstraction, a "society" with a life and force of its own.

The significance of the antithesis between the individual and society will emerge in the analysis of later chapters. But the significance of the concept of society itself merits prior attention, for on that concept hinges much of Mill's doctrine of liberty. It also stands in interesting contrast to Benthamism. For Bentham, society, like community, was a "fictitious body," a term denoting nothing more than a sum of individuals.[18] It was because Bentham's metaphysics was so thoroughly individualistic that his politics could be, on occasion, so thoroughly illiberal. Since the only reality for him was the individual, since there was no such thing as society as such, the only measure of social good, of public interest, or of general will was the sum of individual goods, interests, and wills. That sum was expressed in his famous formula, the greatest happiness of the greatest number. The solution of social and political problems had to be found in some such numerical formula since only numbers were at stake, numbers representing the sums of individuals. By the same token the greater had obviously to prevail over the lesser, the majority over the minority. And nothing was allowed to interfere with this majoritarian formula—neither the idea of liberty nor right nor anything else that could not be subsumed in his calculus. Bentham's hostility to such concepts as liberty and right is often explained semantically, as if he merely objected to their vagueness and abstractness. But his objection went deeper than this. Just as society was meaningless save as it could be reduced to the reality of individuals, so liberty and right were fictitious save as they could

18. Jeremy Bentham, *An Introduction to the Principles of Morals and Legislation* (Dolphin edn.; New York, 1961), p. 18. Bentham was speaking here of community. But the same point obviously applies to society.

be reduced to the reality of power. Moreover, liberty and right were not only fictitious; they were also mischievous, since they might provide a sanctuary for individuals or minorities and thus interfere with the operation of the majoritarian principle.

In order to avoid the majoritarian formula, Mill had not only to restore the reality and primacy of liberty, but also to restore the reality of society as the prime enemy of the individual. If society was consistently thought of, as Bentham did, in terms of its constituent "members,"[19] it would be hard to resist the claims of those members. One would be tempted to calculate, weigh, and balance their competing claims, as Bentham was always doing—and inevitably to the detriment of an individual whose claims, and liberties, would be outweighed by those of the larger number. Only by seeing the enemy in the whole, by abstracting and impersonalizing it, by making of it a single entity, so to speak, could Mill preserve the absolute primacy of the individual. He did, at one point, argue that ultimately the absolute liberty of the individual—absolute on the one condition of his not harming others—would redound to the greatest happiness of the greatest number. But whereas Bentham invoked the interests of the greatest number to decide every problematic case, Mill made it a point never to do so. On the contrary, he insisted that liberty was required above all to resist the pressure of numbers, the pressure of the mass which constituted the tyranny of society.

In the opening paragraph of *On Liberty*, Mill explained that liberty was becoming a new and urgent problem because of the "new conditions," the current "stage of progress" which civilization had entered. Liberty had always been a problem, he said, but previously the problem had manifested itself in the struggle of citizens against tyrannical rulers. In that struggle the aim of liberty had been to estab-

19. *Ibid.*

17

lish a set of "immunities," of "liberties or rights," which would limit the authority of the rulers and thus protect the citizenry from tyranny.[20] More recently liberty had adopted a new strategy. Instead of looking upon the people as opposed to their rulers and seeking to limit the power of the rulers, the aim was rather to identify the people with the rulers, to make the rulers representative of the people and responsible to them. In this case it was no longer necessary to limit power since power was presumably being exercised by the people themselves in their own interests; the only question was how to make power more completely representative and responsive.

This new "mode of thought," which created a new problem for liberty, Mill attributed to "the last generation of European liberalism, in the Continental section of which it still apparently predominates." A similar mode might have prevailed in England, he observed, had there not been a change in the circumstances which "for a time encouraged it."[21] He did not specify which "political thinkers of the Continent" he was referring to; perhaps he had in mind the supporters of the revolutions of 1848—republicans like Lamartine, moderate socialists like Louis Blanc, or the Frankfurt parliamentarians. But it is obvious that English thinkers, much more than Continental ones, expressed and popularized this mode of thought, and did so in a conscious, systematic fashion. This was, in fact, the mode of thought preeminently associated with Bentham and James Mill. One can hear the echo of their words in the passage in *On Liberty* describing the new doctrine:

> *What was now wanted was, that the rulers should be identified with the people; that their interest and will should be the interest and will of the nation. The nation did not need to be protected against its own will. There*

20. *On Liberty*, pp. 65–66.
21. *Ibid.*, p. 67.

was no fear of its tyrannising over itself. Let the rulers be effectually responsible to it, promptly removable by it, and it could afford to trust them with power of which it could itself dictate the use to be made. Their power was but the nation's own power, concentrated, and in a form convenient for exercise.[22]

The sentiments were precisely those of Bentham arguing for a "democratic ascendancy" and an "omnicompetent legislature."[23] They were also those of James Mill in the "Essay on Government," when he insisted that the representative body could not be limited or checked so long as it properly represented the interests and will of the people.

However Mill disguised the object of his attack—it would have been unseemly to quarrel with his father openly—the substance of it was clear enough. The doctrine whose "faults and infirmities" had been exposed by its success was, in England at any rate, unquestionably that of the Philosophic Radicals. It was their "new strategy" that had brought into being the new stage of civilization. And it was the defects of this strategy that Mill was now concerned with. In this sense, *On Liberty* was a rebuttal to his father's philosophy. That philosophy, as Mill now saw it, had effectively triumphed. The "will of the nation" had become the ruling power. In practice this meant the rule of the majority: "the will of the most numerous or the most active *part* of the people; the *majority*, or those who succeed in making themselves accepted as the majority." And the will of the majority threatened to become the "tyranny of the majority," a tyranny that was as much a menace to liberty as any tyrant of old because it was quite as capable of oppressing or suppressing a minority, still more an individual.[24]

22. *Ibid.*
23. Bentham, *Plan of Parliamentary Reform* (London, 1817), p. xxxvi; *Constitutional Code*, in Bentham, *Collected Works*, ed. John Bowring (London, 1843), IX, 119.
24. *On Liberty*, pp. 67–68.

Moreover, the new tyranny, as Mill diagnosed it, was even worse than the old because it made itself felt not only through the actions of public authorities, the government and state, but also through the more insidious mechanism of society.[25] "Society is itself the tyrant—society collectively over the separate individuals who compose it." And the tyranny exercised by society was the most onerous of all, because it could call upon all the resources of "prevailing opinion and feeling," of "moral sentiments" and the *odium theologicum*," to effect its end. "It practises a social tyranny more formidable than many kinds of political oppression, since, though not usually upheld by such extreme penalties, it leaves fewer means of escape, penetrating much more deeply into the details of life, and enslaving the soul itself."[26]

"Society," therefore, was the chief antagonist in *On Liberty*, the great adversary of the individual. The threat to liberty came not from this or that class, faction, interest, monarch, institution, or government agency—the "sinister interests" Bentham had inveighed against. Any one of these or a combination of them could have been dealt with by some legal, constitutional, or institutional reform of the kind Bentham was so ingenious in devising. The threat as Mill conceived it was more formidable: it came from the total social as well as legal and political pressure exerted by the collective whole known as "society." And because that threat was so massive, because the whole of society and all the resources of society were ranged against the single individual, the solution had to be equally drastic. The "principle" of liberty had to be as absolute, as comprehensive, as exigent, as was the threat to liberty. Only by bringing the full weight of this principle to bear upon the side of the

25. In *On Liberty* Mill sometimes used "society" in distinction from "the state," to connote social rather than legal or political mechanisms of control. But he also frequently used "society" as a comprehensive term to include both legal and extralegal mechanisms—the coercion of law as well as of public opinion.
26. *On Liberty*, p. 68.

individual could the overweening power of society be mitigated.

Some commentators have sought to minimize the absoluteness of Mill's principle by suggesting that it was not meant
to apply to everyone, that it was intended only for intellectually mature and rational persons. But Mill's qualifications
were too minimal to carry this interpretation. In limiting the
application of the principle to "human beings in the maturity
of their faculties," he specified that he meant this to exclude
children and minors. And his second qualification was purely
historical, exempting from the operation of the principle
"those backward states of society in which the race itself
may be considered as in its nonage"; and again, as if to forestall misunderstanding, he made it clear that he meant this to
apply to societies in the distant past, the age of "an Akbar or
a Charlemagne." Once mankind had shown itself capable
of being improved by free discussion, the principle became
fully applicable. And this stage of civilization, he added, was
"long since reached in all nations with whom we need here
concern ourselves."[27] Thus Mill clearly intended the principle of liberty to apply to all ordinary adults in the civilized
countries of his time.

In subsequent chapters of *On Liberty*, Mill spelled out the
details and implications of his principle of liberty. In this
first chapter he did little more than state the principle itself.
But that statement was provocative enough. If it does not
provoke the reader as much as it might, this may be because
the doctrine has by now become so familiar that one no
longer attends to it very carefully. And this surface familiarity also brings with it a surface plausibility, thus further

---

27. *Ibid.*, p. 73. Later in the book he parenthetically noted that
the principle applied to persons of "full age, and the ordinary
amount of understanding" (p. 132). In this context, too, the
exclusion can only be interpreted as applying to minors and
mental incompetents—not to adults lacking the kind of "maturity" or "understanding" that other philosophers may have
taken as a prerequisite of absolute liberty.

dulling the critical faculties. Mill himself had no doubt that what he was propounding was a new and radical doctrine. Not that the idea of liberty itself was new; on the contrary, Mill gave it an ancient and honorable lineage. What was new, however, were the circumstances of the age, the "stage of progress" which mankind had entered. In this stage, liberty appeared under "new conditions" and required a "different and more fundamental treatment."[28] And it was this different and more fundamental treatment that Mill provided in *On Liberty*.

Mill never mentioned by name the two parties and ideologies that might have claimed to speak for liberalism in his own time and country. But implicitly he separated himself from both—from the Benthamites in his attack upon the "popular will" that they had made the basis of the new polity and that he took to be the new form of tyranny; and from the Whigs in his insistence upon "one very simple principle" as against the complex structure of history, tradition, and society within which they located liberty. In contrast to these older modes of thought, Mill was quite right to think of his own system as "different and more fundamental."

28. *Ibid.*, p. 65.

LIBERTY OF THOUGHT AND DISCUSSION

THE FIRST SUBJECT dealt with in *On Liberty*, the first area in which the individual was declared to be sovereign and his liberty absolute, was "thought and discussion." In his introductory remarks Mill briefly distinguished between the liberty of thought and the liberty of discussion (verbal or printed), but only to assert that they were "practically inseparable."

> It [*liberty*] *comprises, first, the inward domain of consciousness; demanding liberty of conscience in the most comprehensive sense; liberty of thought and feeling; absolute freedom of opinion and sentiment on all subjects, practical or speculative, scientific, moral, or theological. The liberty of expressing and publishing opinions may seem to fall under a different principle, since it belongs to that part of the conduct of an individual which concerns other people; but, being almost of as much importance as the liberty of thought itself, and resting in great part on the same reasons, is practically inseparable from it.*[1]

1. *On Liberty*, p. 75.

Where his predecessors, he said, had invoked this principle as a security against "corrupt and tyrannical governments," he insisted upon it under all circumstances and all forms of government, the best as well as the worst. Again, his quarrel was implicitly with the utilitarians. "Let us suppose," he wrote—positing a situation in which the utilitarian ideal would have been realized—"that the government is entirely at one with the people, and never thinks of exerting any power of coercion unless in agreement with what it conceives to be their voice." That power, even under those conditions, was as "illegitimate" as the power of the most despotic government. Indeed, the power exercised in accordance with public opinion was "as noxious, or more noxious" than that exercised in opposition to public opinion. "If all mankind minus one were of one opinion, and only one person were of the contrary opinion, mankind would be no more justified in silencing that one person, than he, if he had the power, would be justified in silencing mankind."[2]

At this point, midway in the opening paragraph, the argument took an odd turn. For instead of defending his position on the grounds he was to use elsewhere in *On Liberty*—the importance of preserving individuality against the pressures of social and political conformity—Mill chose to base his case on quite different grounds. It was not for the sake of the individual dissenter that he denied to mankind the right to silence the single dissenting opinion; it was rather for the sake of truth. The suppression of that one opinion would deprive the whole of the human race, "posterity as well as the existing generation," of that opinion. And in the loss of that one opinion, truth itself would suffer: "If the opinion is right, they are deprived of the opportunity of exchanging error for truth: if wrong, they lose, what is almost as great a benefit, the clearer perception and livelier impression of truth, produced by its collision with error."[3]

2. *Ibid.*, p. 79.
3. *Ibid.*

24

The whole of this chapter, "Of the Liberty of Thought and Discussion," is concerned with the subject of truth. And its single thesis is the total dependence of truth upon the free expression of opinion. It is here that Mill developed what is now called the adversary theory of truth: the idea that truth results from a "collision of adverse opinions," a "struggle between combatants fighting under hostile banners."[4] The first part of his argument is most familiar. Its basic proposition is that only by way of the freest expression of conflicting opinions can truth emerge. No opinion can be justifiably suppressed because there is no way of knowing what is true until all opinions have been subjected to full and free inquiry. To suppress any opinion is to risk suppressing what might possibly be true, or what might contain some part of the truth, or what, if not itself true, might contribute to a testing and understanding of the truth. Those who would silence any opinion are guilty of the presumption of infallibility; they assume that *"their* certainty is the same thing as *absolute* certainty."[5]

This first part of Mill's argument resembles a familiar form of relativism. The idea of truth is posited, but only as the abstract, ideal end of inquiry, an end we can never be certain of attaining but which we can pursue only by keeping open every possibility, entertaining every opinion that may take us closer to that end. In practice, the end always eludes us. Even those beliefs we most confidently accept as truth—Mill cited the example of "Newtonian philosophy" —lack that final certainty and must, therefore, be exposed to constant challenge.

The beliefs which we have most warrant for have no safeguard to rest on, but a standing invitation to the whole world to prove them unfounded. If the challenge is not accepted, or is accepted and the attempt fails, we

4. *Ibid.*, pp. 111, 107.
5. *Ibid.*, p. 79.

25

are far enough from certainty still; but we have done the best that the existing state of human reason admits of; we have neglected nothing that could give the truth a chance of reaching us: if the lists are kept open, we may hope that if there be a better truth, it will be found when the human mind is capable of receiving it; and in the meantime we may rely on having attained such approach to truth as is possible in our own day. This is the amount of certainty attainable by a fallible being, and this the sole way of attaining it.[6]

At this point Mill confronted the objection that his argument, while valid for the most part, became questionable when it was "pushed to an extreme" by his refusal to credit any certainties. To this criticism Mill replied that "unless the reasons are good for an extreme case, they are not good for any case," and that it was precisely in those areas where men were most confident of having arrived at the truth that they had to be most wary of the assumption of infallibility.[7] The rebuttal is a curious one because it draws attention to the weakness in Mill's reasoning. The methodological principle enunciated by Mill, that unless the argument holds for the extreme case it does not hold for any case, conflicts with the dictum professed by most legal philosophers, that hard cases (difficult, extreme, exceptional situations) make bad law, and with the common-sense idea that although rules admit of exceptions, the exceptions need not, indeed, should not, be incorporated into the rules.

A more important problem concerns Mill's conception of what constituted the extreme case. Earlier he had cited Newtonian philosophy as an instance where the consensus was so general, the presumption of truth so large, one might think it unnecessary to subject it to further inquiry. But instead of pursuing this question of scientific truths, Mill

6. *Ibid.*, p. 83.
7. *Ibid.*

turned to a consideration of religious beliefs.[8] The belief in God and in immortality, he wrote, were "least favourable to me"; it was there that "the argument against freedom of opinion, both on the score of truth and on that of utility, is considered the strongest."[9] Surely these beliefs, he had his antagonist protesting, were so firmly established that those who held to them could hardly be charged with the fallacy of infallibility; surely they were so necessary to the welfare of society and so "confirmed by the general opinion of mankind" that it was clearly the duty of government to uphold them and to suppress contrary beliefs.[10]

By choosing religious beliefs in illustration of his principle, Mill in effect shifted the grounds of his argument. So far from taking the extreme case, the hard one to prove, that which might be expected to encounter most resistance, he was actually taking the easy path, the path of least resistance. Even in his own day, the area of religious beliefs was least subject to public control; there, more than in any other sphere, the individual was generally regarded to be the keeper of his own conscience; there opinion rather than truth was thought to prevail. (The very expression, "religious beliefs," rather than "religious truths," testifies to this lack of certainty and authority.) If in official pronouncements and on ceremonial occasions, the ideas of God or immortality were invoked, it was with no great conviction or ardor. And on those rare occasions when an attempt was made to suppress dissident religious views, public opinion was hardly zealous in support of that policy; on the contrary, such zeal as was expressed was on the part of enlight-

---

8. Mill did at this point mention moral beliefs as well, but his discussion was devoted entirely to religion.

9. *On Liberty*, p. 85. Here, as elsewhere, Mill used "freedom" and "liberty" synonymously. The present discussion will follow the same practice. The distinctions other philosophers have made between the two words, which may be illuminating for other purposes, would only be confusing in this context.

10. *Ibid.*, p. 84.

ened opinion opposing suppression. On this issue, then, Mill was hardly arguing from the case "least favourable" to him; indeed, here he was comfortably in accord with the *Zeitgeist*. Nor was he being particularly bold in the specific examples he cited: the condemnation of Socrates, the crucifixion of Christ, and the persecutions instigated by Marcus Aurelius. To invoke these in support of the doctrine of liberty was surely to score some rather easy points.[11]

After several pages devoted to such cases—pages containing many unexceptionable sentiments and fine rhetoric but which had the unfortunate effect of dissipating the force of his argument—Mill entertained the obvious objection that these examples were not quite to the point: "It will be said that we do not now put to death the introducers of new opinions: we are not like our fathers who slew the prophets, we even build sepulchres to them." He granted that heretics were no longer killed, that the amount of "penal infliction" which would now be tolerated was insufficient to extirpate even the "most obnoxious opinions.'" But he reminded his readers that the "legal persecution" of opinion still existed: in recent years one man was sentenced to twenty-one months' imprisonment for writing on a gate some offensive words concerning Christianity (in a footnote he noted that several months later the man received a free pardon from the Crown); two men were rejected as jurymen because they declared that they had "no theological belief" (one was the famous atheist George Holyoake); and a third man,

11. In one sense, these might be considered "extreme" cases, cases in which intolerance was pushed to the extreme of persecution and where the persecuted included some of the most eminent thinkers and spiritual leaders in the history of civilization. But this was not "extreme" in the sense Mill had earlier meant—the liberty to dissent from truths as certain as "Newtonian philosophy." The cases of Socrates and Christ represented not the extreme case of liberty but the extreme case of persecution, which most of Mill's contemporaries and all liberals deplored as earnestly as he. To prevent persecution of this kind, one did not need the extreme degree of liberty called for in *On Liberty*.

a foreigner, was "denied justice against a thief," again because he declared himself to be an unbeliever and thus would not take the oath required in the court of law.[12]

These, Mill admitted, were but the "rags and remnants of persecution," evidence of an infirmity of mind rather than a persecuting spirit. But there was no security, he added, that such a suspension of persecution would continue. And in any event what was important, what made England "not a place of mental freedom," was the social stigma attached to unpopular beliefs. "Opinion, on this subject, is as efficacious as law; men might as well be imprisoned, as excluded from the means of earning their bread."[13] Mill did not try to prove that men were, in fact, deprived of their livelihood because of unpopular opinions. In a sense he did not have to prove this, his argument being that the social stigma operated so effectively that few, if any, were ever brought to this test. Among those of independent means, he granted, heretical opinions were not easily discouraged, although they might be disguised or expressed only privately.

At this point Mill returned to the main line of his argument: the moral costs of a society in which opinions were not completely free, and above all the great cost to truth.

Truth gains more even by the errors of one who, with due study and preparation, thinks for himself, than by the true opinions of those who only hold them because they do not suffer themselves to think. Not that it is solely, or chiefly, to form great thinkers, that freedom of thinking is required. On the contrary, it is as much and even more indispensable to enable average human beings to attain the mental stature which they are capable of.[14]

12. *On Liberty*, p. 90.
13. *Ibid.*, pp. 91–92.
14. *Ibid.*, p. 94.

The last quotation suggests a new stage in Mill's argument. For the most part, his argument until then had been predicated upon the assumption that the received opinions which society was upholding, whether by legal penalties or social sanctions, were partly or wholly false and the unpopular opinions partly or wholly true, so that in suppressing the latter, society was also suppressing at least part of the truth. He now addressed himself to the situation in which the received opinions were true, but in which an absence of free discussion would still be fatal to truth. A truth, he said, which is uncontroverted exists as a "dead dogma, not a living truth."[15] In this case, it was not for the emergence of truth that the collision and struggle of opinions was necessary but for the vitality of truth. Truth was no better than superstition when it was not known rationally—that is, by confrontation with opposing opinions.

Mill was so impressed by the need for this collision and struggle, for the competition of opinions in the intellectual marketplace, that he was even prepared, in the absence of competing opinions, to provide for them artificially, to invent them if need be.

So essential is this discipline to a real understanding of moral and human subjects, that if opponents of all important truths do not exist, it is indispensable to imagine them, and supply them with the strongest arguments which the most skilful devil's advocate can conjure up.[16]

Where this advantage [the need to explain or defend truth against its opponents] can no longer be had, I confess I should like to see the teachers of mankind endeavouring to provide a substitute for it; some contrivance for making the difficulties of the question as present to the learner's consciousness, as if they were

15. *Ibid.*, p. 95.   16. *Ibid.*, pp. 97–98.

pressed upon him by a dissentient champion, eager for his conversion.[17]

Mill recommended this strategy of devil's advocate not primarily in the case of scientific truth but rather in regard to "moral and human" truths. Indeed, all his examples were of the latter sort: the Christian precepts to which we pay lip service (that the poor and humble are blessed or that men should love their neighbors as themselves) and the prudential maxims which actually govern our lives. However true these doctrines might be, they required opposition and dissent to elicit their full meaning—contrived opposition and dissent if need be. Mill denied that in proposing this strategy he was perpetuating error—condemning some men to persist in error so that others might better comprehend the truth, or condemning the truth to death as soon as it was universally affirmed. On the contrary, he assumed that the advance of society would reflect a growing consensus about important truths: "The well-being of mankind may almost be measured by the number and gravity of the truths which have reached the point of being uncontested."[18] But he warned that this progress had its drawbacks as well as its benefits. And it was to counteract those drawbacks that he called for contrivances to stimulate—and to simulate—dissent.

The examples Mill offered of such contrivances were anticlimactic, considering the importance he attached to them. In the past, he said, the Socratic dialectic and the disputations of the Schoolmen had served this purpose (the

17. *Ibid.*, pp. 103–4.
18. *Ibid.*, p. 103. A few pages later Mill spoke of the diversity of opinions as continuing to be advantageous "until mankind shall have entered a stage of intellectual advancement which at present seems at an incalculable distance" (p. 105). In that utopian situation, presumably even the doctrine of liberty would be transcended. Mill did not pursue this line of thought, which might have led him into a Comtean universe in which there was no need or room for liberty.

latter, however, having the disadvantage of basing their premises upon authority rather than reason). For the present, he urged a wider use of the method of "negative logic," which exposes "weakness in theory or errors in practice" without feeling obliged to establish positive truths.[19] He did not say what he would do if there were no evident weaknesses or errors. One might suppose that a devil's advocate would be prepared to invent them—in effect, to lie for the sake of the truth. This would seem to be the logical implication of his argument. But this in turn had moral implications which might have been disagreeable.

Instead of elaborating upon this extreme situation, in which the received opinion entirely coincided with the truth, Mill returned the discussion to what he took to be the more common situation, in which the received opinion was neither entirely false nor entirely true but rather a part of the truth, a half-truth. It now appeared that this was the category to which he consigned the "so-called" Christian morality.[20] The defect of Christian morality, he said, was its negative and passive rather than positive and active character; it emphasized innocence rather than nobility, the abstinence from evil rather than the energetic pursuit of good. A more perfect morality would have to supplement the Christian ethic with opposing doctrines drawn from secular traditions.

Having thus established the necessity for dissent in every conceivable situation, Mill took notice of the familiar argument that the freest expression of opinion ought to be permitted on all subjects, on condition only that "the manner be temperate, and do not pass the bounds of fair discussion."[21] He rejected this condition, as he had rejected every other limitation: because it was impossible to prescribe the degree of temperateness or fix the bounds of fairness, be-

19. *Ibid.*, p. 104.
20. *Ibid.*, p. 108.
21. *Ibid.*, p. 112.

cause misrepresentation was more often a matter of unwitting ignorance than willful malice, because the pressure to
control the manner of discussion was more often directed
against those challenging the prevailing opinion than against
those defending it. For these and other reasons he concluded
that "law and authority" could not presume to restrain any
form of misrepresentation, vituperation, or intemperate discussion.[22]

THE PRINCIPLE of absolute freedom of discussion, and its corollary, the dependence of truth upon absolute freedom, are
so prominent a part of *On Liberty* and so commonly associated with Mill that it may come as a surprise to find him
expressing, on other occasions, a quite different view of the
matter.

One might not care to make too much of Mill's first essay
on the subject, an article on the liberty of the press in the
Westminster Review in 1825. For anyone else, an essay
written before the age of nineteen would qualify as juve-
nilia. This essay, however, is as mature a piece of writing as
anything that appeared in that sophisticated journal. It is,
in fact, quite as mature as anything Bentham or James Mill
had written on the subject—perhaps because it derived so
largely from them.

Bentham's earlier essay "On the Liberty of the Press and
Public Discussion," written in 1820–21 in the form of a
letter to the Spanish people, had put the utilitarian argument
in its sharpest form. Liberty of the press was an essential
security for good government, a means of resistance against
a despotic government and a check against abuse in an
"undespotic" one. (Bentham could not bring himself to
speak of a "free" government because in his view no government was free, government being an exercise of power

22. *Ibid.*, p. 113.

and every power being a limitation on freedom.[23]) James Mill elaborated upon this doctrine in an article written shortly after this for the Supplement to the *Encyclopaedia Britannica.* In the course of this essay he raised one point Bentham had not dwelt upon: the relation of opinion and truth.

> *We have then arrived at the following important conclusions,—that there is no safety to the people in allowing any body to choose opinions for them; that there are no marks by which it can be decided beforehand, what opinions are true and what are false; that there must, therefore, be equal freedom of declaring all opinions, both true and false; and that, when all opinions, true and false, are equally declared, the assent of the greater number, when their interests are not opposed to them, may always be expected to be given to the true. These principles, the foundation of which appears to be impregnable, suffice for the speedy determination of every practical question.*[24]

In 1825, when John Stuart Mill undertook to write about the same subject, he consciously assumed the same role in relation to his father that James Mill had towards Bentham —that of disciple and popularizer. Unlike James Mill, however, who necessarily transmitted Bentham's ideas in an *übersetzt und verbessert* form (Bentham's own writings being often abstruse and nearly incoherent), John Mill had little to do but quote and paraphrase. The burden of his argument was the familiar one: the necessity of free speech as a security for good government. A minor theme was the importance of free opinion for the emergence of truth:

23. Bentham, *Collected Works,* II, 287–88. Bentham did at one point use the expression "free government," but he hastily added that the more precise term was "non-despotic government."

24. James Mill, *Essays on Government, Jurisprudence, Liberty of the Press, and Law of Nations* (New York, 1967), p. 23.

"Truth, if it has fair play, always in the end triumphs over error, and becomes the opinion of the world"—a proposition, he added, which "rests upon the broadest principles of human nature."[25] It is not clear whether Mill intentionally altered his father's argument at this point; perhaps after all he too was not above a bit of *übersetzung und verbesserung*. Whatever the case, it is interesting to compare the two formulations. Where James Mill expected only that the "greater number" would give their assent to the truth, John Mill was confident that the "opinion of the world" would coincide with the truth. And where James had predicted that truth would prevail only if the "interests" of the majority were not opposed to it, John derived his universal assent from the "principles of human nature." Perhaps even at this early period, the son was beginning to exhibit the first symptoms of deviation from the utilitarian faith. But even then, he was not prepared to make an absolute of freedom, not even of the freedom of press. Facts, he said, belonged to a different category from that of opinion and therefore did not require the same freedom.

> *False opinions must be tolerated for the sake of the true: since it is impossible to draw any line by which true and false opinions can be separated from one another. There is no corresponding reason for permitting the publication of false statements of fact. The truth or falsehood of an alleged fact, is matter, not of opinion, but of evidence; and may be safely left to be decided by those, on whom the business of deciding upon evidence in other cases devolves.*[26]

This article was written a year before the fateful "crisis" that profoundly altered Mill's life and thought. By 1831,

25. "Law of Libel and Liberty of the Press," *Westminster Review*, III (1825), 291.
26. *Ibid.*, p. 299.

when he had occasion to return to the theme of liberty—liberty of discussion rather than merely the liberty of the press —he treated it in a quite different manner. In a series of articles called "The Spirit of the Age," published anonymously in the *Examiner*, Mill singled out freedom of discussion as one of the chief characteristics of his age. He described this freedom as inevitable and in many respects desirable, but he also dwelt at some length upon its unfortunate consequences. It is no wonder that he later chose not to include these articles among his collected essays, for no amount of editing would have brought them into conformity with the central thesis of *On Liberty*. He had not, however, forgotten them. For while he was writing *On Liberty*, he was also rereading these articles with a view to their possible republication; and at the same time he was explaining, in his *Autobiography*, why he decided not to reprint them. The articles, he said, had made little impression when they were first published. Apart from attracting Carlyle, who saw in them the work of a fellow spirit, a "new Mystic," and made a point of seeking out Mill's acquaintance, they had been generally ignored. As newspaper articles, they were too "lumbering in style" to be effective. They were, moreover, peculiarly ill-timed, having appeared just at the height of the Reform Bill crisis, when men were more preoccupied with the task of enlarging democracy than with guarding against the dangers of democracy.[27]

Mill may well have been right about their lack of impact at the time, but his explanations do not account for his refusal to reprint them almost thirty years later. If their style was inappropriate to a newspaper audience (it was in fact, no more "lumbering" than most of his writings), it was certainly lively enough for the readers of his collected essays. And if it was premature in 1831, it was not so (again by his own standards) in 1859. For "The Spirit of the Age"

27. *Autobiography*, p. 122.

was based upon exactly the same premise as *On Liberty:* both assumed that democratic society, if not democratic government, was the salient fact of contemporary life and that the gravest evil was the overweening influence of public opinion. It is all the more interesting, therefore, to see how the two works, starting from the same point, arrived at quite different conclusions.

"The Spirit of the Age" derived its theme from Saint-Simon and Comte: the alternation in history between "natural" and "transitional" periods.[28] England was then, as Mill saw it, in a transitional stage, the old institutions and doctrines having fallen into disrepute and no new ones having acquired the authority to replace them. It was a time of "intellectual anarchy," a time for the *"diffusion* of superficial *knowledge"* rather than the acquisition of sound knowledge, a time witnessing a great "increase of discussion" without an "increase of wisdom." Men reasoned more about the great questions of the day, but not necessarily better. More men had opinions, but few, "except the very penetrating, or the very presumptuous," had full confidence in their opinions. The current condition, therefore, was "not a state of health, but, at the best, of convalescence," a necessary but temporary transition to a new "natural" state.[29]

Discussion flourished in such a transitional age, Mill explained, because it was a more effective means of exposing error than of establishing truth. A single, simple fact thrown up by discussion could prove a doctrine false. But the truth of a doctrine depended not upon mere discussion but upon analysis: the examination and weighing of an immense

28. These were Mill's terms. Saint-Simon's were "organic" and "critical," Comte's "static" and "dynamic." Mill's choice of words is revealing. To the English ear, "natural" has a more favorable connotation than "organic" or "static"; conversely, "transitional" is more pejorative than "critical" or "dynamic."

29. Mill, *Essays on Politics and Culture*, ed. Gertrude Himmelfarb (Anchor edn.; New York, 1963), pp. 5–6. (All references are to this edition. Italics in quotations are in the original.)

number and variety of facts. Indeed, the mood generated by discussion, which was so propitious for the uncovering of error, was least propitious for the investigation and discovery of truth. Men who were eager to discuss were also inclined to settle too readily for half or less than half of the truth; they were impatient and unequipped for the careful reasoning and slow accumulation of fact by which truth is established. Above all, they were too attached to "the exercise of private judgment," to which discussion had accustomed them, to heed the judgments of those who were wiser or better instructed than they. In the physical sciences, no one invoked the "right" of private judgment unless he had first qualified himself as a man of science—and in the process had come to accept, on the basis of the evidence, the "received opinion." The moral and social sciences, no less than the physical sciences, were "systems of connected truth" in which many propositions had to be understood and agreed upon; yet here "every dabbler . . . thinks his opinion as good as another's." Most political discussions were of an order which one might expect "if the binomial theorem were propounded for argument in a debating society none of whose members had completely made up their minds upon the Rule of Three." Men engaged in discussion with minds "in no degree fitted, by previous acquirements, to understand and appreciate the true arguments: . . . truth, they think, is under a peremptory obligation of being intelligible to them, whether they take the right means of understanding or no."[30]

The "right means of understanding," moreover, were not accessible to all men. Even if there were a great growth of intelligence among the mass of the people—and Mill expected the advance of civilization would lead to such a growth—something more was required, which most people,

30. *Ibid.*, pp. 9–11.

because of the necessary circumstances of their lives, could not attain.

> *I yield to no one in the degree of intelligence of which I believe them to be capable. But I do not believe that, along with this intelligence, they will ever have sufficient opportunities of study and experience, to become themselves familiarly conversant with all the inquiries which lead to the truths by which it is good that they should regulate their conduct, and to receive into their own minds the whole of the evidence from which those truths have been collected, and which is necessary for their establishment. . . . Those persons whom the circumstances of society, and their own position in it, permit to dedicate themselves to the investigation and study of physical, moral, and social truths, as their peculiar calling, can alone be expected to make the evidences of such truths a subject of profound meditation, and to make themselves thorough masters of the philosophical grounds of those opinions of which it is desirable that all should be firmly* persuaded, *but which they alone can entirely and philosophically* know. *The remainder of mankind must, and, except in periods of transition like the present, always do, take the far greater part of their opinions on all extensive subjects upon the authority of those who have studied them.*[31]

The real question, therefore, was not whether to pursue truth or rely on authority, but whether to put confidence in one's own judgment or in that of an authority. The answer to this question depended upon the person asking it: "There are some persons in whom disregard of authority

31. *Ibid.,* pp. 12–13.

is a virtue, and others in whom it is both an absurdity and a vice."[32] Most men fall into the latter category.

If you once persuade an ignorant or a half-instructed person, that he ought to assert his liberty of thought, discard all authority, and—I do not say use his own judgment, for that he never can do too much—but trust solely to his own judgment, and receive or reject opinions according to his own views of the evidence . . . the merest trifle will suffice to unsettle and perplex their minds. There is not a truth in the whole range of human affairs, however obvious and simple, the evidence of which an ingenious and artful sophist may not succeed in rendering doubtful to minds not very highly cultivated, if those minds insist upon judging of all things exclusively by their own lights. . . . You may prevail on them to repudiate the authority of the best-instructed, but each will full surely be a mere slave to the authority of the person next to him, who has greatest facilities for continually forcing upon his attention considerations favourable to the conclusion he himself wishes to be drawn.

It is, therefore, one of the necessary conditions of humanity, that the majority must either have wrong opinions, or no fixed opinions, or must place the degree of reliance warranted by reason, in the authority of those who have made moral and social philosophy their peculiar study. It is right that every man should attempt to understand his interest and his duty. It is right that he should follow his reason as far as his reason will carry him, and cultivate the faculty as highly as possible. But reason itself will teach most men that they must, in the last resort, fall back upon the authority of

32. *Ibid.*, p. 14.

*still more cultivated minds, as the ultimate sanction of
the convictions of their reason itself.*[33]

This, Mill judged, was one of the unfortunate qualities
of a transitional age: the lack of that essential "condition of
humanity" which would ensure the "authority of the best-
instructed." But such a transitional period could not long
prevail and would ultimately give way to a "natural state
of society . . . —namely, the state in which the opinions
and feelings of the people are, with their voluntary acquiescence, formed *for* them, by the most cultivated minds,
which the intelligence and morality of the times call into
existence."[34] And this would happen, Mill predicted, when
the present possessors of wordly power were divested of
their monopoly of power, a monopoly they had used to
prevent uncongenial opinions from becoming established as
the "received doctrine." Once that monopoly was broken
up, a true moral and intellectual authority would reassert
itself: "The most virtuous and best-instructed of the nation
will acquire that ascendancy over the opinions and feelings
of the rest, by which alone England can emerge from this
crisis of transition and enter once again into a natural state
of society."[35]

"The Spirit of the Age" has been quoted at such length
because one might not otherwise believe that Mill was
capable of expressing and sustaining views so antithetical to
those of *On Liberty*. So far from being an absolute good,
freedom of discussion appeared, in these articles, as at best
a very mixed good, at worst a necessary evil; and rather
than furthering the advance of truth, it was seen as hinder-
ing, as often as not, the acquisition of truth and, still more,
of wisdom. Nor were men encouraged to rely on their

33. *Ibid.*, p. 15.
34. *Ibid.*, p. 36.
35. *Ibid.*, p. 44.

"private judgment"; on the contrary, they were urged to recognize the natural moral and intellectual authority of their betters. Finally—and this is a more subtle point of difference but a profoundly important one—there is the question of "received opinion." Whereas in *On Liberty* such opinion was implicitly equated with "public opinion" and, like everything "received," was to be resisted by enlightened and independent individuals, here it represented the best thought of the best minds, a consensus of truth which the educated could arrive at by a process of reasoning and the uneducated by accepting the authority of the educated. In short, where *On Liberty* was confident and unequivocal in its faith in liberty, "The Spirit of the Age" was questioning and ambivalent.

"The Spirit of the Age" was among Mill's earliest writings. But it must not be supposed that it was an aberration of mind or immature fancy which he soon outgrew. On the contrary, themes from this series reappear in almost all his later work, sometimes alluded to casually, at other times developed at some length.

On one occasion, in the course of a discussion of the concepts of "delegate" and "representative," Mill commented on the argument that if legislators were regarded as delegates who merely executed the will of their constituencies, philosophers would be under an obligation to enlighten the multitude so that they would be capable of wise judgments. No one, he protested, was more desirous than he of this kind of popular education. But he was also acutely aware of the limitations of such an education. Political truths were as difficult to understand as they were to discover; they were the result of a "concatenation of propositions," some of which required an entire course of study, others a long process of meditation and much experience of human nature. How could philosophers convey these to the multitude? "Can they enable common sense to judge of science, or inexperience of experience?" In political philosophy, the false view was, as often as not, more plausible than the true one, and most truths were paradoxical to all except those who made a special study of them. The most that could be hoped for would be a growing consensus among the "instructed classes" so that "the many will not only defer to their authority, but cheerfully acknowledge them as their superiors in wisdom, and the fittest to rule."[36]

The following year, in the essay "Civilization," he returned more explicitly to the problems posed by "The Spirit of the Age." The essay opened with a diagnosis of the malady of the times: the increased power of the masses and a corresponding decrease in the power of individuals. The diffusion of property and knowledge, together with the growth of habits and instruments of combination, had conferred upon the masses a formidable amount of physical and intellectual power. Individuals, however, had experienced no similar accession of power, indeed, had suffered a visible decline of moral power. The same qualities that made this a more amiable and humane age also made it a less heroic one. Great vices had become less common, but so had great virtues. The outward decencies of life were better preserved, but at the considerable sacrifice of personal energy and character. The superior refinement of life was accompanied by a growing "moral effeminacy, an inaptitude for every kind of struggle."[37] The individual was thus doubly weakened: as his power was eroded by a mass society, so his character was enervated by the progress of civilization.

So far, in the diagnosis of the malady, "Civilization" resembled *On Liberty*. In one crucial respect, however, the

36. Review of vol. I of Tocqueville, *Democracy in America*, in *London and Westminster Review*, October 1835; reprinted in *Essays on Politics and Culture*, pp. 196–97.

37. "Civilization," *London and Westminster Review*, April 1836; reprinted in *Essays on Politics and Culture*, p. 58.

diagnosis—and with it the prescription—differed. In "Civilization" Mill attributed part of the decline of the influence of individuals, especially of superior individuals, to the vast increase of literature in modern times and the large number of competing ideas in circulation. He quoted a passage from one of his earlier reviews to suggest the inverse relationship between the quantity and quality of intellectual activity.

> *This is a reading age; and precisely because it is so reading an age, any book which is the result of profound meditation is, perhaps, less likely to be duly and profitably read than at a former period. The world reads too much and too quickly to read well. When books were few, to get through one was a work of time and labour: what was written with thought was read with thought, and with a desire to extract from it as much of the materials of knowledge as possible. But when almost every person who can spell, can and will write, what is to be done? . . . The world, in consequence, gorges itself with intellectual food, and in order to swallow the more, bolts it. . . . The public is in the predicament of an indolent man, who cannot bring himself to apply his mind vigorously to his own affairs, and over whom, therefore, not he who speaks most wisely, but he who speaks most frequently, obtains the influence.*[38]

Thus the quantity and competition of ideas, which in *On Liberty* figured as part of the cure for the modern malady, appeared in "Civilization" as a cause and symptom of the malady itself. Similarly, instead of seeking to stimulate discussion and competition, as he did in *On Liberty*, in this earlier essay he sought rather to encourage a "greater and more perfect combination among individuals," a greater "spirit of cooperation." In literature especially such a sys-

---

38. *Ibid.*, pp. 61–62. (The quotation is from Mill's review of John Austin, *Lectures on Jurisprudence*, in *Tait's Magazine*, December 1832.)

tem of cooperation and combination was required, for there "the system of individual competition has fairly worked itself out." The public, presently at the mercy of self-serving advertisements and reviews, had to have some better guidance "to direct them in distinguishing what is not worth reading from what is."[39] Mill suggested that something like a "collective guild" of authors might perform that function: "The resource must in time be, some organized co-operation among the leading intellects of the age, whereby works of first-rate merit, of whatever class, and of whatever tendency in point of opinion, might come forth with the stamp on them, from the first, of the approval of those whose name would carry authority."[40]

In his famous essay on Coleridge, written four years later, Mill went much further in the same direction. Here it was not a collective guild of authors that he recommended but something much more ambitious: a "clerisy" comprehending the learned of all denominations, roughly corresponding to Coleridge's idea of a "national church." This clerisy was to be supported and maintained by the state as an "endowed establishment" with the purpose of cultivating and transmitting not religion (as the common view of the establishment had it) but rather the national culture.[41] A small part of this order, its more distinguished members representing the "fountain heads of the humanities," was charged with preserving and enlarging the stock of knowledge as well as instructing their lesser colleagues. The latter, the ordinary professionals distributed throughout the country, would provide each locality with its "resident guide, guardian, and instructor." Thus knowledge would be diffused to every person in the community.[42]

39. *Ibid.*, pp. 63–65.
40. *Ibid.*, pp. 65–66.
41. "Coleridge," *London and Westminster Review*, March 1840; reprinted in *Essays on Politics and Culture*, p. 157.
42. *Ibid.*, p. 152.

This essay also contained a memorable account of the nature of political society, which had important implications for freedom of discussion. One of the preconditions for a permanent polity, Mill said, was a sense of "allegiance" or "loyalty." The constitution of every state had to make provision for "*something* which is settled, something permanent and not to be called in question."[43] By "constitution" Mill, like Coleridge, meant not a written constitution but rather the "idea" underlying the state. And it was some part of that idea, whether represented by a God, or person, or system of laws, or political principle, which had to be regarded as "*above* discussion."

> *In all political societies which have had a durable existence, there has been some fixed point; something which men agreed in holding sacred; which it might or might not be lawful to contest in theory, but which no one could either fear or hope to see shaken in practice; which, in short (except perhaps during some temporary crisis), was in the common estimation placed above discussion. And the necessity of this may easily be made evident. A state never is, nor, until mankind are vastly improved, can hope to be, for any long time exempt from internal dissension; for there neither is nor has ever been any state of society in which collisions did not occur between the immediate interests and passions of powerful sections of the people. What, then, enables society to weather these storms, and pass through turbulent times without any permanent weakening of the ties which hold it together? Precisely this—that however important the interests about which men fall out, the conflict does not affect the fundamental principles of the system of social union which happen to exist; nor threaten large portions of the community with the*

43. *Ibid.*, p. 137.

*subversion of that on which they have built their cal-
culations, and with which their hopes and aims have
become identified. But when the questioning of these
fundamental principles is (not an occasional disease,
but) the habitual condition of the body politic; and
when all the violent animosities are called forth, which
spring naturally from such a situation, the state is virtually in a position of civil war; and can never long
remain free from it in act and fact.*[44]

The last sentence of this passage might have been written
by a critic of *On Liberty* anticipating a state of affairs in
which the doctrine of that work—the deliberate and constant "questioning of these fundamental principles"—
would have become the "habitual condition of the body
politic."

On LESS FORMAL occasions, in private letters and in his diary,
Mill voiced opinions which were even more dramatically
opposed to *On Liberty*. Here too the evidence ranges over
a longer span of time than might be supposed. One passage,
from a letter to Carlyle in 1833, could have been written by
Carlyle himself: "I have not any great notion of the advan-

44. *Ibid.*, pp. 137-38. This is the passage as it originally appeared
in the *London and Westminster Review*, March 1840. The passage was quoted in this form in the first two editions of Mill's
A System of Logic (1843 and 1846). For the third edition of the
Logic (1851), Mill made small but significant changes in it, and
these were reproduced in the essay as it was eventually reprinted in *Dissertations and Discussions*. In the revised version
the clause in the first sentence, "which it might or might not be
lawful to contest in theory," was altered to read "which, wherever freedom of discussion was a recognized principle, it was of
course lawful to contest in theory." And in the parenthetical
clause in the last sentence, the words "or salutary medicine"
followed "not an occasional disease." (*Essays on Politics and
Culture*, p. 138.) The effect was to weaken slightly Mill's original argument and make some concessions to the doctrine of
On Liberty.

47

tage of what the 'free discussion' men call the 'collision of opinions,' it being my creed that Truth is *sown* and germinates in the mind itself, and is not to be struck *out* suddenly like fire from a flint by knocking another hard body against it."[45]

A short-lived diary of 1854 reverted to the theme of "The Spirit of the Age" written almost a quarter of a century earlier. While Mill was now convinced, as he had not been before, of the intellectual superiority of the present over the past, he was also convinced of its moral and spiritual inferiority—a deficiency of conviction, character, feeling, and the sense of truth. As in those earlier articles, he attributed these defects to the "multitude of thoughts," the variety of opinions which bred uncertainty and a lack of conviction. "Those who should be the guides of the rest, see too many sides to every question. They hear so much said, or find that so much can be said, about everything, that they feel no assurance of the truth of anything. But where there are no strong opinions there are (unless, perhaps, in private matters) no strong feelings, nor strong characters."[46] Where *On Liberty* assumed a continuum of opinion and truth—the vitality of truth dependent upon the freest circulation of opinions—in his diary he testified to exactly the opposite experience: a radical discontinuity between truth and opinion, the very variety and accessibility of opinions undermining any certainty of truth and therefore any strength of feeling and character.

Shortly after this diary entry, at about the time he was writing the first draft of *On Liberty*, Mill was involved in a curious episode which put the doctrine of that work to a practical test. He had been invited to join the "Neophyte Writer's Society," the function of which, as Mill understood it, was not to "promote any opinions in particular"

45. *Earlier Letters*, I, 153 (May 18, 1833).
46. *The Letters of John Stuart Mill*, ed. Hugh S. R. Elliot (London, 1910), II, 359 (Diary, Jan. 13, 1854).

but rather to bring together writers of "conflicting opinions" so that they would become better writers. Mill declined the invitation with some acerbity, protesting that he was not interested in "aiding the diffusion of opinions contrary to my own," but only in promoting those which he considered "true and just."

Now, I set no value whatever on writing for its own sake, and have much less respect for the literary craftsman than for the manual labourer, except so far as he uses his powers in promoting what I consider true and just. I have, on most of the subjects interesting to mankind, opinions to which I attach importance, and which I earnestly desire to diffuse, but I am not desirous of aiding the diffusion of opinions contrary to my own; and with respect to the mere faculty of expression, independently of what is to be expressed, it does not appear to me to require any encouragement. There is already an abundance, not to say superabundance, of writers who are able to express in an effective manner the mischievous commonplaces which they have got to say. I would gladly give any aid in my power towards improving their opinions, but I have no fear that any opinions they have will not be sufficiently well expressed, nor in any way should I be disposed to aid in sharpening weapons when I know not in what cause they will be used.[47]

One would also have difficulty in recognizing the author of *On Liberty* in an episode precipitated by him shortly after the publication of that work. Mrs. Gaskell, in her biography of Charlotte Brontë, had quoted a letter written by Brontë about "Enfranchisement of Women." "When I first read the paper," Brontë had written, "I thought it was

47. *Later Letters*, I, 205 (Apr. 23, 1854).

the work of a powerful minded, clear-headed woman, who had a hard, jealous heart, muscles of iron, and nerves of bend leather; of a woman who longed for power and had never felt affection." Finding out that the essay was by Mill, Brontë conceded its "admirable sense," although she thought Mill would make a "hard, dry, dismal world of it." His head, she concluded, "is, I dare say, very good, but I feel disposed to scorn his heart."[48]

Although the biography had been published two years earlier, Mill came upon this letter only after his wife's death and after he himself had publicly attributed to her this particular essay. He was, therefore, dismayed to read Brontë's remarks about the kind of woman who might have written it, and he was outraged that the letter should have been published. He charged Mrs. Gaskell with disregarding the "obligation which custom founded on reason has imposed, of omitting what would be offensive to the feelings and perhaps injurious to the moral reputation of individuals." He attributed to her the idea that a biographer was justified in publishing whatever might throw light on his subject—a notion, he said, that "the world, and those who are higher and better than the world, would, I believe, perfectly unite in condemning."[49]

Upon receiving this rebuke, Mrs. Gaskell abjectly apologized, denying that she had ever held so misguided a view of the function of the biographer. After reading the dedication to *On Liberty*, she said, she could well understand how deeply wounded Mill would be by any sentiment derogatory of his wife. The answer, however, only incensed Mill more, since it sounded as if he were merely being sensitive on his wife's behalf, whereas his objection, he insisted, was a matter of principle. He then repeated his initial charge that she had "neglected the usual and indispensable duties

48. E. C. Gaskell, *The Life of Charlotte Brontë* (New York, 1857), II, 189-90 (quoting a letter by Brontë, Sept. 20, 1851).
49. *Later Letters*, II, 628-29 (JSM to Mrs. Gaskell, July 1859).

which custom (founded on reason) has imposed of omitting all that might be offensive to the feeling of individuals."[50]

If Mrs. Gaskell had read beyond the dedication to *On Liberty*, she might have been amused—she was a good-natured woman—by the very different tone of that book. Mill did, at one point, grant that "opinion" ought to condemn those who were guilty of "want of candour, or malignity, bigotry, or intolerance of feeling."[51] But in the context in which this phrase appears, it is difficult to believe that Mill intended to prevent the publication of anything that might offend the feelings of any single individual; what he clearly meant to discourage was an intolerance of the order of bigotry—a want of respect for religious, national, racial, or moral sensibilities. Anything else would have been an invitation to censorship on the largest scale. This had been Mill's argument when he rejected the idea that discussion be free only on condition that it be "temperate" and "fair"; any strong statement, he then pointed out, was bound to seem intemperate and unfair, to give "offence," to anyone who disagreed with it.[52] If Mrs. Gaskell were duty-bound to omit the Brontë letter on the grounds that it was "offensive to the feelings or injurious to the reputation" of Mrs. Mill, regardless of how revealing it might be of Brontë's attitude toward a most important subject (Mill implicitly admitted the intrinsic importance of the letter), one wonders what remains of the central argument of *On Liberty*—the need for fearless, frank, candid, bold discussion, uninhibited by conventional opinions and feelings.

Only a few weeks after this affair, Mill expressed himself on another matter in a fashion that was similarly inconsistent with *On Liberty;* and here there was no personal involvement to obscure the issue. When his old friend (and future biographer) Alexander Bain wrote that he thought *On*

50. *Ibid.*, pp. 629–30 (July 1859).
51. *On Liberty*, p. 113.
52. *Ibid.*, p. 112.

Liberty was meant to convert not the world but only an "intellectual aristocracy," Mill disavowed such an elitist intention. On the contrary, he said, he wanted to make "the many more accessible to all the truth by making them more open minded." But he then went on to say that if Bain's remark applied only to the subject of religion, there was some truth in it: "On that, certainly I am not anxious to bring over any but really superior intellects and characters to the whole of my own opinions—in the case of all others I would much rather, as things now are, try to improve their religion than to destroy it."[53]

The reservation was an important one—and appears nowhere in *On Liberty*. If religion enjoyed the special immunity Mill was now giving it, it could only have been because, whatever its other defects, it still functioned as a support for morality. But this implied that something less than the whole truth was more desirable than the whole truth, that a religion based upon intellectual error was preferable to an agnosticism which may have been intellectually sounder. This suggestion is so at odds with the entire argument of *On Liberty* that one can only attribute it to the "other" Mill, a Mill who was sensible of the complexity of the moral life and was aware that prudence was as much a moral imperative as truth.

MILL'S *Autobiography* reveals something of the tension of thought under which he labored while he was writing *On Liberty*. In a revised version of the *Autobiography* (revised in the late 1850s while he was working on *On Liberty*), he purported to describe his state of mind at the time of "The Spirit of the Age":

> *I looked forward, through the present age of loud disputes but generally weak convictions, to a future*

---

53. *Later Letters*, II, 631 (JSM to Alexander Bain, Aug. 6, 1859).

which will unite the best qualities of the critical with the best of the organic periods; unchecked liberty of thought, perfect freedom of individual action in things not hurtful to others; but along with this, firm convictions as to right and wrong, useful and pernicious, deeply engraven on the feelings by early education and general unanimity of sentiment, and so well grounded in reason and in the real exigencies of life, that they shall not, like all former and present creeds, religious, ethical and political, require to be periodically thrown off and replaced by others.[54]

Here, as in so much of the *Autobiography*, Mill was trying to straddle two positions that were further apart than he cared to admit, to have the best of two worlds that were, if not mutually exclusive, at least in important respects antithetical. There is something almost pathetic in his retrospective attempt to superimpose the principles of *On Liberty*—"unchecked liberty of thought, perfect freedom of individual action in things not hurtful to others" (the wording is almost identical with that of *On Liberty*)—upon the Comtean vision of an organic society so firmly based upon reason, morality, and a "general unanimity of sentiment" as to preclude any further change.

The original draft of this portion of the *Autobiography* reflected more faithfully the state of mind that had produced "The Spirit of the Age." In place of the passage quoted above, with its unconvincing synthesis of the critical and the organic, Mill described the logic of ideas which had led him to the vision of an organic society. The organic nature of the physical sciences, he explained, had been familiar enough.

54. *The Early Draft of John Stuart Mill's Autobiography,* ed. Jack Stillinger (Urbana, Ill., 1961), p. 139. With some minor changes, this passage is essentially the same as in the final version of the *Autobiography* (Columbia Univ. Press edn., pp. 116-17).

In mathematics and physics what is called the liberty of conscience or the right of private judgment, is merely nominal: though in no way restrained by law, the liberty is not exercised: those who have studied the subject are all of the same opinion; if any one rejected what has been proved by demonstration or experiment he would be thought to be asserting no right but the right of being a fool: those who have not studied these sciences take their conclusions on trust from those who have, and the practical world goes on incessantly applying laws of nature and conclusions of reasoning which it receives on the faith not of its own reason but of the authority of the instructed.[55]

What had not been generally appreciated, and what he himself had first learned from Comte, was the extent to which the "moral, social, and political sciences" shared the same organic quality—the quality of objective, certain knowledge. When these moral sciences would have advanced to the point presently occupied by the physical sciences, the attitudes appropriate to a critical age—"liberty of conscience or the right of private judgment"—would become as irrelevant as they now were in the case of mathematics or physics.

Prior to his reading of Comte, Mill continued (with a barely veiled allusion to the teachings of Bentham and James Mill), he had "always identified deference to authority with mental slavery and the repression of individual thought." And so it was, in those cases where at least a minority of "thinking and instructed persons" privately disbelieved what they were publicly obliged to avow. But when all such persons would have become as nearly unanimous in their moral, social, and political beliefs as they

55. *Early Draft*, p. 188. This is not part of the final version of the *Early Draft* but of a still earlier version—what the editor calls the "rejected leaves."

presently were in regard to physics or mathematics, they would naturally and properly exercise their "authority" and "ascendancy" over the multitude. It was the desirability of this "united authority" that Comte had impressed upon him.

I did not become one atom less zealous for increasing the knowledge and improving the understanding of the man; but I no longer believed that the fate of mankind depended on the possibility of making all of them competent judges of questions of government and legislation. From this time my hopes of improvement rested less on the reason of the multitude, than on the possibility of effecting such an improvement in the methods of political and social philosophy, as should enable all thinking and instructed persons who have no sinister interest to be so nearly of one mind on these subjects, as to carry the multitude with them by their united authority.[56]

Few critics of *On Liberty* have gone so far as Mill himself, on other occasions, in disputing the absolute value of absolute freedom of discussion. Even more startling is the fact that at the very time he was writing *On Liberty*, he was mindful of everything that could be said, that he himself had said, in qualification of that view. His argument for an intellectual "clerisy" is most familiar in the form he gave it in his essay on Coleridge. But many of his other writings testify to the same conviction that some intellectual authority and consensus were necessary for the sake both of truth and of the well-being of society. If public opinion was ill-informed, he repeatedly argued, it could be enlightened and elevated only under the guidance of the well-informed. Left to its own devices, it could only multiply opinions without providing the means for judging between good and bad

56. *Ibid.*, pp. 188–89.

opinions, between truth and error. Nor was it only reason that suffered from this indiscriminate profusion of opinion. Society suffered as well, for in a natural order of society consensus rather than dissension was the normal state of affairs, and the wise were acknowledged to be the superiors of the ignorant.

It is in contrast to this conception of a natural, organic age that *On Liberty* emerges more sharply than ever as the credo of a critical age. And not of a critical age *faute de mieux*, an age of transition which in the normal and natural course of events would give way to a new organic age; but of a critical age in perpetuity, an age which was represented as both the natural and the ideal condition for mankind. In his other writings Mill analyzed and criticized the critical spirit. In *On Liberty* he celebrated and glorified it.

LIBERTY OF ACTION:
INDIVIDUALITY

THE COROLLARY OF FREEDOM of discussion was freedom of action. For the same reasons that men had to be free to form and express their opinions, they also had to be free to act upon those opinions—"so long as it is at their own risk and peril." The last qualification, Mill admitted, was a limitation upon freedom. In this one respect action was not "as free" as opinion.[1]

The "risk and peril" clause, in the several formulations given it in *On Liberty*, has been the subject of much dispute. Critics have been dissatisfied with Mill's lack of precision at this crucial point in his argument, an imprecision reflected in the variety and vagueness of language used to express this qualification. Sometimes the limitation was said to apply to acts which were "hurtful," "harmful," "evil," "injurious," or "mischievous" to others. Sometimes the acts were described more neutrally, as "affecting," "concerning," or "regarding" others or the "interests" of others. Formulations of the second kind have given rise to a large controversy over the meaning and validity of the distinction between "self-regarding" acts, in which liberty was deemed absolute, and "other-regarding" acts, in which liberty might legitimately be limited.

1. *On Liberty*, p. 114.

57

It is easy to fault Mill for these vagaries of language; it is indeed surprising to find the author of *A System of Logic* so unsystematic and illogical. Yet the linguistic difficulties can be exaggerated. Mill's intent is generally clear even if his language is not always what one might expect from a professional philosopher. If the whole of his discussion is taken into account, his specific examples as well as general formulas, it becomes evident that when he spoke of acts which "concern" or "affect" others, he meant concern or affect them adversely, harmfully. It is also evident that he wanted to circumscribe the limitation as much as possible, generally restricting it, for example, to physical and material rather than moral or spiritual harm. Moreover, it was meant to apply only to freedom of action, not to freedom of discussion, except in the one instance in which discussion constituted a direct and practical call to action—a "positive instigation to some mischievous act"[2]—not a symbolic or potential call to action. Furthermore, the sanctions called for in the event of a harmful action could be either those imposed by public opinion or those exercised by law and authority, depending upon the legal status of the particular action. Those actions which were not harmful were entirely the concern of the individual and could no more be subject to the sanction of public opinion than to that of the law.

Other aspects of this qualification emerge in the following chapter. (He then made it clear, for example, that while an act could in principle be subject to social or legal sanction, it was not always expedient to impose either of these sanctions. His qualification, therefore, turns out to be permissive rather than prescriptive.) What is interesting at this point is the fact that, having stated the qualification in various forms in the opening paragraph of this chapter, he did not choose to explicate or elaborate upon it. Instead he turned the discussion from the qualification to the principle itself, from the

2. *Ibid.*

negative aspect to the positive. Thus the rest of the chapter is an argument for liberty of action in its most comprehensive sense.

The strategy of this chapter is almost identical with that of the preceding one. Just as earlier he had insisted upon absolute freedom of discussion as the necessary precondition for the emergence and vitality of truth, so he now insisted upon the largest possible liberty of action as the precondition for the emergence and vitality of individuality. Earlier it had been differences of opinion that had not only to be tolerated but encouraged for the sake of truth; now it was differences of "plans of life," "experiments of living," that had to be tolerated and encouraged for the sake of a vigorous, individualistic character.[3] In the first case, it was assumed that reason developed only by actively using it to choose among a variety of opinions; in the second, it was assumed that individuality developed only by actively exercising it to choose among varieties of conduct and behavior. And individuality, like truth, was deemed to be of the greatest importance to mankind collectively as well as to individual persons: it was "one of the leading essentials of well-being," "one of the principal ingredients of human happiness, and quite the chief ingredient of individual and social progress."[4]

The idea of individuality was not so much defined as characterized by association with such words as "experiment," "spontaneity," "originality," "variety," "choice," "diversity," "vigour," "desire," "impulse," "peculiarity," and "eccentricity." Its antithesis was represented by "custom," "tradition," "obedience," "conformity," "restraint," "law," and "discipline." One other word expressive of individuality, which recurs throughout the chapter and is

3. *Ibid.,* pp. 117, 115. In the text, "plan of life" is in the singular. Elsewhere Mill spoke of "experiments in [not of] living" (p 137).
4. *Ibid.,* p. 115.

of special interest, is "development." Earlier Mill had used, as the epigraph for *On Liberty*, a quotation from Wilhelm von Humboldt: "The grand, leading principle, towards which every argument unfolded in these pages directly converges, is the absolute and essential importance of human development in its richest diversity."[5] Now he described the main thesis of Humboldt:

> *That "the end of man, or that which is prescribed by the eternal or immutable dictates of reason, and not suggested by vague and transient desires, is the highest and most harmonious development of his powers to a complete and consistent whole;" that, therefore, the object "towards which every human being must cease-*

5. *Ibid.*, p. 62. The work by Humboldt, quoted by Mill in the epigraph and in this chapter, appeared in English translation in 1854, just at the time Mill started to write *On Liberty*. It is interesting that this was a very early work by Humboldt, written originally in 1791–92, when he was only twenty-four. Only short sections of it were published at the time, and the whole did not appear until a complete edition of his works was issued in 1852, seventeen years after his death. In *On Liberty* Mill gave the title of the English translation, *The Sphere and Duties of Government*. The German title was *Ideen zu einem Versuch die Grenzen der Wirksamkeit des Staats zu bestimmen*. It has recently been reissued in English as *The Limits of State Action*, ed. J. W. Burrow (Cambridge, Eng., 1969).

Humboldt's fame in his own time came not from this exceedingly laissez-fairist book but from his activities as Minister of Public Instruction in Prussia. He founded the University of Berlin, reorganized the Prussian *Gymnasium* (the secondary school), and tried to impress upon both his elevated conception of culture. It is this Humboldt whom Matthew Arnold admired, using a quotation from one of Humboldt's educational memoranda as the epigraph to his own book, *Schools and Universities on the Continent* (London, 1868). That quotation read: "The thing is *not* to let the schools and universities go on in a drowsy and impotent routine; the thing is to raise the culture of the nation ever higher and higher by their means." It is curious that Mill and Arnold should have used Humboldt for quite different purposes.

It is also curious that of all philosophers, ancient and modern, the only one Mill chose to quote was the relatively obscure Humboldt. It is as if he were asserting his independence from the entire tradition of philosophical thought.

lessly direct his efforts, and on which especially those who design to influence their fellow-men must ever keep their eyes, is the individuality of power and development;" that for this there are two requisites, "freedom, and variety of situations;" and that from the union of these arise "individual vigour and manifold diversity," which combine themselves in "originality."[6]

Mill also owed to Humboldt—although here he did not make the attribution explicit—the analogy between the development of human nature and the development of other natural organisms: "Human nature is not a machine to be built after a model, and set to do exactly the work prescribed for it, but a tree, which requires to grow and develop itself on all sides, according to the tendency of the inward forces which make it a living thing."[7] And he concluded this part of his argument by repeating that individuality was the "same thing with development," that only the cultivation of individuality could produce "well-developed human beings." "What more or better can be said of any condition of human affairs than that it brings human beings themselves nearer to the best thing they can be?"[8]

The idea of development was crucial to Mill's argument, as it was to Humboldt's. In one sense it was an entirely neutral concept—suggesting any kind of development, development in any direction, for any purpose and toward any end; but in another sense it was a highly charged concept, containing within itself the teleological promise of a higher end, ultimately the highest end. This is why Humboldt could proceed so confidently from the conditions of "freedom and variety," to the "individuality of power and

6. *On Liberty*, pp. 115–16. The citations from Humboldt are from pp. 11–13 of the 1854 translation (pp. 16–17 of the Burrow edition).

7. *On Liberty*, p. 117. This is a brief paraphrase of Humboldt (Burrow edn., pp. 18–19).

8. *On Liberty*, p. 121.

development," and emerge with the "end of man" (the "true end of man," in the original German), which was nothing less than the "highest and most harmonious development of his powers to a complete and consistent whole."[9] And so Mill too could follow a similar easy progression from "development" per se that was simply synonymous with individuality, to the "well-developed" individual, and finally to the "best thing" that an individual could be. Just as the tree could not do better than develop in accord with its "inward forces," so the human being need only consult his own "inclination," his "personal impulses and preferences," "all that is individual" in himself, in order to become a "noble and beautiful object of contemplation."[10]

Implicit in this argument was the dialectical transformation of quantity into quality, the "manifold diversity" of situations, actions, feelings, desires, and impulses all combining to make for a strong and noble character. As life became "rich, diversified, animating," it produced not just a rich and lively diversity of thoughts and feelings but "high thoughts and elevating feelings."[11] Similarly, as the individual was encouraged to cultivate his individuality, the "fulness" of his own existence, so he became more "valuable" to himself and to others. And so too passion was made conducive to virtue. Mill did not explicitly pose the classical problem of the relationship between passion and virtue, but he did attempt to resolve this problem, and in a peculiarly modern fashion.

To say that one person's desires and feelings are stronger and more various than those of another, is merely to say that he has more of the raw material of human nature, and is therefore capable, perhaps of more evil, but certainly of more good. Strong impulses are

9. Humboldt (Burrow edn.), pp. 16–17.
10. *On Liberty*, pp. 119–21.
11. *Ibid.*, p. 121.

but another name for energy. Energy may be turned to bad uses; but more good may always be made of an energetic nature, than of an indolent and impassive one. Those who have most natural feelings are always those whose cultivated feelings may be made the strongest. The same strong susceptibilities which make the personal impulses vivid and powerful, are also the source from whence are generated the most passionate love of virtue, and the sternest self-control.[12]

The transmutation of quantity into quality, of passion into virtue, implied a particular view of human nature. In this passage, for example, Mill assumed that a larger amount of the "raw material" of human nature meant that there was "perhaps" a larger potential for evil but "certainly" a larger potential for good, that energy "may" be used for the bad but that "more" good would come from an energetic than from a passive nature. This assumption runs throughout the chapter: the greater the exercise of "spontaneity and individuality," the greater the quantity and intensity of "desires and impulses," the greater the "variety of situations" upon which the individual could freely act, the more probable it was that all of this activity would add up to good rather than bad.[13]

Although Mill did not explicitly state his own view of human nature, it may be inferred from the view he attributed to his antagonists. Those who did not share his enthusiasm for liberty, he said, were essentially committed to a "Calvinist theory" of human nature. In its strict form, this theory held that since human nature was "radically corrupt," there was no redemption for man until "human nature is killed within him." It deemed "self-will" to be the source of all evil, "obedience" the source of such good as man was capable of. The maxim of this school was

12. *Ibid.*, p. 118.
13. *Ibid.*, pp. 116–18.

"Whatever is not a duty is a sin." Mill admitted that many people held to this doctrine in a "mitigated" form, allowing for some gratification of man's natural inclinations. But even in this form, the manner of gratification was circumscribed, so that obedience continued to dominate over will, and human nature remained "pinched and hidebound," "cramped and dwarfed." It was some version of this Calvinist theory, he insisted, that prevailed in his own day.[14]

In describing the alternative to Calvinism, Mill was also describing something close to his own position. A religion that assumed God to be good, he reasoned, must also assume that God gave man faculties to be cultivated rather than rooted out, a human nature to be satisfied rather than abnegated. "Pagan self-assertion," Mill quoted John Sterling, as much as "Christian self-denial," was "one of the elements of human worth."[15] If it was better to be a John Knox than an Alcibiades, it was better to be a Pericles than either—and in any case, Mill concluded, a latter-day Pericles would contain all that was good in a Knox.

The alternatives, as Mill presented them, were obviously weighted. Instead of attributing to his opponents a conception of individuality that fell short of his own absolute or near-absolute one, he attributed to them a total or near-total denial of individuality. And this total denial permitted him to saddle them with a commensurately negative view of human nature. Even if they held to a "mitigated" form of Calvinism, he assumed that they wanted human faculties "rooted out," human nature "abnegated."[16] In contrast, his own view of human nature was generous and comprehensive. He wanted, in fact, to have the best of both worlds: "Christian self-denial" as well as "pagan self-assertion," a

14. *Ibid.*, pp. 119–20.
15. *Ibid.*, p. 120. The quotation from John Sterling (1806–44), an old friend of Mill's and a disciple of Coleridge, was from his posthumous *Essays and Tales*, ed. Julius Hare (London, 1848), I, 190.
16. *On Liberty*, p. 120.

Pericles with all the virtues (whatever they might be) of a Knox, but none of the vices of an Alcibiades.

If Mill was unwilling to take upon himself as radical a view of human nature as that which he attributed to his opponents—a radical optimism that might have been more in keeping with the radical individuality he was advocating—it was perhaps because such a view of human nature would have contradicted another part of his argument. And it is, significantly, just at this point, just after his remarks upon human nature, that his discussion took a new turn. Until then he had been recommending the largest liberty of action for everyone. Now he addressed himself to the problem of those who "do not desire liberty, and would not avail themselves of it."[17] At this point, the tone as well as the focus of his argument shifted. Mill revealed himself to be almost as pessimistic about people, the majority of the people, as the Calvinists he had previously castigated. Most people, it now appeared, did not desire liberty, would not use it if they had it, did not want others to use it—and, moreover, would not use it well if they did use it.

Some few, however, did desire liberty, would use it, and use it well. It was for their sake that liberty was especially required. And it was they who would derive from it one of its chief benefits, originality. Mill made it clear that he meant by originality not only the discovery of new truths—for that only free speech was needed—but also the discovery of new practices, new ways of living and modes of conduct; it was the latter that required freedom of action, freedom for the cultivation of individuality. Originality, he admitted, could not be expected of most people; nor could most people be expected to turn it to good account. "There are but few persons, in comparison with the whole of mankind, whose experiments, if adopted by others, would be likely to be any improvement on established practice. But

17. *Ibid.*, p. 122.

these few are the salt of the earth; without them, human life would become a stagnant pool."[18] Theirs was the creativity of genius:

> *Persons of genius, it is true, are, and are always likely to be, a small minority; but in order to have them, it is necessary to preserve the soil in which they grow. Genius can only breathe freely in an* atmosphere of *freedom. Persons of genius are,* ex vi termini, *more individual than any other people—less capable, consequently, of fitting themselves, without hurtful compression, into any of the small number of moulds which society provides in order to save its members the trouble of forming their own character.*[19]

Most people, Mill granted, were prepared to pay lip service to the importance of genius. But they took it to be important only in the creation of a fine poem or painting. They did not see it in terms of "originality in thought and action."[20] To this kind of genius most people were either indifferent or hostile. And here Mill returned to one of the themes of his introductory chapter: the "public opinion" that rules the world. Earlier he had decried public opinion as a threat to liberty and individuality; now he saw it as a threat to originality and genius. "The general tendency of things throughout the world is to render mediocrity the ascendant power among mankind."[21] Public opinion ruled even though it was not always the same public: in America the public was the whole white population, in England it was chiefly the middle class. But in both cases, the opinion was that of the "mass," which is to say, of a "collective

18. *Ibid.* In other metaphors, life without originality was portrayed as mechanical and dead—a sad commentary on the lives of all but the very few.
19. *Ibid.*
20. *Ibid.*, p. 123.
21. *Ibid.*

mediocrity." This collective mediocrity could be transcended only when gifted individuals were given their head, when "the sovereign Many have let themselves be guided (which in their best times they always have done) by the counsels and influence of a more highly gifted and instructed One or Few."[22]

It was these gifted "One or Few," the "exceptional individuals," who had to be permitted and encouraged to be individuals—that is, to act differently from the mass. In other ages, before the ascendancy of the mass, the "tyranny of opinion," there was no advantage in individuals acting differently from the mass "unless they acted not only differently but better."[23] Now, the "mere example of nonconformity," the simple fact of "eccentricity," was itself a virtue in breaking through this social tyranny. And the larger the quantity of nonconformity and eccentricity, the greater was the likelihood of genius: "Eccentricity has always abounded when and where strength of character has abounded; and the amount of eccentricity in a society has generally been proportional to the amount of genius, mental vigour, and moral courage it contained."[24]

The genius, then, was an object of special solicitude; it was his individuality that was most precious. But since he could only thrive in an "atmosphere of freedom," all men had to share the same degree of liberty. And they all had to share it for their own sakes as well as for the sake of genius. After his paean to genius, Mill hastened to add that it was not only "persons of decided mental superiority" who had to be encouraged to live their lives in their own way. The "average man" should also be encouraged to adopt an individual mode of life. And not because that mode would be "the best in itself, but because it is his own mode."[25]

22. *Ibid.*, p. 124.
23. *Ibid.*
24. *Ibid.*, p. 125.
25. *Ibid.*

In theory, this argument for individuality, for the largest "independence of action and disregard of custom,"[26] applied equally to the genius and to the ordinary man. The genius would elevate the ordinary man, and the ordinary man would elevate himself by the fullest exercise of his individuality. Yet there is a tension which Mill never satisfactorily resolved between the nature of genius and the nature of the ordinary man. This tension first appears in his discussion of human nature, when Mill stopped far short of the optimism that his theory would seem to require. It appears again in his discussion of the collective mediocrity of the mass. For if there was a larger potential for good than for evil in human beings, why did human beings in the mass—who were, after all, only a collectivity of individuals—exercise so baneful an effect upon society? Mill did not here, or anywhere else, propose anything like a theory of the "crowd" or "mob," which would have individuals en masse act differently from the way they act separately. Nor did he propose anything like the Benthamite theory, which assumed that people acted against their own interests only when they were manipulated by the "sinister interests" of particular men or groups. Mill seemed rather to believe that ordinary people, individually or en masse, were themselves fearful of individuality, more comfortable with custom, tradition, conventional modes of behavior. But this has the paradoxical implication that men, ordinary men, violated their own nature, their individuality, by virtue of another aspect of their nature, their impulse to conformity.

A similar tension appears in Mill's suggestion that the "sovereign Many" could not do better than be guided, as they were in the "best times," by the "counsels and influence of a more highly gifted and instructed One or Few"; and by the tribute, immediately following this, to the "average man" who was willing to take direction from the excep-

26. *Ibid.*

tional man. "The initiation of all wise or noble things comes and must come from individuals; generally at first from some one individual. The honour and glory of the average man is that he is capable of following that initiative; that he can respond internally to wise and noble things, and be led to them with his eyes open."[27] Mill was careful to say that it was by the "counsels and influence" of the "One or Few" that the average man should be guided and that he should follow the initiative of his betters "internally" and "with his eyes open." Yet did not the average man, in following that initiative, abdicate the individuality that Mill, only a paragraph later, urged upon him? In that second paragraph, the average man was urged to follow his own mode of life not because "it is the best in itself but because it is his own mode."[28]

The tension appears once more in Mill's attempts to relate individuality to the general progress, advancement, and improvement of mankind. On the one hand, he had no difficulty in arguing that the progress of all depended upon the liberty of each. "In proportion to the development of his individuality, each person becomes more valuable to himself, and is therefore capable of being more valuable to others."[29] Liberty and improvement might, in the short run, seem to be antithetical, but in the long run they were dependent upon each other.

The spirit of improvement is not always a spirit of liberty, for it may aim at forcing improvements on an unwilling people; and the spirit of liberty, in so far as it resists such attempts, may ally itself locally and temporarily with the opponents of improvement; but the only unfailing and permanent source of improvement is liberty, since by it there are as many possible inde-

27. *Ibid.*, p. 124.
28. *Ibid.*, p. 125.
29. *Ibid.*, p. 121.

pendent centres of improvement as there are individ-uals.[30]

Yet in the very next paragraph, he described the present condition of England as one in which improvement had turned out to be inimical to liberty and individuality. The most dramatic advances of the past century, he pointed out, had the unfortunate effect of decreasing the "variety of situations" upon which human development depended. Political reforms, improvements in transportation and communication, the increase of manufactures and commerce, the extension of education, even the refinement of morals, all contributed to the elimination of differences—material, moral, cultural, and social differences. Now more than ever, as the result of the wider distribution of goods, the growth of affluence, education, and democracy, people tended to live similar lives, see the same things, read the same books, obey the same moral code, aspire to the same goals, share the same hopes and fears, even enjoy the same "rights and liberties." The tendency of the age was to raise the low, but by the same token, it also lowered the high; it reduced social eminences, thereby rendering everything level and uniform. Against this overwhelming tendency, Mill could only try to persuade the "intelligent part of the public" to appreciate the value of difference per se, "to see that it is good there should be differences, even though not for the better, even though, as it may appear to them, some should be for the worse."[31]

On this note, Mill concluded this chapter. Having earlier made individuality a necessary condition of improvement, he now depicted a situation in which improvement was undermining individuality itself. He did not say that the improvements were wrong or misguided; he could hardly quarrel with the greater affluence, education, or even polit-

30. *Ibid.*, p. 128.
31. *Ibid.*, pp. 130-31.

ical power of the masses, with the improvement in their morals and sensibility, the raising of their ambitions, the satisfaction of their needs and wants. But he had to acknowledge that all these goods had a deleterious effect upon individuality. He finally rested his case by simply making a virtue of difference for the sake of difference, even if particular differences should appear to be not for the better but for the worse. At the end of the chapter as at the beginning, Mill was committed to individuality as a good in itself, indeed the highest good. But whereas at the beginning individuality seemed to be unambiguous and unproblematic, a necessary and sufficient means of progress and improvement, by the end it was caught up in a profound ambiguity and a tragic paradox. Improvement, he discovered, might militate against individuality—in which case individuality would have to stand on its own right, the right to be worse rather than better.

THIS CHAPTER may well be regarded as the heart of *On Liberty*. Individuality was above all a claim to liberty of action, and this claim was Mill's unique contribution to the history of thought. Liberty of speech (although not absolute liberty of speech) was a familiar and respectable idea long before Mill. But liberty of action was not. Or if it was familiar, it was certainly not respectable. It existed, even as an ideal, only on the outer fringes of intellectual thought, in the recurrent impulses towards millenarianism, antinomianism, and varieties of anarchism. But while these movements might occasionally impinge on the rest of the world, they rarely exercised any significant intellectual influence on it, such thinkers as they produced being generally looked upon as eccentrics or irresponsibles.

Those who spoke out most loudly and effectively for freedom of speech—Milton, Locke, the Founding Fathers—were careful to distinguish that freedom from freedom of action. Kant put the distinction in its extreme form in his famous dictum, "Argue . . . but obey."[32] This proposition almost suggests an inverse relationship between liberty of speech and liberty of action: the greater the liberty of speech, the more circumscribed was the liberty of action. Liberty of speech could only be assured if obedience (to rulers and laws) was assured. Ultimately, Kant reasoned, the liberty of speech would alter the state of the law, so that the realm of action would be enlarged. But the need to obey the law remained a condition for the exercise of free speech.

Many liberals have been uncomfortable with the Kantian formula. They have preferred to think of liberty of speech and of action as having a direct rather than inverse relation to each other. But most would agree with Kant that liberty of speech was primary and that it could be claimed in far larger measure than liberty of action. Even the Founding Fathers, who came closest to an absolutist position regarding liberty of speech, avoided any implication that the same logic held for action. They valued liberty of action, but only in moderation, insofar as it was consistent and coexistent with other values. By the same token, they valued individuality, insofar as the individual's character and behavior were good, not insofar as they were individualistic or merely different. And to the extent to which authority, law, public opinion, and all the other resources of society could contribute to the improvement of character and behavior, these too were valued.

It is in this liberal tradition that the "other" Mill belongs, the tradition in which liberty of action is good, but not an absolute or ultimate end, and in which individuality is good, but again not absolutely, in all forms and under all conditions. Mill had always been concerned with the prob-

---

32. Immanuel Kant, "What Is Enlightenment?" in *The Philosophy of Kant*, ed. Carl J. Friedrich (Modern Library edn.; New York, 1949), p. 139.

lem of developing a strong and energetic character. But elsewhere he kept clearly in mind the particular kind of character he wanted to see developed—a character that was not simply strong and energetic in pursuit of its individuality, but was strong and energetic in pursuit of the good. And that good was something other than the individual's desires, impulses, passion, and will. There was a virtue that transcended these, an order of goods which might not accord with desire and impulse and which might require the subordination of passion and will. It was the promotion of these goods that was Mill's preoccupation during most of his life.

This is where *On Liberty* differed so markedly from most of Mill's other writings. In *On Liberty* the immediate and direct objects of his attention were liberty and individuality. If in the course of this work he sometimes spoke as if liberty and individuality were proximate ends, the ultimate ends being truth and the highest development of human nature, he always assumed that the latter would be the necessary and automatic consequences of the former.[33] He could therefore concentrate entirely on the promotion of liberty and individuality, could direct all his principles and policies to these ends, confident that the others would follow in their wake. Thus the practical effect of his doctrine was to exalt liberty and individuality as goods in themselves, while denigrating authority and conformity as evils in themselves.

THE DOCTRINE OF *On Liberty* would have been as little congenial to the young Mill, the Benthamite Mill, as it

33. At one point, for example, Mill spoke of "great energies guided by vigorous reason, and strong feelings strongly controlled by a conscientious will" (*On Liberty*, p. 127). But it was the "great energies" and "strong feelings" that were directly furthered by his doctrine of liberty, while the "vigorous reason" and "conscientious will" were taken for granted as the natural concomitants of powerful energies and feelings.

would have been to the older, Coleridgean Mill—although for different reasons. In one respect it was closer to the Benthamite position, which reduced all human motives to questions of passion and will (in Benthamite terminology, interest and power). But the working out of the utilitarian calculus, the greatest happiness of the greatest number, required an abnegation of some individual passions and wills. It was for this reason that Bentham refused to make a right of liberty, indeed denied the meaningfulness of the concept of liberty. Every law, every act of government, he insisted, was a limitation on liberty. And since laws and acts of government were the instruments for bringing about the greatest happiness of the greatest number, liberty had neither meaning nor value in itself. What was required was not liberty, whatever that might be, but good government.[34]

This was exactly the position Mill took in his first article for the *Westminster Review* in 1824. It was an attack on the *Edinburgh Review* for, among other things, judging every law by the standard of liberty rather than good government.

> *Liberty in its original sense, means freedom from restraint. In this sense, every law, and every rule of morals, is contrary to liberty. A despot, who is entirely emancipated from both, is the only person whose freedom of action is complete. A measure of government, therefore, is not necessarily bad, because it is contrary to liberty; and to blame it for that reason leads to confusion of ideas.*[35]

This confusion of ideas, Mill suspected, was precisely what the Whigs wanted, for it enabled them to enact small reforms in the name of liberty and to resist large ones under the same pretext.

34. E.g., *Three Tracts on Spanish and Portuguese Affairs* (1820), in Bentham, *Collected Works*, VIII, 478; *Constitutional Code*, in Bentham, *Collected Works*, IX, 123.
35. "Edinburgh Review," *Westminster Review*, I (1824), 508.

If the concept of liberty was anathema to the Benthamite, the concept of individuality, in the sense in which Mill presented it in *On Liberty*, was anathema to the Coleridgean. The first public intimation of the Coleridgean strain in Mill's thought came in a speech on "Perfectibility" in 1828, delivered before the debating society that he and his friends had organized. His ostensible subject was perfectibility, his real subject virtue. In effect, he was asking the Platonic question: Is virtue teachable? In the modern idiom he used, the question emerged as: Can moral character be improved? His answer was that character could be improved if two forces were brought to bear upon individuals: a sound moral education in their early years and the "insensible influence of the world, of society, and public opinion upon their habits and associations in after life."[36] If some men were morally inferior to others, it was either because their education had been faulty or because the influence of public opinion had been insufficient. And Mill interpreted public opinion in the largest terms, as representing the opinion not of the group immediately surrounding the individual but of society at large. He advised that men be removed from the "opinion of their separate and private coteries" and made "amenable to the general tribunal of the public at large." Only if that were done, if public opinion itself were elevated to a higher moral level by a proper system of education, and if that public opinion exercised the influence it was capable of, could a "high state of general morality" be attained.[37]

Ten years later, in his essay on Bentham, Mill systematically exposed the assumptions and principles of utilitarianism, including its concept of the individual and of society. He criticized Bentham for reducing human nature to the level of interests and passions at the expense of conscience, char-

36. "Speech on Perfectibility," reprinted in *John Stuart Mill's Autobiography*, ed. Harold J. Laski (World's Classics edn.; London, 1958), p. 293.
37. *Ibid.*, pp. 297-98.

acter, and moral sense and for subverting those forces in society which might have inspired a sense of morality. Thinking logical clarity to be everything, Bentham had dismissed as "vague generalities" the entire moral history and experience of mankind. "It must be allowed," Mill rebuked him, "that even the originality which dares think for itself, is not a more necessary part of the philosophical character than reverence for previous thinkers, and for the collective mind of the human race."[38] Lacking respect for tradition, the mind of the past, Bentham also failed to recognize the existence of "national character," that collective spirit which alone "enables any body of human beings to exist as a society," which causes one nation to succeed and another to fail, one to "aspire to elevated things, another to grovel in mean ones." Bentham's philosophy might be appropriate for the "business" part of life; but it was totally inadequate for the moral and spiritual side.[39]

In his essay on Coleridge, Mill carried these ideas still further, criticizing not only Bentham but the French *philosophes* for adopting a totally critical and negative stance toward society. Instead of attacking the old regime for failing to provide the essential conditions of a durable order, for "sapping the necessary foundations of society," the *philosophes* exulted in the fact that these foundations were being destroyed.

In the weakening of all government they saw only the weakening of bad government; and thought they could not better employ themselves than in finishing the task so well begun—in expelling out of every mind the last vestige of belief in that creed on which all the restrain-

38. *Essays on Politics and Culture*, p. 92. In the revised version of this essay printed in *Dissertations and Discussions*, "reverence" was replaced by the somewhat feebler phrase "a thoughtful regard."

39. *Essays on Politics and Culture*, p. 102.

ing discipline recognised in the education of European countries still rested, and with which in the general mind it was inseparably associated; in unsettling everything which was still considered settled, making men doubtful of the few things of which they still felt certain; and in uprooting what little remained in the people's minds of reverence for anything above them, of respect to any of the limits which custom and prescription had set to the indulgence of each man's fancies or inclinations, or of attachment to any of the things which belonged to them as a nation, and which made them feel their unity as such.[40]

It was in opposition to this negative, subversive philosophy that Mill posited the three essential conditions for a permanent political society. One of these—"allegiance" to the fundamental tenets of a society, tenets which were "above discussion"—has been mentioned in connection with the freedom of discussion.[41] The other two, "nationality" and "education," have a more direct bearing upon the idea of individuality.[42] By a "strong and active principle of nationality," Mill did not mean, he hastened to say, a senseless antipathy to foreigners, or a cherishing of "absurd peculiarities" merely because they were those of one's own nation, or a refusal to take what was good from other countries. The principle of nationality was a positive idea; it expressed a sense of sympathy rather than hostility, of union rather than separation. It was the "feeling of common

40. *Ibid.*, pp. 141–42.
41. See above, pp. 46–47.
42. *Essays on Politics and Culture*, pp. 136 ff. In the opening sentence of the paragraph on nationality in the *Dissertations* version, the word "nationality" was replaced by "cohesion among the members of the same community or state." But in the following sentence the original word was permitted to stand. Like most of the other changes in this essay, this had the effect of slightly muting Mill's meaning without essentially altering it.

interest" which tied together those with a common polity, history, and geography, which made them cherish that tie, feel that they were one public indissolubly bound together.[43]

If this principle of nationality was at variance with the individuality Mill was to emphasize in *On Liberty*, the principle of education was even more diametrically opposed to it. For in the Coleridge essay, Mill represented as the aim of education precisely those qualities that in *On Liberty* he was to deprecate as the unfortunate heritage of Calvinism. The education he was speaking of was that which began in infancy and "continued through life." Whatever else it might include, its "main and incessant ingredient," Mill emphasized, must always be a *"restraining discipline."*

> *To train the human being in the habit, and thence the power, of subordinating his personal impulses and aims, to what were considered the ends of society; of adhering, against all temptation, to the course of conduct which those ends prescribed; of controlling in himself all the feelings which were liable to militate against those ends, and encouraging all such as tended towards them; this was the purpose, to which every outward motive that the authority directing the system could command, and every inward power or principle which its knowledge of human nature enabled it to evoke, were endeavoured to be rendered instrumental.*[44]

Reading this passage after *On Liberty*, one might be tempted to think that Mill was criticizing the kind of education described here. The very words evoke everything Mill deplored in *On Liberty*: "restraining discipline," "subordinating his personal impulses and aims," "controlling in himself all the feelings which were liable to militate against those [social] ends." But the rest of the paragraph and the essay as a whole make it clear that he regarded such an

43. *Ibid.*, p. 139.
44. *Ibid.*, pp. 136–37.

education as essential and praiseworthy. Without it, he said, no polity had ever been able to sustain itself. When this system of discipline failed, the polity failed:

> *Whenever and in proportion as the strictness of this discipline was relaxed, the natural tendency of mankind to anarchy reasserted itself; the state became disorganized from within; mutual conflict for selfish ends, neutralized the energies which were required to keep up the contest against natural causes of evil; and the nation, after a longer or briefer interval of progressive decline, became either the slave of a despotism, or the prey of a foreign invader.*[45]

It might also be supposed that in presenting these principles—education, allegiance, and nationality—as the necessary conditions of a viable society, Mill was simply reporting on Coleridge's view of the matter, reporting on it sympathetically, perhaps, but essentially expounding rather than commending it. This is not, however, the case. For one thing, these conditions were not originally formulated by Coleridge but by Mill himself, and where he did quote Coleridge (on the function of the clerisy, for example), it was with entire approval. (Mill's only reservations concerned Coleridge's epistemology and economics.) More important is the fact that Mill chose to reprint the whole of this discussion of the "essential conditions" of society, some fifteen hundred words, in his *System of Logic*, which was first published in 1843 and reissued in seven other editions in the course of his lifetime (one of them at the time he was working on *On Liberty*).[46] The passage appears in the final

45. *Ibid.,* p. 137.

46. The only substantive change in the passages quoted above (pp. 78–79) was introduced in the 1851 edition of the *Logic* and reproduced in *Dissertations and Discussions.* In the first sentence of the second passage, "this discipline" was changed to "the restraining discipline." (Appendix to *Essays on Ethics, Religion and Society,* p. 505.)

book of the *Logic*, in the section on the "Logic of the Moral Sciences." Mill had spoken of the need for a "political ethology," a science of "national character," which would determine the causes of the opinions, feelings, and habits making up the character of a people in any particular time and age.[47] He then presented the passage from the Coleridge essay (apologizing for quoting himself but not mentioning Coleridge or even giving the title of the essay, so that the ideas appear entirely as his own) as an example of the kinds of sociological laws which such a science might be expected to produce. And having reprinted the long passage, he then repeated his conviction that social existence was made possible only by a "disciplining of those more powerful propensities" (the selfish ones) and "subordinating them to a common system of opinions." "The degree of this subordination," he added, "is the measure of the completeness of the social union, and the nature of the common opinions determines its kind."[48]

In 1859, at the very time *On Liberty* was being published, Mill expressed similar views in endorsing a principle advanced by the famous jurist John Austin. Reforms, Austin had said, should always be adapted, if at all possible, to the framework of the existing constitution. Mill observed that this was a subject on which the "knowledge of mankind" spoke most wisely—that even good institutions "cannot dispense with the support afforded by traditional sentiment." The principle of utility, he quoted Austin, generally leads to an "invincible diversity of views." It was therefore all the more necessary to have an "attachment resting on authority and habit to the existing constitution 'in and for itself'." Such an attachment, Mill agreed, was "an almost indispensable condition of the stability of free government."[49]

47. *A System of Logic* (London, 1949), pp. 590–91.
48. *Ibid.*, p. 605.
49. *Essays on Politics and Culture*, p. 346. Apart from "invincible diversity of views" and "in and for itself," the other quotations are from Mill, not Austin.

National character, the principle of allegiance, and the moral discipline of education were not the only means by which Mill sought to curb the selfish propensities of individuals, to elevate the individual character by making it part of a larger consciousness. In some of his early essays, he gave to social classes the same function—and not only the learned and professional classes, the "clerisy," but also the landed and leisured classes.

In his review of the first volume of *Democracy in America*, in 1835, Mill had criticized Tocqueville for exaggerating the dangers of democracy. Five years later, reviewing the second volume, he criticized him for having "confounded the effects of Democracy with the effects of Civilization," for having attributed to democracy the dangers inherent in any modern commercial society.[50] It may seem that Mill was making essentially the same point in both instances, that he was trying to moderate Tocqueville's thesis in order to remove from democracy some of the onus Tocqueville had placed upon it. If this was the implication of the first essay, it was not of the second. For in the latter Mill was in fact extending rather than contracting Tocqueville's thesis. Without making democracy any less onerous, he was making all of modern society onerous for the same reason that democracy was. In England as in America, he pointed out, there was the same tendency toward a leveling and uniformity of condition, a despotism of public opinion, a growing insignificance of individuals relative to the mass. Yet in England this was due not to a democratic, classless society dominated by the mass of the people, but rather to a society which still contained within it distinct classes—an aristocracy and working class as well as a middle class—and in which the middle class, not the mass, was dominant. What England had, in fact, was a "Democracy of the middle

50. *Ibid.*, p. 257.

class."[51] And by its nature the middle class, embodying a bourgeois, commercial spirit, was inimical to a speculative frame of mind, fearful of eccentricity and originality.

So far, in diagnosing the evil of the time, the essays on Tocqueville anticipated some of the themes of *On Liberty*. But at some points they diverged from the later work, and not only in prescribing a cure for the modern malady but in diagnosing the disease itself. In the earlier essays Mill agreed with Tocqueville that one of the baneful aspects of democracy was its tendency to make each man, as Mill put it, "retire within himself, and concentrate his interests, wishes, and pursuits within his own business and house-hold."[52] In effect Mill was suggesting, as Tocqueville had, that individuality was as much a consequence and a fault of democracy as equality:

> *The members of a democratic community are like the sands of the sea-shore, each very minute, and no one adhering to any other. There are no permanent classes, and therefore no esprit de corps; few hereditary fortunes, and therefore few local attachments, or outward objects consecrated by family feeling. A man feels little connexion with his neighbours, little with his ancestors, little with his posterity.*[53]

There were hardly any ties among individuals, Mill continued, save the common bond of country. And in a large country that bond was not sufficient to hold men together. Certainly it was no substitute for the bonds of locality, community, and heritage which had held men together in previous times.

The remedy for this excessive individualism, Mill suggested, was not the denigration of public opinion but rather

51. *Ibid.*, p. 261.
52. *Ibid.*, p. 245.
53. *Ibid.*

the improvement of public opinion, the creation of the "best public opinion." And this would require developing a "great social support for opinions and sentiments different from the mass."[54] Such a support could be found in three classes: the agricultural, the leisured, and the learned classes. The ways in which the leisured and learned classes served to counteract the tendencies of modern society were too obvious, Mill said, to require elaboration. But he did dwell at some length upon the function and importance of the agricultural class. If in America, he pointed out, that class did not have a salutary effect, it was because American farmers were, to all intents and purposes, a commercial class, sharing the mobility and rootlessness of the rest of the population. But in an old country like England, farmers were largely unaffected by the commercial spirit. Attachments were still strong—attachments to particular places and persons, to traditional occupations and the customary rewards and modes of life. Farmers were less impatient than town people, less mobile and restless, less eager for gain and change. They represented the "counterbalancing element" in the national character. As opposed to the commercial classes, they were content with "moderate wishes, tranquil tastes, cultivation of the excitements and enjoyments near at hand, and compatible with their existing position."[55]

Mill used the term "commercial spirit" as distinguished from Tocqueville's "democratic spirit." But he could as well have spoken of it as the individualistic spirit. For much of the commercial spirit, as he described it, derived from the separateness of individuals, the sense that each man was on his own, could determine his own conditions and mode of life, was not bound by ties either to the past or to the present. To a considerable extent, Mill was decrying in the commercial class the very qualities he was to make so much of in *On Liberty:* the "freedom and variety of situa-

54. *Ibid.*, p. 264.
55. *Ibid.*, p. 265.

tions" that were the "two requisites" of individuality.[56] In the Tocqueville essay, freedom and variety—freedom from all ties, a restless desire for change, and the ability to satisfy that desire—were precisely the features of modern society that made for the unfortunate mediocrity of life. And it was to counterbalance these tendencies that he wanted to give greater support to the class which embodied the opposite virtues: moderation, tradition, a resistance to change, a contentment with things as they were.[57]

In some respects, the contrast between *On Liberty* and Mill's other work is so obvious as to require little comment. One need only juxtapose the essential conditions of *On Liberty*—freedom and variety—with the essential condi-

---

56. *On Liberty*, p. 116.

57. In *Dissertations and Discussions* Mill appended to this essay on Tocqueville part of a review written five years later in which he had characterized the democratic spirit in terms similarly at variance with the message of *On Liberty*: "Want of appreciation of distant objects and remote consequences; where an object is desired, want both of an adequate sense of practical difficulties, and of the sagacity necessary for eluding them; disregard of traditions, and of maxims sanctioned by experience; an undervaluing of the importance of fixed rules, when immediate purposes require a departure from them." (*Dissertations and Discussions* [London, 1859], II, 81.)

Mill's argument for a "stationary state," in his *Political Economy*, echoes some of the sentiments of the Tocqueville essay. The ceaseless striving for wealth, the competitive struggle to acquire more of the goods of life, the continual growth both of population and of capital were qualities of a "progressive" economy which then seemed to him to be anything but admirable. In defending the idea of a stationary state, he insisted that this implied "no stationary state of human improvement"; on the contrary, there would be as much, perhaps more, opportunity for mental, moral, and social progress. (*Principles of Political Economy*, ed. V. W. Bladen and J. M. Robson [vols. II–III of *Collected Works*, Toronto, 1965], II, 752–57.) Mill did not specify what limitations on individual liberty would be required to keep in check the striving for wealth, material goods, and status; he was more specific about the limitations necessary for keeping the population in check (see below, pp. 117–18). His favorable attitude toward the stationary state in the *Political Economy* may be compared with the abhorrence he expressed in *On Liberty* (p. 129) for the "stationary" condition of China.

tions of the Coleridge essay—education, allegiance, and nationality; or the virtues celebrated in *On Liberty* with the "counterbalancing" virtues of the agricultural class in the Tocqueville essay. Other points of contrast—his view of human nature, for example—are less immediately obvious but no less important.

In *On Liberty* "desires and impulses," "personal impulses and preferences," "desires and feelings," "natural feeling" and "inclination," "energy" and "strong susceptibilities" constituted the "raw material of human nature." The person with the greater amount of raw material had the larger capacity for "good"; one with the largest stock of "natural feeling" had the greatest potential for "cultivated feeling"; the strongest impulses and susceptibilities were the source of the "most passionate love of virtue" and the "sternest self-control."[58] The metaphor of development had similar implications: a nature that was most abundantly developed, that availed itself most fully of the conditions of freedom and variety, would also be "best" developed, developed to the "highest and most harmonious," the most "complete and consistent whole."[59] And the God whom Mill preferred to the Calvinist God was similarly well disposed to human nature: a benevolent God could only have intended man to use and develop all his natural faculties, not to suppress or deny them.[60]

A quite different conception of human nature emerges from the essay "Nature," written in 1853–54, only months before *On Liberty* although published posthumously. (Per-

58. *On Liberty*, pp. 118–19.

59. *Ibid.*, p. 115. Elsewhere Mill was less tolerant of the idea of development. After reading Sterling's book on Hegel in 1867, Mill wrote to Bain that "conversancy" with Hegel "tends to deprave one's intellect." For some time after finishing Sterling's book, he complained, "all such words as *reflexion, development, evolution*, etc., gave me a sort of sickening feeling which I have not yet entirely got rid of." (*Later Letters*, III, 1324 [Nov. 4, 1867].)

60. *On Liberty*, p. 120.

haps it was because of this discrepancy that Mill chose not to publish it.) In this essay Mill placed human nature in the context of the larger natural order, the order of the physical universe. And the nature of that universe, as Mill then described it, was anything but good. Indeed, it had an infinite, awesome capacity for evil. If the God who created this nature could be presumed to be good, Mill reasoned— in an exact reversal of the argument he used in *On Liberty* —his goodness could only consist in his intention of having that nature "amended, not imitated, by Man."[61] To the extent to which men were rational creatures, they could only try to correct and counteract nature. To do otherwise, to accept nature as good, to take it as a guide or model, would make men as capricious, selfish, mean, and cruel as nature itself.

If it was the duty of man to amend nature, so it was also his "paramount duty . . . to amend himself."[62] For his own natural impulses were no more trustworthy, no more admirable or commendable, than the forces of physical nature. Again—as if to refute in advance his own argument in *On Liberty*—Mill protested against the fallacious reasoning which assumed that because God had endowed men with "impulses" and "stimuli," He therefore "intended, and approved, whatever human beings do." It was a peculiarly modern form of sentimentality, he observed, which "exalts instinct at the expense of reason" and gives greater authority to "unreflecting impulses" than to rationally controlled actions. Against this modern heresy Mill gave it as his own view that "nearly every respectable attribute of humanity is the result not of instinct, but of a victory over instinct." What was valuable in natural man was not his impulse or instinct but his "capacities." And the latter could be realized only by an "eminently artificial discipline." The idea that goodness was natural could only have developed in a

61. *Essays on Ethics, Religion and Society*, p. 391.
62. *Ibid.*, p. 383.

"highly artificial" society, because only after a long course of "artificial education" did good sentiments become so habitual as to arise spontaneously when they were needed.[63] In short, man became civilized not by following nature and his natural impulses but by overcoming nature, by restraining and disciplining his impulses.

Mill carried this argument very far, attacking not only the view that all impulses and instincts were naturally good and therefore worthy of being fully realized, but also more moderate versions of this optimistic position. He criticized those who, while admitting the superiority of reason, were nevertheless sufficiently deferential to nature to think that "every natural inclination must have some sphere of action granted to it, some opening left for its gratification," that "all natural impulses, all propensities sufficiently universal and sufficiently spontaneous to be capable of passing for instincts, must exist for good ends, and ought to be only regulated, not repressed." Against this view he argued that some instincts were simply bad and had to be not "regulated" but "extirpated." Even those instincts which represented the most elementary impulses, instincts necessary to life itself, needed to be "tamed and disciplined"; without some such "artificial training" the most natural and spontaneous impulses would reduce the world to a state of misery, violence, and tyranny, the like of which was found only in the animal kingdom.[64] Virtue was not natural; it was eminently unnatural and notoriously difficult: "The acquisition of virtue has in all ages been accounted a work of labour and difficulty, while the *descensus Averni* on the contrary is of proverbial facility; and it assuredly requires in most persons a greater conquest over a greater number of natural inclinations to become eminently virtuous than transcendently vicious."[65]

63. *Ibid.*, pp. 392–93.
64. *Ibid.*, pp. 397–98.
65. *Ibid.*, p. 401.

If Mill at this time gave no more credence to orthodox religion than to nature as a guide to morality, he did recognize the need for some religion to elevate men above their private passions and wills. In the essay "Utility of Religion," written immediately after "Nature" and before *On Liberty*, Mill defined religion as "the strong and earnest direction of the emotions and desires towards an ideal object, recognized as of the highest excellence, and as rightfully paramount over all selfish objects of desire."[66] That ideal Mill found best expressed in Comte's "Religion of Humanity."

Mill never went so far as Comte in prescribing the structure of the Religion of Humanity—the forms of worship, ritual, and hierarchy which would support it. Nor did he allow to it the degree of authority that Comte did, making it binding upon all members of society and giving it a decisive role in the system of social controls. But he did share with Comte a sense of the urgent need for the transcendence of self. And this purpose the Religion of Humanity admirably served. "It carries the thoughts and feelings out of self, and fixes them on an unselfish object, loved and pursued as an end for its own sake." The "unselfish object" to which it directed men was the good of other men, the community as a whole. The function of morality had always been the "amelioration of human nature," the subordination of selfish feelings to unselfish ones. The Religion of Humanity performed this function more adequately than any mere system of morality; and it had the advantage over conventional religion in making mankind rather than God the object of unselfish feelings.[67]

In his diary at this time Mill noted that the only doctrine worth laboring at was a "Philosophy of Life" that would provide a better alternative than orthodox religion to a doctrine of mere "self-indulgence." The best thing, indeed the only good thing he found in Comte's second treatise, the

66. *Ibid.*, p. 422.
67. *Ibid.*, pp. 422–23.

System of Positive Polity, was his rigorous attempt to supply such an alternative in the form of the Religion of Humanity. This religion would cultivate to the highest degree the "sentiments of fraternity with all our fellow beings, past, present, and to come." It would make the "happiness and dignity of this collective body" the standard for all actions and judgments, for imagination and noble ideals. Mill could only hope that this religion managed to obtain as firm a hold on mankind, "as great a power of shaping their usages, their institutions, and their education," as other religions had done.[68]

Years later, in his book on Comte written in 1865, Mill tempered his criticism of the *System* with an appreciation of the impulse behind that work. Comte, he said, had wanted to direct all education and moral discipline to the single object of making "altruism" (a word of Comte's invention, Mill pointed out) predominate over "egoism." If Comte had merely meant by this that "egoism is bound, and should be taught, always to give way to the well-understood interests of enlarged altruism," no one who "acknowledges any morality at all" could object to it. Unfortunately, Comte went further than this, seeking not only to "strengthen the social affections by constant habit and by referring all our actions to them, but, as far as possible, to deaden the personal passions and propensities by desuetude."[69] It was only the negative proposition that Mill found objectionable; the positive one—the strengthening of "social affections"—he entirely endorsed. Still later, in his last completed essay, "Theism," Mill went so far as to suggest that the Religion of Humanity be strengthened by incorporating into it some elements of conventional religion, including a belief in the deity. Religion would then better serve its purpose, which was to make the welfare of all of humanity an "obligatory limit to every selfish aim, an end for the

68. *Letters* (Elliot edn.), II, 362–63 (Diary, Jan. 23–24, 1854).
69. *Essays on Ethics, Religion and Society*, p. 335.

direct promotion of which no sacrifice can be too great."[70]

In *On Liberty*, by contrast, Comte appeared simply and unqualifiedly as the arch example of the despotic reformer. After writing the first draft of the essay, Mill explained why it should be expanded and published as a volume: "Almost all the projects of social reformers in these days are really *liberticide*—Comte, particularly so."[71] This distrust of Comte, was reflected in *On Liberty*, where he was described as aiming at "establishing (though by moral more than by legal appliances) a despotism of society over the individual, surpassing anything contemplated in the political ideal of the most rigid disciplinarian among the ancient philosophers."[72]

In one sense it is odd that Mill should have singled out Comte in this fashion; no other contemporary thinker was criticized by name. It is especially odd since just about the time Mill was writing the first draft of the essay on liberty, he wrote a letter to a French disciple of Comte explaining that the "practical doctrines" of Comte had not made "the least headway" in England. "He is not known, esteemed, even attacked as a philosopher. On social questions he is simply not taken into account."[73] In actual fact, then, it would seem that Comte was hardly the menace—or at least that Mill himself did not take him to be such—that he was made out to be in *On Liberty*.

Yet it is fitting that Mill should have treated Comte as he did in *On Liberty*, for this work was totally incompatible not only with the extremes of Comte's position but with the whole of it, with everything Comte was attempting to do— much of which Mill himself, on other occasions, praised so highly. The very idea of a Religion of Humanity, even

70. *Ibid.*, p. 488.
71. *Later Letters*, I, 294 (to Harriet Mill, Jan. 15, 1855).
72. *On Liberty*, p. 76.
73. *Later Letters*, I, 237 (JSM to Barbot de Chément, Aug. 7, 1854).

shorn of its authoritarianism, was antithetical to a philosophy which recognized no higher, no more worthy subject than the individual, which made the individual the repository of wisdom and virtue, and which made the freedom of the individual the sole aim of social policy. Where the Religion of Humanity besought individuals to subordinate their selfish, egotistical interests to the good of others, the collective good of humanity, *On Liberty* encouraged them to prize and cultivate their personal desires, impulses, inclinations, and wills, to see these as the source of all good, the force behind individual and social well-being.

Just as Comte in the *System* carried his doctrine to one extreme, so Mill in *On Liberty* carried it to another. If Comte was not content to "strengthen the social affections" but strove instead to "deaden the personal passions and propensities," Mill tried so strenuously to enliven the personal passions and propensities that he did little to strengthen the social affections; certainly he did nothing to encourage them "by constant habit and by referring all our actions to them." *On Liberty* did not teach, as Mill had counseled elsewhere, that egoism should "give way to the well-understood interests of enlarged altruism." It did not make an "ideal object" paramount over "all selfish objects of desire." It did not offer a creed of "fraternity" in place of the prevailing creed of "self-indulgence."[74] It represented, in short, not merely a rejection of all that, from Mill's point of view, was worst in Comte; it represented a rejection of all that Mill elsewhere took to be the best in Comte—community, fraternity, and morality.

74. See above, footnotes 66–69, pp. 88–89.

THE LIMITS OF INDIVIDUALITY
AND SOCIETY

Having gone so far, in the first three chapters of *On Liberty*, in extending the liberty of the individual to its outer limit, Mill now returned to a more detailed and systematic examination of the limit itself. What, he asked, is the "rightful limit to the sovereignty of the individual over himself?"[1] What part of life should be assigned to individuality and what part to society?

Mill's initial answer was unexceptionable: to individuality belonged that part of the individual's life in which the individual was chiefly interested, to society that part in which society was chiefly interested. It was a formula most liberals, including the "other" Mill, could happily endorse. In elaborating upon it, however, Mill introduced concepts and distinctions which were meant to bear out the specific doctrine of *On Liberty* but which, as often as not, raised problems of their own. The present analysis of his argument, while trying to respect its logic and coherence, inevitably reflects some of the confusion in Mill's own thought.

In specifying the limits of individuality, Mill allowed society to impose two conditions upon the individual: the individual's conduct must not injure the interests of another

1. *On Liberty*, p. 131.

—"or rather, certain interests, which either by express legal provision or by tacit understanding, ought to be considered as rights"; and each individual had to bear his share of the "labours and sacrifices incurred for defending society or its members from injury and molestation." These two conditions society was justified in enforcing "at all costs"—that is, by an exaction of either legal or social penalties. In addition, society could proceed (although in this case only by social penalties, not by law) against actions which were "hurtful to others, or wanting in due consideration for their welfare," but which did not actually violate their "constituted rights."[2]

Society, in short, had jurisdiction over any part of a person's conduct which "affects prejudicially the interests of others." It remained "open to discussion" whether society should, in any particular case, exercise this jurisdiction. What was not open to discussion, and what never came under society's jurisdiction, was that part of an individual's conduct which "affects the interests of no persons besides himself, or needs not affect them unless they like (all the persons concerned being of full age, and the ordinary amount of understanding)." Here the individual enjoyed "perfect freedom, legal and social," to do what he wanted to do and to take the consequences of his actions.[3]

The conditions upon which society could intervene obviously hinged upon the definition of "right," "interest," and "injury." But these were either not defined by Mill or were only vaguely defined in terms of each other. Thus, "certain interests" were "rights" either by "legal provision" or by "tacit understanding."[4] But "legal provision" and

---

2. *Ibid.*, p. 132. Earlier, Mill had claimed to "forgo any advantage which could be derived to my argument from the idea of abstract right, as a thing independent of utility" (p. 74). "Constituted rights" were presumably legal rather than "abstract"—i.e., metaphysical or "natural."

3. *Ibid.*, p. 132.

4. *Ibid.*

"tacit understanding" beg the question, which was precisely the problem of what the law should undertake to prohibit and what society should tacitly understand as being prohibited. At one point Mill gave examples of "acts injurious to others": "encroachment on their rights; infliction on them of any loss or damage not justified by his own rights; falsehood or duplicity in dealing with them; even selfish abstinence from defending them against injury." These, he said, were "fit objects of moral reprobation, and, in grave cases, of moral retribution and punishment."[5] But why did the first instance—"encroachment" on the rights of others—call only for moral sanctions and not for legal ones? And did the second—an injury "not justified by his own rights"— imply that one's own rights always took precedence over those of another even to the injury of the other? And did not the final example—"abstinence from defending" another against injury—come under the earlier provision requiring every individual to share in the "labours and sacrifices" of defending others from injury, in which case was it not subject to legal as well as moral punishment?

Even the principle of "perfect freedom, legal and social," in all matters not affecting others, was more equivocal than it might at first seem. For in denying that his was a doctrine of "selfish indifference," in which people concerned themselves with others only so long as their own interests were involved, Mill proceeded to allow for so large an expression of concern for others that it threatened to impinge upon that "perfect freedom." His doctrine, he insisted, required more rather than less "disinterested exertion to promote the good of others." "Disinterested exertion," however, should take the form of "conviction and persuasion" rather than "compulsion." Men should "help," "encourage," and "stimulate" others to distinguish the better from the worse and to choose the former in preference to the latter. But no one

5. *Ibid.*, p. 135.

was warranted in "saying" to another that he should do otherwise than as he chose to do. Considerations and exhortations might be "offered" to another, even "obtruded" on him, but not so as to "constrain" him. We should all feel free to judge one another, to warn one another of our judgment (indeed, this "good office" should be more freely rendered than was customary), to act on that judgment (by avoiding his society or favoring another over him), even to caution others against him if we think his conduct or conversation likely to have a "pernicious effect" upon them. In all these ways, Mill admitted, an individual might "suffer very severe penalties at the hands of others for faults which directly concern only himself." But so long as these penalties were the "spontaneous consequences of the faults themselves" rather than "purposely inflicted on him for the sake of punishment," they were entirely proper and the individual had no cause for complaint.[6]

Mill further distinguished between "moral vices" and "self-regarding faults." Moral vices were the "dispositions" which led to acts injurious to others—cruelty, malice, ill nature, envy, dissimulation, insincerity, irascibility, resentment, pride, love of domination, egotism. These dispositions, since they affected others, were as much subject to moral reprobation and retribution as the acts themselves. Self-regarding faults, on the other hand, were not "immoralities" because they affected only oneself, one's own dignity, or respect, or development, or prudence. The distinction, Mill insisted, was not merely "nominal." Self-regarding faults may be displeasing to us, may cause us to express our displeasure or stand aloof from another, but would not justify us in making the other's life "uncomfortable." We may regard the other as an object of "pity" or "dislike" but not of "anger" or "resentment." We may leave him to himself but not look upon him as an "enemy of society." We may

6. *Ibid.*, pp. 132–34.

inflict upon him no suffering "except what may incidentally follow from our using the same liberty in the regulation of our own affairs which we allow him in his."[7]

At this point Mill took cognizance of the basic difficulty in his position. There were those, he said, who would deny the possibility of distinguishing between that part of a person's life which affected only himself and that part which affected others. No one, it could be argued, was an isolated being; anything harmful to one person was bound to affect others as well. A man who injured his own property necessarily injured those who derived their support from it and the community whose resources were thereby diminished. A man who permitted his bodily or mental faculties to deteriorate visited that deterioration upon his dependents and upon the community to which he had obligations. A man who indulged himself in vices and follies that were not directly harmful to others harmed them indirectly by his example.

Mill also confronted the more serious argument that even if the consequences of an action were entirely confined to an individual, even if there were such a thing as a completely self-regarding action, society might be supposed to have a responsibility for those doing harm to themselves, just as it had a responsibility for children and minors. This argument is so central to Mill's doctrine that it deserves to be quoted at length. For here was the real alternative to his doctrine. It was not the absolute denial of liberty and individuality (as he had earlier implied); nor the imposition of conformity by means of legal penalties and physical force; but rather the use of social sanctions whose legitimacy derived from long experience and an accepted body of "moral or prudential truth." In stating the counterposition so clearly, Mill pointed to the essential difference be-

7. *Ibid.*, pp. 135-36.

tween his doctrine of liberty and the conventional one. He
described the reasoning behind the familiar liberal position:

> *And even . . . if the consequences of misconduct should*
> *be confined to the vicious or thoughtless individual,*
> *ought society to abandon to their own guidance those*
> *who are manifestly unfit for it? If protection against*
> *themselves is confessedly due to children and persons*
> *under age, is not society equally bound to afford it to*
> *persons of mature years who are equally incapable of*
> *self-government? If gambling, or drunkenness, or in-*
> *continence, or idleness, or uncleanliness, are as injuri-*
> *ous to happiness, and as great a hindrance to improve-*
> *ment, as many or most of the acts prohibited by law,*
> *why (it may be asked) should not law, so far as is*
> *consistent with practicability and social convenience,*
> *endeavour to repress these also? And as a supplement to*
> *the unavoidable imperfections of law, ought not opin-*
> *ion at least to organise a powerful police against these*
> *vices, and visit rigidly with social penalties those who*
> *are known to practise them? There is no question here*
> *(it may be said) about restricting individuality, or im-*
> *peding the trial of new and original experiments in*
> *living. The only things it is sought to prevent are things*
> *which have been tried and condemned from the begin-*
> *ning of the world until now; things which experience*
> *has shown not to be useful or suitable to any person's*
> *individuality. There must be some length of time and*
> *amount of experience after which a moral or pruden-*
> *tial truth may be regarded as established: and it is merely*
> *desired to prevent generation after generation from*
> *falling over the same precipice which has been fatal to*
> *their predecessors.*[8]

8. *Ibid.*, p. 137.

This passage represents a turning point in the chapter. For until this point it might have appeared that Mill was proposing a looser construction of his doctrine, allowing a larger latitude to society, at least in respect to social sanctions, than had been evident in the preceding chapters. But now, confronted with a prudent and plausible alternative to his doctrine, he rejected this alternative and he retreated to a strict construction of his doctrine. The case of drunkenness and the other examples which occupy the rest of this chapter were designed to distinguish his doctrine of liberty from the more conventional one. These examples might more logically have been included in the final chapter, "Applications." Their inclusion here suggests that Mill wanted to shift the weight of his argument back where it had originally been—on the side of the individual as against society.

Drunkenness, Mill now insisted, was properly subject to "moral disapprobation" (legal punishment was never at issue) only when it resulted in the violation of a "distinct and assignable obligation" to another person—the inability of the drunkard to pay his debts or to support his family.[9] But in this case, it was not drunkenness itself that was morally reprehensible but only its consequences. Had the same consequences been caused by a socially acceptable act —had a man neglected his family, for example, in order to invest all his money in business—he would have been equally culpable. For the same reason, the soldier or policeman drunk on duty should be punished, while the ordinary drunkard should not.

The general principle Mill deduced from this example helps elucidate his idea of injury. Only, he said, when there was a "definite damage, or a definite risk of damage" to another person or to the public could the drunkard be subject to society's sanctions, moral or legal. Short of that, if

9. *Ibid.*, p. 138.

the injury were "merely contingent," violating no "specific duty" to the public and occasioning no "perceptible hurt to any assignable individual except himself," it was not, within the terms of his definition, an injury at all. Rather it was an "inconvenience," one which society could afford for the sake of the "greater good of human freedom."[10] By qualifying the idea of injury in this way—"definite," "specific," "perceptible," "assignable"—Mill did not entirely eliminate the ambiguity from it, but he did try to construe it as strictly as possible. It may also be noted that in the course of this definition of injury, the word "interests" disappears, being too vague, too elastic, for his purpose.

The example of drunkenness also prompted Mill to comment on, and reject, the argument that society had a duty to encourage its members to observe the "ordinary standard of rational conduct." Society, he said, had "absolute power" over individuals in the entire period of their childhood and minority. If it could not make them rational then, it had only itself to blame and should not now be permitted to do by sanctions or punishment what it could not earlier do by means of education. Nor did he credit the argument that society had to be protected from the bad example of the vicious and self-indulgent. He admitted that such an example might have a "pernicious" effect on others, "especially" when the example was of wrongdoing committed with impunity. But the latter case, coming under the category of other-regarding conduct, would in any event be punished. Where there was no actual wrongdoing to others, where the person was only harming himself by his vicious conduct, society had no cause to interfere. Besides, Mill added, the visible evidence of the harm he was inflicting on himself, would, "on the whole," be more salutary than injurious to those observing it.[11] He did not explicitly deal with those cases which escaped his "especially" and "on the

10. *Ibid.*
11. *Ibid.*, pp. 139-40.

whole" qualifications—where the bad example was not of
wrongdoing to others or where the evidence of self-harm
was not such as to have a salutary effect on the observer.
Such cases, presumably, came under the category of "in-
conveniences" which society had to tolerate for the sake
of the greater good of freedom.

An incidental but interesting aspect of Mill's argument is
the assumption that vicious or self-indulgent conduct would
generally have such "painful or degrading consequences" to
the individual as to be clearly visible to others and serve as
a warning to them. The benign view of human nature, evident at one point in the preceding chapter,[12] has its parallel
here in a providential view of human conduct, in which
immorality redounds immediately, directly, and manifestly
to the disadvantage of the perpetrator himself. If Mill did
not believe in an avenging God, he seems to have believed,
at least "on the whole," in an avenging moral order.

Having rejected one or another reason for the intervention of society in self-regarding affairs, Mill went on to
what he took to be the strongest argument against such
intervention—the fact that when society did intervene, it
tended to do so on the wrong side. Public opinion was in
no position to judge what was wrong or right. It could
only apply to the individual its own standards, the standards of the majority, and it tended to be unduly offended
by any deviations from those standards. Nor did it limit
itself to those judgments which could be said to be the
products of "universal experience"; it always assumed that
its own experience was universal. What was universal, Mill
found, was the propensity to "extend the bounds of what
may be called moral police, until it encroaches on the most
unquestionably legitimate liberty of the individual."[13] It was
this "moral police" that had at all costs to be resisted.

The examples Mill gave of the operation of a "moral

12. See above, p. 64.
13. *On Liberty*, p. 141.

police" may seem odd to the reader; with one exception they were all concerned with religious rather than moral practices. The exception was the temperance societies which sought to prohibit the sale of liquor on the grounds that drinking was not a private but a social act involving the "social rights" of others. Mill condemned the doctrine of social rights as a monstrous violation of liberty since anything could be prohibited in its name: "The doctrine ascribes to all mankind a vested interest in each other's moral, intellectual, and even physical perfection, to be defined by each claimant according to his own standard."[14]

Apart from this, his other examples were drawn from religion and had little to do with morality in the usual sense.[15] He cited the Moslem prohibition against the eating of pork, the Catholic persecution of Protestant sects, the Puritans' enforcement of Sabbatarian decrees, and the refusal to acknowledge the legality of Mormon polygamy. Each of these represented a deeply held belief on the part of the majority of the society, and each resulted in the imposition of that belief on the entire population. If society was at all justified in encroaching upon the private sphere, Mill reasoned, it was justified in enforcing a religious orthodoxy even to the point of persecution.

By choosing these cases, Mill was assured of an easy victory. In his own time (still more, of course, in ours), religion was generally regarded as the most private area of life. The complicated nature of other beliefs and practices, the difficulty of drawing a line between self-regarding and other-regarding acts, applied least of all to religion. To argue persuasively, as Mill did, against a "moral police" in religious matters, like arguing against religious persecution in a secular age, required no great feat of imagination or

14. *Ibid.*, p. 146.
15. The only other example, apart from temperance legislation, which might be regarded as non-religious was the sumptuary legislation favored by some democrats—but even this was quasi-religious in the context of Puritanism.

courage. Above all, it did not require a doctrine of liberty such as Mill was proposing.[16]

Earlier, Mill had raised more serious theoretical objections to his doctrine, objections dealing with the gray area in which the interests of the individual and society were not sharply demarcated, where the exercise of individual liberty did impinge upon others, not to the extent of violating their legal rights or causing visible injury but in more subtle and profound ways. But the examples he now cited were not of this nature. They belonged rather to an area that was least controversial, where the issues could most easily be drawn in black and white. And even his one example of "social rights," the example of the temperance societies, was grossly oversimplified. Whatever the merits of temperance as a solution to the problem of drunkenness, the problem itself was surely, in Mill's time, of great social urgency. To speak of the attempt to curb drunkenness—not an occasional bout of excessive drinking nor the isolated case of the habitual drunkard, but drunkenness on a widespread scale and to an inordinate degree—as the imposition of a standard of "perfection" is surely a travesty of the issue.

Mill concluded this chapter on a note that seems equally bizarre. For two pages he engaged in an impassioned protest against the "persecution" of the Mormons. Not that he himself, he made it clear, had anything but abhorrence for the institution of polygamy, which was itself a violation of liberty, half the community being enchained to the other half with no recognition of reciprocal obligations. But to outlaw polygamy, he insisted, was to make of the Mormons martyrs of liberty. By a process of reasoning which is rather obscure, he concluded that a civilization which was afraid of succumbing to barbarism (presumably the barbarism of the Mormons) must have become too degenerate to save itself or to be worth saving. "It can only go from bad to

---

16. Cf. Mill's use of religious examples in connection with the freedom of discussion (above, pp. 27–29).

worse, until destroyed and regenerated (like the Western Empire) by energetic barbarians."[17] If one is surprised to find the example of the Mormons looming so large in Mill's case for liberty, one is even more startled by so apocalyptic a conclusion.

SINCE THE SUBJECT of this chapter, the proper limits of individuality and of society, overlaps with other chapters, some of the points raised elsewhere would be pertinent here as well. One issue, however, is especially relevant, and that is the distinction between self-regarding and other-regarding actions.

In *On Liberty* Mill alluded to those critics of his doctrine who would "refuse to admit" the distinction between conduct affecting only oneself and conduct affecting others.[18] Elsewhere Mill himself objected precisely to this distinction. In his *Logic*, for example, he recognized that the great difficulty in discovering moral and social laws was the fact that all the phenomena in any society were inextricably interrelated with each other. No part of society could be adequately described in isolation from any other part since whatever affected one part affected every other as well.

> *Whatever affects, in an appreciable degree, any one element of the social state, affects through it all the other elements. . . . We can never either understand in theory or command in practice the condition of a society in any one respect, without taking into consideration its condition in all other respects. There is no social phenomenon which is not more or less influenced by every other part of the condition of the same society, and therefore by every cause which is influencing any other of the contemporaneous social phenomena.*[19]

17. *On Liberty*, p. 149.
18. *Ibid.*, p. 136.
19. *A System of Logic*, p. 586.

In *Utilitarianism* Mill confronted a different problem, but one which similarly undermined the distinction between a self-regarding and an other-regarding sphere. Within the framework of a much modified and qualified utilitarianism, he had to derive a principle of social morality from the principle of private utility. And rejecting, as he did, the idea of an intuitive or innate moral sense, he had to find some other basis for moral obligation. His solution was to claim that the moral sense, although not intuitive or innate, was nonetheless "natural" since it was a "natural outgrowth" from man's nature. If it were not to that degree natural, morality might be inculcated and nurtured by a careful system of education, but it could also be destroyed by the corrosive effect of analysis. Fortunately, however, man possessed a "powerful natural sentiment" which provided a firm foundation for the development of morality.

> *This firm foundation is that of the social feelings of mankind; the desire to be in unity with our fellow creatures, which is already a powerful principle in human nature, and happily one of those which tend to become stronger, even without express inculcation, from the influences of advancing civilization. The social state is at once so natural, so necessary, and so habitual to man, that, except in some unusual circumstances or by an effort of voluntary abstraction, he never conceives himself otherwise than as a member of a body; and this association is riveted more and more, as mankind are further removed from the state of savage independence.*[20]

As society developed, this feeling of unity increased. Each person came to see the interests of others as his own; he recognized in himself a "collective interest" which he

20. *Utilitarianism,* in *Essays on Ethics, Religion and Society,* p. 231.

increasingly acted upon. This collective interest, in turn, fostered a sense of collective feeling. Not only did each individual develop a strong interest in promoting the good of others; he also came to "identify his *feelings*" with the good of others. "He comes, as though instinctively, to be conscious of himself as a being who *of course* pays regard to others. The good of others becomes to him a thing naturally and necessarily to be attended to, like any of the physical conditions of our existence." Every step in civilization advanced these sentiments of common interests, feelings, and sympathy. At every point they became more natural, so that more and more the opposition of interests gave way to a feeling of unity. The optimum condition was one in which this feeling of unity was taught as a "religion," with the "whole force of education, of institutions, and of opinions" directed to this end, so that every person from infancy was "surrounded on all sides both by the profession and by the practice of it."[21]

But even in the present less ideal state of affairs, Mill was confident that there was enough "social feeling" to make individuals think themselves something other than "struggling rivals" for happiness. "The deeply-rooted conception which every individual even now has of himself as a social being, tends to make him feel it one of his natural wants that there should be harmony between his feelings and aims and those of his fellow creatures." He might still have a larger stock of selfish feeling than of social feeling. But whatever the degree of social feeling, it was experienced by him as natural, not something "despotically imposed by the power of society."[22]

Earlier in this study of utilitarianism, Mill had arrived, by a curious amalgam of Bentham and Jesus, at the conclusion that the principle of utility was nothing other than the golden rule. "To do as one would be done by, and to love

21. *Ibid.*, pp. 231–32. Italics are Mill's.
22. *Ibid.*, pp. 232–33.

one's neighbour as oneself, constitute the ideal perfection of utilitarian morality." The golden rule could be promoted by two means: "laws and social arrangements" which would make the interests of individuals conform to those of society as a whole; and "education and opinion," which would inculcate in the mind of every individual an "indissoluble association between his own happiness and the good of the whole; especially between his own happiness and the practice of such modes of conduct, negative and positive, as regard for the universal happiness prescribes." This dual strategy—the manipulation of legislation and institutions on the one hand and of education and public opinion on the other—would have a dual effect: the negative effect of making it impossible for the individual to conceive of his own happiness in conduct opposed to the general good; and the positive effect of making him want to promote the general good. By these means, it would come about that a "direct impulse to promote the general good may be in every individual one of the habitual motives of action, and the sentiments connected therewith may fill a large and prominent place in every human being's sentient existence."[23]

It may be argued that there is no real contradiction between *Utilitarianism* and *On Liberty*—that in the first he was describing the principles of morality and that in the second he was not denying those principles but only denying to society the right to impose them upon the individual. Unfortunately, this view of the matter is not borne out by the works themselves. For in *Utilitarianism* Mill clearly gave to society a large and positive role in the promotion of morality. Morality may have had its beginnings in the nature of man, but it required all the resources of society—laws and institutions, education and public opinion—to bring it to fruition. Since it was not innate, morality had to be developed, and its development was the result of

23. *Ibid.*, p. 218.

"external" as well as "internal" sanctions.[24]

In *On Liberty*, morality had also to be developed, but here it was presumed to develop internally, by the unfolding of the individual's nature. And here the development was furthered not by encouraging a sense of unity, sympathy, common interests, and common feelings, but quite the contrary—by encouraging variety, diversity, individuality, all that was unique to each individual, that differentiated him from other men and from society at large. Moreover, so far from seeking legal and social sanctions—laws and institutions, education and public opinion—to promote morality, to develop the social sense, Mill would have withdrawn such sanctions as currently existed (apart from those required to prevent injury).

The primary goods in *Utilitarianism* were morality and a sense of unity; the primary goods in *On Liberty* were liberty and individuality. In *Utilitarianism* Mill's purpose was precisely to overcome the separateness of individuals, to make the "social state" as natural, habitual, and compelling as the individual, private state was in *On Liberty*. One of the happy effects of an advancing civilization, he found in *Utilitarianism*, was the tendency to "rivet" the bonds of association and remove man from a state of "savage independence," to make him other than a "selfish egotist" whose concerns were centered in his own "miserable individuality."[25] It was not thus that he spoke of independence and individuality in *On Liberty*.

Another passage in *Utilitarianism* is so far from the spirit of *On Liberty* as to be reminiscent of Hegel:

> *For the truth is, that the idea of penal sanction, which is the essence of law, enters not only into the conception of injustice, but into that of any kind of wrong. We do not call anything wrong, unless we mean to*

24. *Ibid.*, p. 228.
25. *Ibid.*, pp. 231, 216.

*imply that a person ought to be punished in some way
or other for doing it; if not by law, by the opinion
of his fellow creatures; if not by opinion, by the reproaches of his own conscience. This seems the real
turning point of the distinction between morality and
simple expediency.*[26]

By associating morality with punishment, Mill was giving
morality an existential—"actual," Hegel would say—reality;
he was rooting it in the institutions of society and the state,
ratifying and validating it as only the law and popular opinion could do. In *On Liberty* he deliberately dissociated
morality and punishment, leaving morality dependent on
nothing more than the "reproaches" of the individual's
conscience.

Earlier, in his *Logic*, Mill had posed even more sharply
the ethical doctrine that was in such dramatic contrast to
On Liberty: "Hence it is said with truth, that none but a
person of confirmed virtue is completely free."[27] If this
sentiment (and much else in this section of the *Logic*)
evokes echoes of Spinoza, the discussion of morality in
Utilitarianism recalls the famous dictum of Aristotle: "The
best man is not he who exercises his virtue toward himself;
but he who exercises it toward another."[28]

The fact that Mill's other works are so richly evocative
of other philosophical traditions is yet another indication of
the pronounced difference between the "other" Mill and the
Mill of *On Liberty*. It is also suggestive of the profound
tension of thought under which Mill himself labored.
Whatever difficulties one may find in the internal logic of
Utilitarianism or in that of *On Liberty*, the problem of reconciling the two works might well take priority over all
those other difficulties.

26. *Ibid.*, p. 246.
27. *Logic*, p. 551.
28. Aristotle, *Ethics*, bk. V, chap. I.

V

APPLICATIONS

THE FINAL CHAPTER of *On Liberty* was meant to clarify Mill's doctrine by providing concrete "applications" of it. If some of the examples introduced new qualifications and complications, these are often as revealing as the doctrine itself. For the examples were borderline ones, and Mill's reasons for assigning them to the sphere of the individual or to that of society bring his purpose and principle into clearer focus.

The first example drew attention to one aspect of the doctrine he had not earlier dwelt upon. Conduct injurious to the interests of others, he had consistently maintained, came within the province of society. He now considered a circumstance which was exactly of that order and yet which did not warrant the interference of society. This was the case of the individual who succeeded in a competitive situation—an examination or profession—to the necessary disadvantage of another; yet society did not try to prevent or punish that injury, because the loser in that competitive situation did not have a "right, either legal or moral," to immunity from the consequences of his loss.[1]

Another category of actions was analyzed in quite differ-

1. *On Liberty*, p. 150.

ent terms. This comprised the entire field of trade. "Trade is a social act," Mill flatly asserted. Since it necessarily involved the interests of several persons, sometimes society as a whole, it properly came within the province of society.[2] For this reason, governments had once thought it their duty to fix prices, regulate the manufacture of goods, and otherwise determine the conditions of trade. More recently people had come to believe that the price and quality of goods were better left to the free determination of the marketplace. But this doctrine of free trade rested on grounds "different from, though equally solid with," the principle of liberty: "Restrictions on trade, or on production for purposes of trade, are indeed restraints; and all restraint, *qua* restraint, is an evil: but the restraints in question affect only that part of conduct which society is competent to restrain, and are wrong solely because they do not really produce the results which it is desired to produce by them."[3]

The governing principle here, Mill seemed to be suggesting, was not liberty but expediency. Society had the right to interfere in matters of trade, but should exercise that right only if that happened to be the best way to attain the desired results. It was this consideration, he said, that determined such questions as how much government control was necessary to prevent fraud by adulteration or to protect the health and safety of workers in dangerous occupations. The issue of liberty entered these cases only insofar as it was always better, other things being equal, to leave people alone than to control them. Other restraints on trade, however, Mill condemned as violations of liberty: temperance laws, the prohibition of the import of opium into China, restrictions on the sale of poisons. In these latter cases, the intention of the law was to make it impossible or difficult to obtain a commodity. These restraints Mill ob-

2. *Ibid.*
3. *Ibid.*, pp. 150–51.

jected to "not as infringements on the liberty of the producer or seller, but on that of the buyer."[4]

This paragraph, dealing with a large and crucial aspect of the relations of the individual and society, raises more problems than it solves. If trade was a social act within the legitimate province of society, in what sense was a restraint of trade "*qua* restraint," an "evil"? Would Mill also have called it "evil" for society to exercise restraints in other social situations—for example, in imprisoning a convicted criminal? Why, in any case, did he call trade a "social act," thus excluding it from the governance of the principle of liberty, only to reintroduce that principle in certain aspects of trade (such as the purchase of poison)? Would it not have been more consistent to say that the doctrine of liberty operated in trade as in all matters and that society's intervention was warranted only in cases of injury? Would this not have covered the situations of adulteration and safety regulations? Why, furthermore, was a restraint on the buyer an infringement of liberty whereas a restraint on the seller or producer was not? And was it not a restraint on the buyer, and therefore "evil," to prevent him from purchasing an adulterated product, assuming it was properly labeled and he knew what he was buying? Would not the principle of *caveat emptor* have been more in accord with the doctrine of liberty?

Mill's reasoning on this subject seems so tortuous, his distinctions so arbitrary, one suspects them of being completely *ad hoc*, contrived to legitimize the particular restraints he had decided in advance were necessary and to illegitimize all other restraints as evil. In principle, Mill could not have denied to trade the status of a "social act"; if there was any warrant for a distinction between self-regarding and other-regarding activities, trade had to fall in the latter category. But in practice Mill wanted to re-

4. *Ibid.*, p. 151.

strict that area as much as possible. Thus his initial bold statement, "trade is a social act," which seemed to augur so large an amount of social control, was whittled down until it allowed only for limited and specific controls on producers and sellers. The buying side of the trade transaction —even when the commodity was potentially dangerous, as in the case of liquor, opium, and poison—remained firmly within the province of the individual and therefore entirely governed by the principle of liberty. Whatever logical inconsistencies there were in his argument, Mill's intention was clear: to permit government to intervene in specific instances without making of intervention a general principle or practice—without, in fact, making of trade a "social act."

In his analysis of specific cases, Mill went to great lengths to preserve the liberty of the individual even at the risk of injury (possibly even death) to the same individual whose liberty was being so carefully protected. Allowing in general that government had the duty to prevent crimes and accidents, he found this preventive function so frequently abused that he sought to restrict it as much as possible. In the case of poisons, for example, which had legitimate as well as illegitimate uses, he thought it proper to require labeling and a register of sale (neither of which interfered with the liberty of the buyer), but not medical prescriptions (which might make the product too expensive or difficult to obtain and thus constitute an infringement of liberty). Similarly, a man crossing an unsafe bridge could be forcibly restrained only if there was no time to warn him of the danger; "for liberty consists in doing what one desires, and he does not desire to fall into the river."[5] But if there was time to warn him, he could not be prevented from taking whatever risk he chose to take, provided he was an adult in possession of his senses. In the latter instance, Mill

5. *Ibid.*, p. 152.

noted that a warning would suffice if there were a danger rather than a certainty of mischief. But he did not say what his position would be if there were a certainty of mischief. What if a person desired to fall into the river, to commit suicide? Was he not at liberty to do what he desired?

Mill did cite one case that might have a bearing upon the question of the liberty of the suicide. No contract, he declared, however freely entered into, was binding if it sold a man into slavery. "The principle of freedom cannot require that he should be free not to be free. It is not freedom to be allowed to alienate his freedom."[6] This could be extended to mean that a man should not be free to alienate his own being, to take his life. But it is not clear that Mill intended this. It might be significant that he chose, as the "extreme case,"[7] slavery, the denial of freedom, rather than suicide, the denial of life. Given the value he attached to freedom, it is likely that suicide may have seemed to him to be a less extreme form of self-denial.

The same logic that left a man free to cross an unsafe bridge if he so desired, also left him free to drink whatever and as much as he desired, so long as he caused no injury to another. Such "self-regarding misconduct" was not to be "meddled with," either by way by punishment or prevention.[8] Earlier, Mill had specified the conditions under which drunkenness ceased to be self-regarding and could be punished: if, for example, it led to injury to others or the failure to meet one's legal obligations. Now he added other forms of permissible control: for instance, someone already convicted of a crime committed under the influence of liquor might be placed under a special legal restriction which would subject him to punishment if he were found drunk. On the subject of temperance laws, however, Mill was as adamant as before, rejecting not only the prohibition of

6. *Ibid.*, p. 158.
7. *Ibid.*, p. 157.
8. *Ibid.*, p. 153.

liquor but also any attempt to discourage drinking by making it more costly or difficult to obtain. Thus to tax liquor for the purpose of regulation was to penalize individuals for "gratifying a particular taste," and this society had no authority to do. On the other hand, liquor could be taxed for the sole purpose of raising revenue. To the question of why liquor rather than another commodity should be taxed, Mill replied that the state was justified in taxing commodities the consumer could best spare, especially those which, consumed in excess, were deemed "positively injurious." Similarly, he approved of the licensing of drinking houses for the purpose of maintaining order, since "offences against society are especially apt to originate there."[9] But he disapproved of licensing designed to limit the number of public houses or to make them inaccessible. Such legislation was an insult to the working classes, for it treated them as "children or savages" who had to be placed under an "education of restraint, to fit them for future admission to the privileges of freedom."[10]

Each case Mill cited involved him in further distinctions: between misconduct committed in private and injuring only the individual himself and the same acts committed in public, at which time they became a "violation of good manners," an "offence against others" or "against decency," and therefore properly indictable.[11] He also distinguished between personal misconduct—fornication or gambling—and instigating others to misconduct—procuring or keeping a gambling house. His treatment of the latter cases is particularly instructive. Since they clearly fell into the other-regarding class, he might have been expected to subject them to social control. Instead, he put one difficulty after another in the way of this solution. "Whatever it is permitted to do," he declared, "it must be permitted to advise

9. *Ibid.*, p. 156.
10. *Ibid.*, p. 157.
11. *Ibid.*, p. 153.

to do."[12] Thus the procurer could not be forbidden to advise someone to do what it was legal to do—fornication, indeed prostitution, being legal. Moreover, if it was legal for one person to try to dissuade another from committing a personal act of misconduct, it must also be legal for another person to try to persuade him to commit the same act. At one point Mill suggested that this argument might be negated by the fact that the procurer was not merely advising another but was deriving personal financial benefit from that advice; in promoting what "society and the State consider to be an evil," the procurer had an interest "opposed to what is considered as the public weal."[13] But Mill was dubious about this last argument too, for if an activity was legal, how could it be made criminal merely by making a living out of it? Finally, after more arguments and counter-arguments in this vein, Mill concluded that there was much to be said on both sides and that he himself could not choose between them: "I will not venture to decide whether they are sufficient to justify the moral anomaly of punishing the accessary [*sic*], when the principal is (and must be) allowed to go free; of fining or imprisoning the procurer, but not the fornicator—the gambling-house keeper, but not the gambler."[14] Even in his irresolution, however, Mill was clearly leaning to the permissive side. Having stated the "moral anomaly" in these terms, it is difficult to see how he could do otherwise than let both the accessory and the principal go free.

The doctrine of liberty also meant that people should be completely free to make or break contracts concerning only themselves. From this doctrine Humboldt had deduced that marriage should be dissolvable at the will of either party. Mill objected that this was too simple a view of the matter, that it overlooked the moral obligations entered into

12. *Ibid.*, p. 154.
13. *Ibid.*
14. *Ibid.*, p. 155.

with marriage. He therefore qualified Humboldt's principle by suggesting that while people should be legally free to end a marriage, their "moral freedom" was not so unlimited.[15] (He did not say, however, whether that moral limitation carried with it a social sanction.) Within the marriage relationship, he added, it required no special doctrine of liberty to abolish the "almost despotic power" exercised by husbands over wives; all that was needed was to give wives the same rights and protection of the law enjoyed by everyone else.[16]

In two cases Mill argued that "misapplied notions of liberty" had left individuals with powers that should have been exercised by the state.[17] Both involved children, and in both cases the children were commonly regarded as an extension of their parents. The first case concerned the education of children. Was it not, Mill asked, almost a "self-evident axiom, that the State should require and compel the education, up to a certain standard, of every human being who is born its citizen?" Surely it was "one of the most sacred duties" of parents, and "unanimously" affirmed as such, to give to every child brought into the world an education "fitting him to perform his part well in life towards others and towards himself." Yet few people, he complained, agreed with him that if the parents did not fulfill that duty, "the State ought to see to it that it was fulfilled, at the charge, as far as possible, of the parent."[18] The government did not have to provide that education; it only had to insist that parents provide it from whatever source they pleased, and, in the case of the poor, defray the costs of that education. This would preserve the diversity in education while guaranteeing the education itself.

But Mill proposed to do more than provide for education

15. *Ibid.*, p. 159.
16. *Ibid.*, p. 160.
17. *Ibid.*
18. *Ibid.*

as such. He was also prepared to enforce standards of education by means of an elaborate system of public examinations to be taken by all children. At a given age, every child would be expected to read; if he failed this test, the parent, unless he had a sufficient excuse, would be fined and the child put to school at the parent's expense. Annual examinations would be given in a gradually extended range of subjects, "so as to make the universal acquisition, and what is more, retention, of a certain minimum of general knowledge virtually compulsory."[19] Beyond this minimal, compulsory level, voluntary examinations would be given in all subjects leading to certificates of proficiency. To prevent the state from exercising an undue influence over opinion, the examinations would be purely factual and scientific—an examination in religion, for example, turning on the particular doctrines held by various sects rather than on the supposed truth of those doctrines. The certificates themselves would have no legal standing, although they would carry whatever weight was attached to them by "public opinion."[20]

If the education of children was a moral obligation enforceable by the state, so also, Mill reasoned, was the bearing of children. To bring into the world a child lacking the ordinary chance of a "decent existence" was a "crime" against that child. And in a country threatened with overpopulation, it was also an "offence" against all who lived by their labor. To prevent this crime and offense, the state had the legitimate power to pass laws similar to those on the Continent which "forbid marriage unless the parties can show that they have the means of supporting a family." Whether such laws were expedient or not was a question to be determined by local circumstances. But they did not constitute a violation of liberty since they were intended to "prohibit a mischievous act—an act injurious to others."

19. *Ibid.*, p. 162.
20. *Ibid.*, p. 163.

Even when legal punishment was not expedient, improvident marriage ought at the very least to be "a subject of reprobation and social stigma."[21]

The final cases Mill discussed were of a different order: those in which interference by the state would constitute no restraint upon the individual and therefore no violation of liberty, but were only intended to help the individual. Mill devoted the last half dozen pages of his book to the kinds of situations where there was no threat to liberty and yet where it was inadvisable for the state to intervene for the purpose of helping its citizens. These included affairs which individuals were better fitted to deal with than was the state (industrial matters, for example); where individuals were less well fitted than the state but where it was desirable for them to retain responsibility "as a means to their own mental education" (local government);[22] or where the evil of adding to the powers of government would outweigh whatever advantages might be derived from it (where, for example, the assumption of control over roads, railways, or banks would lead to the enlargement of the apparatus of government). It was no argument in favor of bureaucracy that it was efficient and intelligent; on the contrary, the more efficient and intelligent a bureaucracy was, and the more it concentrated within itself the efficient and intelligent part of the population, the more fatal it was to the "mental activity and progressiveness" both of the bureaucracy itself and of those ruled by it. Mill formulated a principle for the optimum degree of government intervention: "the greatest dissemination of power consistent with efficiency; but the greatest possible centralisation of information, and diffusion of it from the centre."[23] The state, he concluded, did no service to its citizenry when it tried to do

21. *Ibid.*
22. *Ibid.*, p. 164.
23. *Ibid.*, p. 168.

the work of individuals, to postpone their "mental expansion and elevation" for the sake of some immediate benefit.[24]

The range of subjects covered in this final chapter suggests how far-reaching were the implications of Mill's principle of liberty, how varied the situations it had to deal with, how many problems it raised, and how many qualifications and distinctions were needed for their solution. By the time the reader has worked his way to the last of Mill's "applications," he may well wonder about the "one very simple principle" that was thought to comprehend such a variety of occasions and needs.

HOWEVER VALID OR COGENT Mill's disposition of each of these problems, his intention was clear: to make the principle of liberty a practical, decisive guide to social affairs. At least this was his intention in all but two conspicuous cases—the bearing of children and their education. And these exceptions may prove as interesting as the rule itself.

Mill did not present these as exceptions. And in one sense they were not. From the beginning he had said that the principle of liberty did not apply to children and minors, so that when he now proposed to bring them for certain purposes under the control of the state rather than of their parents, he could represent this as a transfer of authority rather than a diminution of liberty. In another sense, however, the issue of liberty was clearly involved. For unless Mill was prepared to entertain views of a very radical kind toward the family (which he was not), he had to accept the principle of parental authority. If parents had a moral and legal obligation to their children, as he maintained in his discussion of the marriage contract, they also had to have the authority and power to discharge that obligation. Their

24. *Ibid.*, p. 170.

liberty, to be sure, was limited by this obligation but no more than in other situations involving obligations.

There was, in fact, no logical reason for treating parental responsibilities in any special or exceptional way. Mill could have argued here, as he did in the case of drunkenness, that punishment should follow the violation of a "distinct and assignable obligation,"[25] that it was only the consequences of a man's actions, not the moral character of those actions, that were the proper concern of society. In the case of children, this would have meant punishing parents only when they had manifestly failed to fulfill their obligations, rather than anticipating that failure and preventing them in advance from bearing children. Indeed, the preventive procedure would seem to be less appropriate here than in the case of drunkenness, where Mill specifically rejected it. In the latter the visible evidence of drunkenness was so clear, the connection between cause and effect, drunkenness and irresponsibility, so immediate, that one could reasonably hope to forestall the effect by preventing the cause. But in the case of children, there was no such certainty of evidence and no such predictability of cause and effect. Two sets of parents in exactly the same material circumstances could obviously discharge their responsibilities in very different fashion. The difficulty of determining what constituted a "decent existence" for children or "adequate means of supporting a family," the additional difficulty of passing laws incorporating such vague concepts and of administering and enforcing those laws, would give pause to the most ardent statist, let alone liberal. And the problems are compounded when that determination had to be made, as Mill was proposing, at the time of marriage, when the means of support might be more meager than later, when it could not be known what were adequate means because it was not known how many children would require support, when it

25. *Ibid.*, p. 138.

could not, in fact, be known that any "crime" or "offence" would be committed.

In view of everything Mill had said earlier in praise of individuality and nonconformity, eccentricity and experiments of living, and in view also of his warnings against bureaucracy and benevolent government, it is hard to credit his protests that laws prohibiting marriage constituted no violation of liberty. Something else was clearly at stake here, something so urgent, in Mill's estimate, that it warranted this very considerable departure from his principle of liberty.

What was at stake was an issue that had occupied Mill all his life—the problem of overpopulation. Nowhere in his *Autobiography* did Mill mention what must have been one of the most memorable events of his youth. He was then seventeen, working as a clerk under his father at India House. Walking to the office one morning through St. James's Park, he discovered the dead body of a newly born infant wrapped in rags; continuing on his way, he passed the Old Bailey where he saw the hanging bodies of several criminals. The dramatic conjunction of these experiences reenforced the lesson he had already learned from Malthus: that overpopulation was the cause of untold misery and vice. It also convinced him that something more was required than the "moral restraint" Malthus had counseled, that birth control of a positive kind was a virtue and necessity rather than the vice Malthus had made it out to be. Equipped by Francis Place with tracts containing practical advice about birth control, Mill and a friend proceeded to distribute them in working-class neighborhoods and at the servants' entrances of houses. The two young men were arrested, charged with obscenity, and jailed overnight. To a proper, even prudish seventeen-year-old like Mill, the affair could hardly have been a trivial one. Half a century later he still could not bring himself to mention it in an autobiography which he knew would be published only after his death. It is a curious omission in an account which otherwise exhibits evidence of almost total recall.[26]

The episode only adds a personal dimension to an intellectual position Mill firmly adhered to throughout his life. In that half century, while the theoretical validity and practical import of Malthusianism were being increasingly challenged, Mill continued to regard population control as one of the most important conditions of economic and social well-being. Again and again the need for restraints on population—voluntary restraints if possible, legal ones if necessary—appeared in the course of his analysis of a variety of problems: the poor laws, the Irish famine, the condition of the working classes, the social and legal status of women, the allotment system and land laws, the distribution of wages, rent, and profits.[27]

And repeatedly Mill coupled the issue of overpopulation with that of education. In his private letters as in his public writings, he insisted that the melioration of intellectual and social life lay in the "extension and improvement of education" and in "the grand source of improvement, repression of population."[28] No reform of social institutions, he wrote

26. The other notable omission in the *Autobiography* is similarly significant—the failure to mention the breakdown which coincided with his father's fatal illness.

That the birth control episode had not been forgotten by others is attested to by the allusions to it in the obituaries of Mill. Reminded of it, Gladstone, despite his professed admiration for Mill (it was he who dubbed Mill the "Saint of Rationalism"), was moved to withdraw his name from the memorial to Mill.

27. It was almost certainly this obsession, as it seemed to some of his friends, that lies behind an elliptical remark by Bain. Mill had told another friend, the historian George Grote, that *On Liberty* was about "what things society forbade that it ought not, and what things it left alone that it ought to control." Grote repeated this to Bain, adding: "It is all very well for John Mill to stand up for the removal of social restraints, but as to imposing new ones, I feel the greatest apprehensions." Bain commented, with no further explanation: "I instantly divined what the new restraints would be." (Alexander Bain, *John Stuart Mill* [London, 1882], pp. 103–4.)

28. *Earlier Letters*, II, 713 (JSM to John Austin, Apr. 13, 1847).

in his *Political Economy*, could effect a real improvement in the circumstances of the mass of mankind in the absence of two conditions: "universal education" and a "due limitation of the numbers of the community." Without these conditions even a reform of the magnitude of communism would not suffice to render the masses "other than degraded and miserable"; given these conditions, however, even within the framework of present institutions, "there could be no poverty."[29] And the two conditions were causally related. In his *Autobiography* he explained that it was the hope of "universal education, leading to voluntary restraint on population," that sustained him during the period when he despaired of all other attempts to relieve poverty.[30]

Mill's faith in education, like his apprehensions about population, had deep roots in his personal life. Whatever changes of mind and heart he experienced in other respects, he never wavered in this. In a sense, education was the very condition of his being. He might later quarrel with the kind of education he received, but he never doubted its efficacy in making him the kind of person he was, in fashioning, for good and bad, his emotional as well as intellectual character. In his *Autobiography* he described in great detail the remarkable experiment in education which had him reading Greek at the age of three and progressing through the conventional classical studies to a mastery of logic, political economy, and history—all by the age of fourteen. With the wisdom of hindsight and maturity, he concluded this extraordinary account with the still more extraordinary statement: "What I could do, could assuredly be done by any boy or girl of average capacity and healthy physical constitution: and it is most encouraging to the hopes of improvement for the human race, that education can do so much for persons of not more than the ordinary natural gifts."[31] If there is a

29. *Political Economy*, I, 208.
30. *Autobiography*, p. 162.
31. *Early Draft of the Autobiography*, p. 54.

suspicion of disingenuousness in his modesty, there is no doubt of his genuine belief in the redemptive powers of education. And he carried that belief with him through every stage of his mental progress, from his Benthamite period when education had an entirely individual character, to his Coleridgean stage when it assumed a social and national character, and finally to *On Liberty* when, in the interests of education, he permitted so large a deviation from the principle of liberty.

The departure from the principle of liberty, in the cases of education and population, is all the more conspicuous because logically both could have been left to the responsibility of the individual. If the individual had an unlimited right to publish falsehoods, why not also to teach his children whatever he pleased, in the assurance that truth would eventually emerge? If to engage in "experiments in living," however idiosyncratic or offensive they might seem to the rest of society, why not also to bring up his children in poverty, in defiance of conventional notions of a "decent existence"?

Once Mill abandoned this mode of argument, he went much further in denying liberty than those of his contemporaries who had never pretended to be great liberals. In *On Liberty* he referred in passing to the "many countries on the Continent" which legally forbade marriage without adequate means of support.[32] Earlier, in the *Political Economy*, he had specified the places where there were such laws—not so many, as it happened: Norway, some of the smaller German states, and several Swiss cantons.[33] But no prominent Englishman was recommending the passage of similar laws. Even the authors of the *Poor Law Report*, from which Mill obtained this information, did not advocate the legal prohibition of marriage; they only hoped to discourage the increase of population among the poor by restricting

32. *On Liberty*, p. 163.
33. *Political Economy*, I, 346–48.

poor relief and making the conditions of relief (in the workhouse, for example) unfavorable to procreation.[34] Nor, with the notable exception of Matthew Arnold, were there many Englishmen, even among the proponents of public education, who called for a system of national examinations such as that proposed in *On Liberty*. And even Arnold, for all of his attempts to create a system of "accountability" in education, did not go so far as Mill in holding parents to account if their children were unable to read by a given age.

It is surely significant that on these two issues about which he felt most deeply, Mill chose not to rely upon liberty for the achievement of his ends. It is as if he had decided that education and population were too crucial for the welfare of mankind to be left to the circuitous workings of liberty. Truth, he was confident, would eventually emerge from the free expression of opinion, genius from individuality, and morality from the freedom to choose between good and bad. But this confidence deserted him when it came to education and population. On these critical issues he favored the direct intervention of the state—and without the elaborate qualifications and reservations that accompanied all his other admissions of public control.

ON THE GENERAL SUBJECT of government intervention, *On Liberty* invites comparison with the work in which Mill most explicitly and systematically addressed himself to this problem, the *Principles of Political Economy*. Unfortunately, the *Political Economy* was itself inconsistent on this

34. In the preface to the appendix to the *Poor Law Report*, which Mill quoted as his authority, Nassau Senior did not recommend that England adopt such laws. Instead he looked to the example of those countries where the population was kept down by the simple device of having no system of poor relief. (*Report from His Majesty's Commissioners for Inquiring into the Administration and Practical Operation of the Poor Laws, 1834* [London, 1834], appendix F, pp. lxxxvi–vii; the preface is dated May 1835.)

issue. But even its inconsistencies are illuminating in comparison with *On Liberty*.

The most flagrant contradiction within the *Political Economy*, and the point of greatest divergence from *On Liberty*, was Mill's treatment of communism and socialism.[35] For the most part, in the first edition of the *Political Economy*, he regarded the doctrine of free trade, or laissez-faire, as the most practical and desirable mode for the conduct of economic affairs. But in successive editions of the *Political Economy*, he made so many concessions toward socialism and communism that he came close to abandoning the orthodox doctrine.

In the first edition of the *Political Economy*, published in 1848, Mill cited as the decisive objection to communism (a term which he then used synonymously with socialism) the fact that it would totally destroy liberty: "The perfection of social arrangement would be to secure to all persons complete independence and freedom of action, subject to no restriction but that of not doing injury to others: but the scheme which we are considering [communism] abrogates this freedom entirely, and places every action of every member of the community under command."[36]

In 1849 this was qualified by adding, after "the scheme which we are considering," the parenthetical clause "(at least as it is commonly understood)"[37]—thus implying, if tentatively, that communism in some other sense might not be inimical to liberty. In the third edition of 1852, which was the most extensively revised one, the second part of the sentence was entirely deleted and replaced by a warning against the temptation to exchange liberty for comfort, affluence, or equality. But having issued that warning, Mill

35. In the earlier editions of the *Political Economy*, Mill used "communism" and "socialism" almost interchangeably. In the later editions he distinguished between the two, although not entirely consistently.
36. *Political Economy*, II, 978.
37. *Ibid.*

went on to a very different conclusion from his initial one regarding the relationship between liberty and communism. "It remains to be discovered how far the preservation of this characteristic [liberty] would be found compatible with the Communistic organization of society. No doubt this, like all the other objections to the Socialist schemes, is vastly exaggerated."[38]

One after another of his initial objections to communism and socialism was reconsidered in the same fashion and in each instance the conclusion was similar: the objection was not as fatal as he had earlier thought; in some forms of socialism (Fourierism, for example), it had already been overcome and as other socialist schemes were perfected it might be obviated there too; besides, the same or other objections could be raised against the present individualistic, competitive system. Where he had originally argued that the present system for all its faults was better than any of its alternatives, the weight of the argument in the later editions shifted to the point where the alternative systems, for all their faults, were better than the present one.

If, therefore, the choice were to be made between Communism with all its chances, and the present state of society with all its sufferings and injustices; . . . if this or Communism were the alternatives, all the difficulties, great or small, of Communism would be but as dust in the balance.[39]

The restraints of Communism would be freedom in comparison with the present condition of the majority of the human race.[40]

While conceding that the practical efforts of economists would continue to focus on the improvement rather than

38. *Ibid.*, I, 209.   39. *Ibid.*, p. 207.   40. *Ibid.*, p. 209.

the subversion of the present system, he also intimated that socialism, particularly of the Fourierist variety, had a larger potentiality for good than the present system even in its most improved state. This last conclusion was arrived at by a typically negative mode of reasoning: "The impossibility of foreseeing and prescribing the exact mode in which its [communism's] difficulties should be dealt with, does not prove that it may not be the best and the ultimate form of human society."[41] The emergence of even a tentative superlative from this string of negatives may have seemed to Mill sufficiently odd, upon a subsequent rereading of that sentence, to prompt him to remove it from later editions.[42] But even without this sentence the argument remained a strained, somewhat tortuous attempt to give communism and socialism every possible benefit of the doubt, while keeping in mind the objections—"difficulties," as he more often called them in the later editions—which might be brought against them.[43]

The largest difficulty, as Mill admitted, was the question of the compatibility of socialism with liberty and individuality. This was a problem even in Fourier's model, which professed to be cooperative rather than statist in nature. For even there, as Mill pointed out in one edition, the plan could not rest with the creation of isolated communities. "Nothing less would be requisite for the complete success of the scheme, than the organisation from a single centre, of the whole industry of a nation, and even of the world."[44] Although the sentence was deleted from the later editions of the *Political Economy*, its substance could not so easily have been erased. The probability that even Fourierism would require a total, universal organization of the economy

41. *Ibid.*, p. 207.
42. This sentence appeared only in the 1852 edition. It was removed from all subsequent editions (i.e., the fourth through the seventh).
43. E.g., *Political Economy*, I, 206.
44. *Ibid.*, II, 985. This was the 1849 edition.

must have lurked behind all the negatives, conjectures, and hypothetical propositions which Mill resorted to at decisive points of his argument:

> *It would be extremely rash to pronounce it incapable of success, or unfitted to realize a great part of the hopes founded on it by its partisans.*[45]

> *It is yet to be ascertained whether the Communistic scheme would be consistent with that multiform development of human nature, those manifold unlikenesses, that diversity of tastes and talents, that variety of intellectual points of view, which . . . are the mainspring of mental and moral progression.*[46]

> *We are too ignorant either of what individual agency in its best form, or Socialism in its best form, can accomplish, to be qualified to decide which of the two will be the ultimate form of human society.*[47]

The most positive note in this largely negative defense of socialism had the paradoxical effect of making more acute the problem of liberty and individuality. In countering the objection that communism would do away with any incentive to work, Mill adduced one motive that might be more effective than the present system of private property and wage labor: the development of a "public spirit" which would encourage men to exert themselves not for their "separate and self-regarding interests" but rather in the "pursuit of the general benefit of the community." This public spirit would exist as naturally in a communist community as in a religious order. But it would also be stimulated by one of the most powerful resources available to communism: "the most universal, and one of the strongest, of personal motives, that of public opinion."[48]

45. *Ibid.*, I, 213. 46. *Ibid.*, p. 209. 47. *Ibid.*, p. 208.
48. *Ibid.*, p. 205.

Mill also invoked public opinion to satisfy another objection commonly raised against communism: that under communism, as under a system of poor relief, there would be no reason for self-restraint in procreation and that there would be therefore an inordinate increase of population. This was a serious problem for Mill, and he resolved it by suggesting that in place of the present motives for self-restraint—the pressures of wages and subsistence—communism would rely on the force of public opinion. In a communist system more than in any other, "opinion might be expected to declare itself with greatest intensity against this kind of selfish intemperance." With no other excuse for an excessive number of children, "opinion could not fail to reprobate, and if reprobation did not suffice, to repress by penalties of some description, this or any other culpable self-indulgence at the expense of the community."[49] Several paragraphs later, having left behind the subject of overpopulation, Mill wondered whether "public opinion would not be a tyrannical yoke; whether the absolute dependence of each on all, and surveillance of each by all, would not grind all down into a tame uniformity of thoughts, feelings, and actions." But he felt it an open question, one that was "yet to be ascertained," whether public opinion under communism would indeed have that effect.[50]

That Mill made large concessions to socialism in the *Political Economy* can hardly be doubted. Nor can it be doubted that these concessions had significant implications for the doctrine of *On Liberty*. But there may be some question of how seriously one should take the entire subject of socialism as it appeared in the *Political Economy*. One might be inclined to minimize it on the grounds that it involved only one chapter of that work—an important chapter, to be sure, but only one. Or one might discount

49. *Ibid.*, p. 206.
50. *Ibid.*, p. 209.

it as the contribution more of Harriet Taylor than of Mill.[51] But the rest of the *Political Economy* cannot be so easily discounted. And it is in other parts of this work, not merely in this one chapter, that one finds attitudes far removed from those of *On Liberty*.

Socialism itself, as Mill conceived of it, was part of the larger subject of the distribution of wealth. And it was a fundamental thesis of the *Political Economy*—and the point on which Mill diverged most sharply from Ricardo and James Mill—that the laws governing the distribution of wealth were of a different character from those governing the production of wealth. Whereas the production of wealth obeyed its own natural laws, the laws of the market-place, the distribution of wealth obeyed whatever laws society chose to impose on it. In that considerable area of life, it was society, not the individual, that was sovereign. Whatever products of labor and wealth the individual possessed, he did so upon the sufferance of society. "In the social state, in every state except total solitude, any disposal whatever of them [the products of wealth] can only take place by the consent of society."[52] Even what an individual produced by his own labor, unaided by anyone else, he could only keep with the permission of society. And not only its tacit, passive permission—the fact that society itself refrained from taking his goods—but also its active assistance, its interference with others who might try to gain possession of them. It is in this context that Mill gave to socialism and communism a prima facie justification; they might be properly rejected on other grounds, but they had a right to consideration as alternative modes, alternative social arrangements, for the distribution of wealth.

In giving to the distribution of wealth this distinctive character, Mill made of the *Political Economy* something other than the conventional laissez-fairist doctrine. He also

51. See below, chap. IX.
52. *Political Economy*, I, 200.

went much further than he did in *On Liberty* when he pronounced trade to be a "social act." For it was not only trade but a large portion of life that was brought within the jurisdiction of society. The final book of the *Political Economy*, "On the Influence of Government," is far more complicated in its treatment of the individual and society than *On Liberty*. Indeed, Mill's opening remarks in this section stand almost as a rebuke to *On Liberty*. Having criticized those "impatient reformers" who, finding it easier to get control of the instruments of government than of the minds of the people, sought to extend the province of government beyond its proper limits, he went on to quarrel with the opposing faction: those who, reacting against the unwise interference of government and the injudicious proposals of reformers, developed an automatic "spirit of resistance" to government and a "disposition to restrict its sphere of action within the narrowest bounds."[53] The first tendency Mill found to be more prevalent on the Continent, the second in England. And it was the second he took to task for not appreciating the "multifarious character of the necessary functions of government."

> *In attempting to enumerate the necessary functions of government, we find them to be considerably more multifarious than most people are at first aware of, and not capable of being circumscribed by those very definite lines of demarcation, which, in the inconsiderateness of popular discussion, it is often attempted to draw round them. We sometimes, for example, hear it said that governments ought to confine themselves to affording protection against force and fraud: that, these two things apart, people should be free agents, able to take care of themselves, and that so long as a person practises no violence or deception, to the injury of others*

53. *Ibid.*, II, 799.

in person or property, legislators and governments are in no way called on to concern themselves about him. But why should people be protected by their government, that is, by their own collective strength, against violence and fraud, and not against other evils, except that the expediency is more obvious?[54]

It might be *On Liberty* itself that Mill was refuting in this passage. For there he did precisely what here he objected to: he circumscribed the government within "definite lines of demarcation," confining it to the task of "protection against force and fraud"; he insisted that, apart from this, "people should be free agents"; and above all he asserted as his central principle the idea that "so long as a person practises no violence or deception, to the injury of others in person or property, legislators and governments are in no way called on to concern themselves about him." The very words are familiar—except that here, in the *Political Economy*, they described the position Mill was criticizing, and in *On Liberty* the position he so ardently defended. The irony is even more pointed when one considers the original version of this passage. For in place of the phrase, "legislators and governments are in no way called on to concern themselves about him," the earlier editions read: ". . . he has a claim to do what he likes, without being molested or restricted by judges and legislators."[55] It was in the edition of 1857, the first edition of the *Political Economy* to appear after the drafting of *On Liberty*, that Mill deleted that telling phrase "he has a claim to do what he likes"—an expression almost identical with that in *On Liberty*, except that in the latter it was used approvingly and in the *Political Economy* disparagingly.

After arguing in the *Political Economy* for a more "multifarious" view of the functions of government, Mill

54. *Ibid.*, p. 800.
55. *Ibid.*

proceeded to give examples of functions that did not come within the category of protection against injury: laws governing inheritance, the use of common property, rules of contract, the adjudication of disputes even when there was no question of bad faith, the keeping of public records, the coining of money, prescribing standards of weights and measures, and the like. These were not optional but necessary functions of government, he insisted. Yet they had no justification in the principle of injury. Their only justification, and a sufficient one, was that they contributed to the "general convenience." There was, in fact, he concluded, no single "restrictive definition," no "universal rule," limiting the role of government, save the "simple and vague" one of strong expediency.[56]

In the course of the final section, Mill did propose that government be restricted to the narrowest compass within the realm of expediency, that laissez-faire be the "general practice" or "general rule," every departure from it, "unless required by some great good," being a "certain evil."[57] And much of his discussion about specific areas in which government could properly intervene—education, the care of the young and the insane, contracts in perpetuity—was in substance consistent with *On Liberty*. But even here there were differences, the *Political Economy* being noticeably more

56. *Ibid.*, pp. 803–4. Mill made the same point in a letter written soon after the completion of the first draft of the *Political Economy*. Not only, he said, was there no single principle applicable to the "province of government"; there was no general set of principles, no "axiomata media": "I suspect there are none which do not vary with time, place, and circumstance. I doubt if much more can be done in a scientific treatment of the question than to point out a certain number of *pro's* and a certain numbers of *con's* of a more or less general application, and with some attempt at an estimation of the comparative importance of each, leaving the balance to be struck in each particular case as it arises." (*Earlier Letters*, II, 712 [JSM to John Austin, Apr. 13, 1847].)

57. *Political Economy*, II, 945–47. See also his praise of "complete independence and freedom of action," quoted above, p. 126.

relaxed in its application of the general rule, more willing to entertain exceptions to it. Unlike *On Liberty*, for example, where roads and railways appear as examples of activities in which the government should not become involved because the advantages of control were outweighed by the disadvantages of an enlarged bureaucracy, the *Political Economy* took exactly the opposite position; here Mill argued that whatever was done by joint-stock companies could as well be done by the government, that much of the objection to government intervention in these cases was really an objection to the "bad organization" of government and could be obviated by a better organization.[58] Similarly, the *Political Economy*, while maintaining that in general products and services were best left to those who had the most direct interest in them and were the best judges of them, provided for government intervention in cases where the consumer might not be a competent judge and where the product or service in question was one "in the quality of which society has much at stake."[59] It also allowed for intervention where it was a question not of overruling the judgment of the people involved but of giving effect to their judgment, as in the regulation of working hours. (The *Political Economy* did not actually endorse such legislation, but it did grant its legitimacy.[60])

The differences between the *Political Economy* and *On Liberty* become more significant when one considers the subjects of the two books. Mill had always maintained that the doctrine of laissez-faire was more appropriate to the "business part" of life than to the moral part.[61] In that case, one might have expected a more rigorous adherence to the principles of laissez-faire in the *Political Economy*. Yet it

58. *Ibid.*, pp. 940–41.
59. *Ibid.*, p. 947.
60. *Ibid.*, pp. 956–57. Mill dissociated himself from this proposal more strongly in the later editions (from 1862 on—i.e., after *On Liberty* had appeared).
61. "Bentham," *Essays on Politics and Culture*, p. 102.

was here Mill eschewed any "restrictive definition" or "universal rule," allowing a larger latitude to government than the classical political economists had. *On Liberty*, by contrast, was more concerned with the moral, spiritual, and intellectual aspects of life. Yet there he tried to apply a single, absolute principle, a kind of moral laissez-fairism, which would be binding upon the whole of society as well as government.

IN HIS PRIVATE CORRESPONDENCE Mill raised another issue which he had not mentioned in the *Political Economy* but which, had he done so, would have heightened the contrast to *On Liberty*. One of the reasons he had given in the *Political Economy* for favoring Fourierism was that this system of socialism relied more upon the motive of individual self-interest and was thus both more practical and more compatible with liberty than any other socialist scheme. But at the very time he was amending the *Political Economy* to praise Fourierism on this account, he wrote a letter suggesting that precisely this feature of the system might prove to be its most serious defect. The pivot of any education, he said, should be the cultivation of a *"moral sense—*a feeling of duty, or conscience, or principle, or whatever name one gives it—a feeling that one *ought* to do, and to wish for, what is for the greatest good of all concerned." Instead of supplying that moral sense, Fourier entirely excluded it, relying rather on social arrangements which, without any inculcation of ideas of duty or "ought," would make people zealous for the interests of the whole merely by the "spontaneous action of the passions." Under Fourierism, "nobody is ever to be made to do anything but act just as they like," on the assumption that in the *phalanstère* (the Fourierist community), everyone would always "like what is best." This system, Mill observed, "of course leads to the freest notions about personal relations of all sorts, but is it, in other respects, a foundation on which people would be able to live and act together?" The Fourierists, he regretfully concluded, professed to make people perfect while leaving out "one of the most indispensable ingredients" for perfection.[62]

In his *Autobiography* Mill reflected upon the tension between the socialist and the individualist strains in his thought. He did not speak of it as a tension, still less a contradiction; on the contrary, he gave the impression of having harmonized the two strains. Yet his ambivalence is unmistakable. In this "third period" of his mental progress, he explained (the period which included both the *Political Economy* and *On Liberty*), he was less of a democrat than he had been before and more of a socialist.

> *While we repudiated with the greatest energy that tyranny of society over the individual which most Socialistic systems are supposed to involve, we yet looked forward to a time when society will no longer be divided into the idle and the industrious . . . when the division of the produce of labour, instead of depending as in so great a degree it now does, on the accident of birth, will be made by concert on an acknowledged principle of justice, and when it will no longer either be, or be thought to be, impossible for human beings to exert themselves strenuously in benefits which are not to be exclusively their own, but to be shared with the society they belong to. The social problem of the future we considered to be, how to unite the greatest individual liberty of action with a common ownership in the raw material of the globe, and an equal participation of all in the benefits of combined labour.*[63]

62. *Later Letters*, I, 22 (JSM to Harriet Taylor, Mar. 31, 1849).
63. *Autobiography*, p. 162. One of the changes suggested by Harriet Taylor would have made the internal conflict even more obvious. Her penciled annotation in the manuscript of the *Early Draft* would have had the first sentence of this passage

A social transformation of this order, Mill continued, would have to be accompanied by an equivalent transformation of character. Both the laboring masses and their employers would have to learn to work for "public and social purposes," rather than, as was now the case, "solely for self interested ones."[64] An "interest in the common good" would have to become as strong a motive as the interest in the "personal good" was at present.[65] "Selfishness" would have to be uprooted, "self-interest" minimized. If the common good was now so weak, Mill suggested, it was because "the mind is not accustomed to dwell on it as it dwells from morning to night on things which tend only to personal good," because all of modern institutions tend to generate selfishness, and because there are so few opportunities for the individual to act for the public without being paid to do so. Education and habit, social pressures and social institutions could refashion the minds of men and redirect their energies. "In this direction," Mill concluded, "lies assuredly the course of future progress.[66]

---

read: "While we repudiated with the greatest energy the tyranny of society over the individual, we yet looked forward to a time when the voice of Society on the great fundamental questions of social and political morals should be the voice of all" (p. 173). Mill chose, understandably, not to use her formulation.

64. The last phrase is in the *Early Draft* (p. 173); in the final version of the *Autobiography* it was changed to "narrowly interested ones" (p. 163).

65. "Personal good" in the *Early Draft* (p. 173) became "personal advantage" in the final version (*Autobiography*, p. 163).

66. *Early Draft*, p. 174. This last sentence was deleted in the final version and replaced by one that started: "These considerations did not make us overlook the folly of premature attempts to dispense with the inducements of private interest in social affairs, while no substitute for them has been or can be provided . . ." (*Autobiography*, pp. 163-64). This and similar changes made after the writing of *On Liberty* suggest Mill's awareness of the conflict between the individualistic doctrine of *On Liberty* and the broader social orientation of his other works.

This long passage of the *Autobiography*, appearing toward the end of the first draft, is eloquent and moving. But it is not entirely persuasive. For it does not, in fact, succeed in reconciling the fear of the "tyranny of society over the individual," the desire for the "greatest individual liberty of action," with a mode of social organization which would make men act in "concert" and which would ensure an equal ownership and participation in the resources of the world. The philosopher Henry Sidgwick remarked how surprised he and his friends were to read, in the *Autobiography*, that "our master, the author of the much-admired treatise 'On Liberty,' had been all the while looking forward to a time when the division of the produce of labour should be 'made by concert.' "[67]

It was not only the socialist mode of organization that was at variance with *On Liberty*; it was also the reform of human nature required by the new social organization. In his other works the "course of future progress" was seen to lie in the development of the social character of man; in *On Liberty* Mill looked for it in precisely the opposite direction, the development of man's individuality. Elsewhere he invoked the force of public opinion to encourage man's social propensities and discourage his private and personal ones; in *On Liberty* public opinion was the great evil that had to be resisted in order to free man to pursue his private passions and impulses. In his *Autobiography* Mill deplored those institutions in modern society and daily life which had the unfortunate effect of making people selfish, encouraging them to dwell on their individual selves and personal interests. But the kind of individual and mode of life celebrated in *On Liberty* would have exacerbated precisely these tendencies in modernity.

67. Henry Sidgwick, *Miscellaneous Essays and Addresses* (London, 1904), p. 242.

PART TWO

On Liberty:
The Biography of an Idea

MRS. GRUNDY AND THE EMINENT
VICTORIANS

T HE CASE OF Mill *contra* Mill could be brought to a close
at this point. One could introduce other witnesses on
both sides—contemporary reviewers and later critics and
commentators. But these would largely repeat what Mill
has already testified to. Moreover, there is a certain dramatic
satisfaction in having Mill appear as both defendant and
prosecutor. Who can speak to the issue of *On Liberty* better than Mill himself? Whose testimony can be more
enlightening, whose pronouncements more authoritative?
The burden of disputation may well rest with Mill alone.

One large question, however, remains open. Why does
Mill lend himself to these curious proceedings? Why can
he so readily be summoned to speak on both sides? The
question is of more than biographical curiosity—although
if it were only that, it would still be legitimate. It is also a
matter of great intellectual consequence. For the answer
must have an important bearing not only upon the entire
corpus of Mill's work, the substance and value of his thought,
but also upon *On Liberty* itself, the meaning and validity
of the doctrine that is now a permanent part of our heritage.

The simplest answer is that Mill changed his mind, that
On Liberty represented a later, more mature stage of his

thought. To the extent to which the evidence in the case has been drawn from his early writings, there would seem to be some validity for this supposition. Yet one is confronted not only with the fact that Mill chose to reprint those early writings but also with the fact that he expressed similar sentiments at the very time he was working on *On Liberty* as well as afterward. It is not enough, then, to speak of an "early" and "late" Mill; to a considerable extent the two Mills overlap and coexist—and both conflict with the Mill of *On Liberty*.

Another explanation has already been disposed of—the possibility that Mill was not fully aware of the conflict between *On Liberty* and his other writings. The care with which he read and revised not only his essays but also the *Logic* and *Political Economy* belies this explanation. In addition, there is the evidence of the *Autobiography*, which was one long, if not always entirely candid, attempt to describe and account for his changes of opinion. This explanation is not only untenable in itself, it is also unworthy of Mill—as if he could be supposed to be ignorant of what is so abundantly evident to an attentive and critical reader.

Still another possibility is that in *On Liberty* Mill was addressing himself to a single, specific, and limited problem which could be resolved in terms of a single principle, while elsewhere he was dealing with other problems requiring other, more complicated solutions. His famous statement, "The object of this Essay is to assert one very simple principle . . . ," might conceivably be read in this sense. But this is to take it out of its context. In the book itself that principle was clearly intended to apply to a problem of the greatest magnitude. From the outset and throughout the work, Mill insisted upon the centrality and gravity of the subject at issue. The opening paragraph described the question of "Civil, or Social Liberty" as nothing less than "the nature and limits of the power which can be legitimately exercised by society over the individual"; this was the issue that lay behind the "practical controversies of the age" and would soon emerge as the "vital question of the future." It was the new form of the age-old struggle between liberty and authority, a struggle which had always been "the most conspicuous feature" of human history and was now entering an even more momentous stage.[1] What was at stake, then, in *On Liberty*, was not an isolated or limited problem but rather one that had the largest implications and was of the greatest importance.

It is at this point that the most plausible explanation suggests itself—the possibility that it was the momentousness and urgency of the problem in his own time that caused Mill to adopt, in *On Liberty*, a stance very different from his usual one. If he did indeed feel the social tyranny of mid-nineteenth-century England to be so oppressive, he might have deliberately proposed a bold and dramatic mode of dealing with that problem. The balanced appraisal of alternatives, the judicious weighing of individual rights and social responsibilities, the complicated view of the individual in relation to the polity, the considerations of prudence, moderation, propriety, stability—all these, which were Mill's normal way of approaching social problems, might have seemed, even to himself, inappropriate to a situation calling for prompt and radical redress.

That Mill may have been motivated by some such sense of the situation is suggested by our own impressions of Victorian England.[2] The popular connotation of "Victorian" is

---

1. *On Liberty*, p. 65.

2. Only a few years ago, the lead review in the *Times Literary Supplement* (a review of the new edition of James Fitzjames Stephen's book) stated: "It is a well-known fact that Mill was prompted to prepare his essay *On Liberty* for publication after a visit to Naples, where he found the statues in the local galleries being subject to a 'fig-leaf' censorship. This made him feel that the spirit of Puritan interference was becoming altogether too ubiquitous and aggressive, and that it needed to be countered by a reasoned appeal to mankind's love of freedom" (Oct. 3, 1968). Like many a "well-known fact" this is not a fact at all. It was while en route to Rome that Mill first announced

precisely of the kind of social tyranny described in *On Liberty*—a massive conformity which was inimical not only to every expression of individuality but to the most natural human impulses. We associate the Victorian age with genteel manners and hypocritical morals, with affectations, pretensions, equivocations, and inhibitions fatal to spontaneity, vitality, and individuality. We are reminded of such memorable characters as Mrs. Grundy, Podsnap, and Pecksniff, of piano legs clothed in pantaloons and human legs referred to as "limbs," of a *Family Shakespeare* purged of indelicacies, and of country-house libraries in which male and female authors dwelt chastely upon separate shelves.

But if this is what Mill had in mind, he must also have been aware of the derision with which such "Victorianisms" were regarded even then. One measure of the greatness of the Victorian novelists—and there was no greater age of the novel—was the brilliant light they shed on the absurdities and grievances of their own time. If Pecksniff and Podsnap are taken seriously as typical specimens of their time (caricatures, to be sure, but caricatures of real types), one must also take seriously the fact that it was another contemporary, Dickens, who exposed these types so mercilessly —exposed them not to a small coterie but to a large reading public, who evidently shared his contempt, or at least could see the point of his satire. Moreover, the more absurd and objectionable of the practices associated with Victorianism long predated the period of *On Liberty* and were by then in visible decline. Both Bowdler and Mrs. Grundy were products not of Victorian puritanism but of eighteenth-century evangelicalism: Mrs. Grundy was a fictional character, which suggests that from the start evangelicalism had

---

his desire to expand his essay into a volume; and his visit to Rome preceded his trip to Naples with its "fig-leaf" statuary. (Nor was Mill writing *On Liberty*, as this review has it, in the 1860s.)

its satirists; and Bowdler, a gentleman of indubitable historicity and self-righteousness, died well before Queen Victoria came to the throne. And while Bowdler's heritage survived in the form of the *Family Shakespeare*, there were fewer enterprises of that sort as the century progressed.

As much a Victorian phenomenon as any particular Victorian convention was the critic or novelist who attacked that convention. Mill was no lone prophet preaching in the wilderness. He had a goodly number of colleagues engaged in the same task. And like him, they were respected and influential. Conservatives and liberals alike declaimed against materialism, philistinism, and mindless conformity. Arnold, Ruskin, Carlyle, Bagehot, Kingsley, Newman, Froude, and Buckle were agreed upon this, if upon little else. Nor was Dickens alone among the novelists to attack cant and hypocrisy; Thackeray, Trollope, Charlotte Brontë, George Eliot, Meredith, Mrs. Gaskell, and a host of lesser writers wrote scathing novels of manners and, occasionally, works of great moral sensibility.

One might suppose that if there were so many critics of convention, so many dissenters from the prevailing culture, there must have been much to criticize and dissent from. And so there was. But criticism and dissent, as Mill well knew, flourish most readily in ages of weak beliefs; they are less provoked by powerful, well-entrenched creeds and institutions than by faltering and vulnerable ones. Later generations might be impressed, or appalled, by what appeared to be the security and certainty, the self-righteousness and pomposity of that "age of equipoise," as it has been called.[3] But most thoughtful contemporaries were painfully aware of the insecurities and uncertainties lurking just below, sometimes breaking through, the surface of private and public life. If they complained of the complacency of others, it was because they felt that to be a particularly

3. W. L. Burn, *The Age of Equipoise: A Study of the Mid-Victorian Generation* (London, 1964).

unsuitable response to their troubled condition. And if others defended themselves against this charge, protesting that there was reason for some measure of self-satisfaction, it was because they felt themselves to be under attack, their values derided, and their accomplishments belittled.

In their personal lives as well as in their public pronouncements, the great Victorians were hardly models of conventionality; the liberties they took would be worthy of gossip even in our own more permissive times. Mill himself, in his relationship with Harriet Taylor, was only one of many who openly and with impunity (social impunity, that is; the self-inflicted pains of conscience were another matter) flouted the conventions. George Eliot and G. H. Lewes, William Fox and Eliza Flower entered into blatantly extra-marital arrangements, while others indulged more casually in passing affairs. Sarah Austin, the wife of the famous jurist, was actually blackmailed because of her amorous letters to a visiting German prince. Another of Mill's friends, George Grote, celebrated the completion of his thirty-year-long work on ancient Greece and the fortieth anniversary of his marriage by having an affair with a young woman whose career as a sculptor seems not to have suffered as a result of this peccadillo. There were also those who managed to offend the proprieties by an unseemly celibacy: Ruskin and Carlyle, for example, whose marriages were unconsummated. Nor were marital improprieties the only offense. Swinburne applied his talents to the composition of poetry and pornography alike; and Monckton Milnes (Lord Houghton), Member of Parliament, man of letters, and man about town, collected pornography with the same zeal that he cultivated the friendship of the great. Even Gladstone, that model of rectitude, felt free (perhaps because he was so confident of his own rectitude) to engage in his own pet philanthropy: bringing home a prostitute and lecturing her, over tea, on the error of her ways.

The examples can be multiplied to the point where one

wonders whether there were any proper Victorians. The "other Victorians"—and not only those professionally or pathologically involved with the underworld of prostitution and perversion[4], but also those who indulged their fancies more privately—were sufficiently numerous to make any stereotype suspect. This is not to deny some validity to the stereotype, allowing for all the variations, exceptions, anomalies, and aberrations which attach to all stereotypes. Nor is it to minimize the considerable pressure for social conformity in Victorian England, the greater severity of the moral code and the greater rigors of convention as compared with the preceding and following centuries. But it does suggest that the pressures were not as effective, as totally repressive of individuality, eccentricity, even perversity, as might be thought.

Nor was it only the "great" Victorians who could successfully resist the constraints of conformity and prudery. Proper middle-class young ladies devoured the novels (especially those of George Sand) which some of their elders decried as the height of sensuality and immorality. Moreover, these novels were not acquired or read surreptitiously; they circulated freely in the lending libraries and were talked about openly at the tea table. In addition to such novels there was a genre of sex manual, half exhortatory and half expository, which would be not unworthy of our own time. Five years before *On Liberty* a book was published with the curious title, *The Elements of Social Science: Physical, Sexual, and Natural Religion.* It was as candid in its argument for sexual liberty—"if a man and a woman conceive a passion for each other, they should be morally entitled to indulge it, without binding themselves together for life" —as in its demonstration of the most effective techniques of

---

4. Steven Marcus, *The Other Victorians: A Study of Sexuality and Pornography in Mid-Nineteenth Century England* (New York, 1964).

contraception.[5] The title apparently deceived no one, for the book went through a dozen editions in twenty years.

The lower classes, of course, were even more exempt from the code of morality that we think of as peculiarly Victorian. Prostitution was so common as to earn the title of "The Great Social Evil." And apart from professional prostitution, the general condition of sexual laxity revealed itself in a startling number of illegitimate births even among those regarded as the "respectable" laboring poor. Nor were the lower classes as universally devoted to the "work ethic" as the conventional image of Victorianism would have us suppose. Indeed, a sizable portion seems to have subscribed, sometimes consciously, to something that might be described as a non-work ethic. Henry Mayhew, author of *London Labour and the London Poor*, divided his subject into three categories: "Those that *will* work, those that *cannot* work, and those that *will not* work."[6] Whatever the historian may think of this classification as social typology, he cannot deny its utility for an understanding of the social ethic.

There is an obvious relationship between the sexual ethic and the social ethic, between sexual prudery and economic prudence. The proper Victorian is said to have husbanded his sexual energies as he did his financial resources. On this theory, the wanton waste of semen (as in masturbation) was as sinful as the wanton waste of money; sexual activities were to be scheduled and regulated as carefully as working or business activities; spontaneity in the household or bedroom was as deplorable as in the factory or workroom. Yet if there is some truth in this analogy, one must also take

5. Quoted by Walter E. Houghton, *The Victorian Frame of Mind, 1830–1870* (New Haven, 1957), p. 363.

6. Henry Mayhew, "Labour and the Poor," *Morning Chronicle*, Oct. 19, 1849. The three categories also appear in the subtitle to Mayhew's *London Labour and the London Poor* (London, 1861). In the opening pages of the fourth volume, another work-shy category is introduced to provide for the rich: "Those that need not work" (IV, 3).

seriously the social deviancy that went hand in hand with sexual deviancy. Again Mayhew's work is revealing, the fourth volume being entirely devoted to "Those That Will Not Work, comprising Prostitutes, Thieves, Swindlers, and Beggars." The names contemporaries assigned to this non-working population—the "undeserving poor," the "residuum," "outcasts," "aliens"—confirm the prevalence of the puritan work ethic. But they also confirm the existence of a significant number of poor whose lives, whether by necessity or choice, were not governed by that ethic.

If, then, it is to the spirit of "Victorianism" that we look for the explanation of *On Liberty*, if we assume that Mill's inordinate fear of social conformity derived from the coercive ethic of his time, then we must recognize that the pressure to abide by that ethic was less compelling than we might suppose, that not only individuals but entire social groups seem to have evaded it. From the perspective of later generations, the sexual and social ethic seems totally binding and totally repressive. But what impressed and often dismayed contemporaries was the extent to which that ethic was being violated, and with impunity. It may also be that our own sense of that ethic derives as much from *On Liberty* as from any other source. Indeed, *On Liberty* is often quoted as evidence of the intolerable pressure for social conformity—evidence of unimpeachable authority.[7]

7. E.g., Houghton, pp. 134, 338, 395 ff., 426. Kathleen Tillotson maintains that compared with the 1840s and '50s, the '60s witnessed a return to some of the severity and prudery of early evangelicalism. But her evidence for such regression consists of the occasional admonitions of reviewers and editors (Thackeray, most notably, in the *Cornhill*). And she herself points out that such admonitions were probably the result of the growing habit of reading novels aloud to the family—a circumstance which would give pause even to the most liberal-minded householder. She also notes that "one notorious social abuse, the uncontrolled sale of corrupting literature" (i.e., pornography) had the paradoxical effect of restraining the serious novelist, who did not want his work to sink to the "Holywell Street" level. (*Novels of the Eighteen-Forties* [Oxford, 1954], p. 63.) I suspect that a close study of the literature of the 1860s would confirm what

More important, in this context, than the objective situation is Mill's attitude toward it. And that can only be described as ambivalent. For all his dislike of conformity, his praise of individuality, dissent, and eccentricity, he had no great liking for the more serious forms of social or sexual deviancy. His criticism of Calvinism did not imply any radical departure from what we take to be the puritan ethic either in its social or sexual connotation. His positions on Malthusianism and poor relief suggest that he was as committed to the work ethic as any proper Victorian. This was the meaning of his extraordinary proposal to prohibit the marriage of those who lacked adequate means of support. It was also the reason he was so enthusiastic about the Poor Law of 1834—a law restricting relief for the express purpose of preventing pauperism—and so defensive of it long after it had become the subject of widespread criticism.

Nor, in spite of the anomaly of his personal position— his "affair," if it can be called that, with Harriet Taylor— did Mill approve of libertinism or sensualism. He was, as will be seen, much concerned with questions of marriage and the status of women. But he was not much (if at all) exercised over the question of sex as such. Greater sexual liberties, greater tolerance for sexual deviations (perhaps homosexuality), even a greater latitude for what he clearly regarded as sexual immoralities (prostitution and promiscuity) may have been implied in his doctrine. But it is hard to believe that it was these issues that provoked him to write *On Liberty*, that it was for the sake of these liberties that he felt his doctrine to be urgently required. To judge by his attitude in *On Liberty* itself toward prostitutes and procurers, one might say that it was in spite of such sexual

---

Tillotson observed of the '40s: that in spite of occasional evidence of squeamishness, there was far more latitude in the treatment of moral and sexual themes than one normally associates with "Victorianism."

liberties, rather than because of them, that he advanced his doctrine. It is also significant that neither in *On Liberty* nor, so far as is known, elsewhere did Mill mention, still less criticize, the Obscene Publications Act of 1857, which facilitated judicial proceedings against pornography. (The act, and the debate in Parliament preceding its passage, testify as much to the thriving state of pornography as to this single attempt to curb it.) Even Mill's treatment of divorce was more cautious, less permissive than might have been expected. When he spoke of "experiments in living," there is nothing in *On Liberty* to suggest that sexual experiments were what he had in mind; certainly there is nothing in it remotely suggestive of what was even then being spoken of as "free love."

Mill's own predilections, in fact, were quite the reverse. He believed the "force of natural passions" to be grossly exaggerated—originally, he suggested, by the Catholic Church in order to glorify the "grace of God." And he confidently expected that the progress of civilization would bring with it—indeed, that a mark of progress would be— a diminution of sexuality.

I think it most probable that this particular passion will become with men, as it is already with a large number of women, completely under the control of the reason. It has become so with women because its becoming so has been the condition upon which women hoped to obtain the strongest love and admiration of men. The gratification of this passion in its highest form, there- fore, has been, with women, conditional upon their restraining it in its lowest. It has not yet been tried what the same conditions will do for men. I believe they will do all that we wish, nor am I alone in think- ing that men are by nature capable of as thorough a control over these passions as women are. I have known

*eminent medical men, and lawyers of logical mind, of
the same opinion.*[8]

IF, THEN, IT WAS NOT in respect to the social or sexual ethic
that Mill found his age to be intolerably conformist, if it
was not for the sake of social or sexual liberation in these
senses that a radically new conception of liberty was required, what kind of conformity was it that he thought to
be "enslaving the soul itself"?[9] From some remarks in *On
Liberty* one might suspect it was religious conformity that
especially troubled him. One might also suspect this from
a superficial acquaintance with the time. The common image
of the Victorian is of a church-going, Bible-reading, Sab-
bath-observing worthy who either never questioned the
tenets of his faith or suppressed such doubts as he might have.

That there was even less truth in this religious stereotype
than in the sexual one was demonstrated in the census
of 1851, which showed that there were far fewer regular
church attendants than had been suspected even by those
who were complaining of the growing religious laxity. And
contemporary literature, so far from exuding a sense of
religious convictions and orthodoxy, was obsessed with
doubt and crisis; indeed, the "religious crisis" was a common

8. *Later Letters,* IV, 1693 (JSM to Lord Amberley, Feb. 2,
1870). In his *Autobiography* Mill attributed almost exactly the
same opinion to his father:

> He looked forward, for example, to a considerable increase
> of freedom in the relations between the sexes, though without
> pretending to define exactly what would be, or ought to be,
> the precise conditions of that freedom. This opinion was con-
> nected in him with no sensuality either of a theoretical or of
> a practical kind. He anticipated, on the contrary, as one of the
> beneficial effects of increased freedom, that the imagination
> would no longer dwell upon the physical relation and its
> adjuncts, and swell this into one of the principal objects of
> life; a perversion of the imagination and feelings, which he
> regarded as one of the deepest seated and most pervading evils
> in the human mind. [P. 75.]

9. *On Liberty,* p. 68.

theme of the popular novel. Even among believers the range of creeds and practices was such as should have amply satisfied Mill's criteria of "variety and diversity." Dissenters displayed a remarkable aptitude for sectarianism and separatism; the Established Church had its familiar divisions of Low, Broad, and High, with all the possible gradations in between; and even the supposedly monolithic Roman Catholic Church was torn between Liberal Catholics and Ultramontanes, between the quiescent old Catholic families and the new zealous converts. Non-believers were no less diverse, ranging from militant atheists, troubled agnostics, and placid indifferentists to varieties of disbelief that constituted new forms of belief: Comtean positivism, Feuerbachian humanism, and religious socialism. And all these alternatives were available to all classes of the population in all parts of the country. While London intellectuals were imbibing atheism in the form of George Eliot's translation of Strauss's *Life of Jesus*, working men of Leeds were being circularized with leaflets issued by the Society of Rational Pioneers. That there was nothing either surreptitous or subtle about the latter is evident from a typical title: *Twenty-Five Reasons for Being an Atheist.*

The fluid state of religious belief can perhaps best be seen in the progress of Darwinism. Published in the same year as *On Liberty*, the *Origin of Species* was received with dismay by those who saw it as a threat not so much to the biblical account of creation—that had long since been interpreted metaphorically—as to any teleological system in which God functioned as a first cause, a prime mover. Yet within a decade Darwin's theory had triumphed to the point where, some of its defenders ruefully observed, the new heresy had become the new orthodoxy. This new orthodoxy had revolutionary implications not only for science and religion but also for ethics, politics, and society. Yet it was with a full awareness of these implications that Darwinism came to prevail so rapidly and completely.

There remained, to be sure, religious practices that secular-minded liberals could well object to: the requirements of the religious oath for official posts and legal proceedings, and all the subtle and not so subtle ways in which an established church and a traditionally religious society impinge upon people's lives and liberties. But such causes for offense were fewer in Mill's day than at any time before. Even while he was writing *On Liberty*, a grievance that was especially vexing to intellectuals was eliminated when Parliament abolished the religious requirements for admission to Oxford and Cambridge. If anyone had reason for complaint, it was someone like Matthew Arnold who saw the religious foundations of the state being systematically undermined not only by one after another concession to secularism but by a deliberate subversion of the very idea of an established church.

Mill himself, in *On Liberty*, while harping on the problems of religious liberty, could cite only rather exotic or limited instances of the violation of that liberty: Moslems prohibiting the eating of pork, Americans forbidding the Mormons to practice polygamy, or in England examples of intolerance which Mill himself called the "rags and remnants of persecution."[10] Earlier, in his introductory chapter, he had gone so far as to admit that religion was the one area where the principle of liberty had been unequivocally asserted: "The higher ground has been taken on principle and maintained with consistency"; "the rights of the individual against society have been asserted on broad grounds of principle, and the claim of society to exercise authority over dissentients openly controverted."[11] In practice, he added, society still attempted to exercise that authority when it felt deeply about a particular issue. But the principle at least had been clearly formulated.

In his *Autobiography* Mill went further in conceding the

10. *Ibid.*, p. 91.
11. *Ibid.*, p. 71.

advances that had taken place in recent years in the discussion of religion and other controversial issues. He recalled his own youth when his father, himself a firm disbeliever who had inculcated in his son the same thoroughgoing skepticism, cautioned the boy to be prudent in his disbelief, not to express it openly to those who would be offended by it. The time for such prudence, Mill noted, was happily over, and not only in respect to religious beliefs but to all opinions about which men felt deeply.

The great advance in liberty of discussion which is one of the points of difference between the present time and that of my childhood, has greatly altered the moralities of this question; and I think that few men of my father's intellect and public spirit, holding with such intensity of moral conviction as he did, unpopular opinions on religion or on any other of the great subjects of thought, would now either practise or inculcate the withholding of them from the world; unless in those cases, becoming rarer every day, in which frankness on these subjects would risk the loss of means of subsistence.[12]

IF, THEN, FREEDOM OF RELIGION was not an urgent issue, if, in Mill's own experience, it was becoming "rarer every day" for men to lose their livelihood by speaking out openly on this subject, in what areas of life was social conformity

12. *Early Draft*, p. 61. *On Liberty* gave the impression that the loss of means of subsistence was not so rare an occurrence. Those who had no independent means were represented there as being very much at the mercy of public opinion: "Men might as well be imprisoned, as excluded from the means of earning their bread" (p. 92). Perhaps it was this contradiction that led Mill to add, in the final version of the *Autobiography*, another possible penalty inflicted on the dissenter—"exclusion from some sphere of usefulness peculiarly suitable to the capacities of the individual" (p. 31). But this penalty too, it was implied, was "becoming rarer every day."

becoming more pressing? That it was not becoming so in intellectual affairs he himself suggested in the same statement when he testified to the greater tolerance for "unpopular opinions" on all the "great subjects of thought." For this view there is ample evidence at every level of intellectual life. Respectable men openly pronounced themselves socialists, declared their sympathy for revolutionary movements abroad, and gave comfort and praise to the émigrés who took refuge in England in the forties and fifties. While some men celebrated the "railway age" and looked forward to a mechanized, rationalized modernity, others yearned for the certitudes and beatitudes of a romanticized, idealized medieval past. Disputes raged then, as they still do today, about the "condition of the people" question: whether industrialism had a progressive or regressive effect upon the standard of living of the working classes and whether improved material conditions signified any moral or spiritual progress.[13] Ample occasions for controversy were provided by science and what we now regard as pseudo-science: Alfred Wallace, the co-founder of the theory of natural selection, was one of many reputable thinkers who took seriously the claims of phrenology and spiritualism.

So far from being an age of intellectual conformity, it is the contrasts and paradoxes of that time that may impress us. If some heroes of Victorian novels now bore us with their sobriety and virtuousness, others stand comparison with the great Gothic creations, the grotesque extravagances, of modern literature. Pious tracts competed with salacious song sheets, and the great quarterlies flourished together with "penny dreadfuls." From one side men were besieged by new ideas and inventions, while from the other

13. The Crystal Palace Exhibition of 1851 elicited a chorus of praise for the material and moral state of the nation. But even at the height of these celebrations there were accounts of the condition of England that were anything but complacent—indeed, that today provide much of the ammunition for the "pessimists" in this historical controversy.

they were exhorted to abide by the old ways and beliefs. Mechanics' institutes inculcated the principle of self-help and, wittingly or not, encouraged an independence of thought that went beyond the practical purposes of self-help. Indeed, many of the institutes were of an intellectually higher caliber than one might expect—while the universities were far more inept and incompetent than one would have thought possible. Amateurs made a serious avocation of science (fossil hunting was a favorite pastime of men and women of all ages and classes, and Mill himself was an enthusiastic botanizer); and scientists were so often amateurish in their training and methods as to qualify them, by later standards, as bumbling amateurs. One prominent politician wrote novels, another went in for theological disquisitions; these eccentricities did not prevent them from attaining the highest positions in the land. Nor were they hindered by such other oddities as the distinctly Jewish heritage and appearance of Disraeli and the ambiguous social status of Gladstone ("Oxford on the surface, Liverpool below").

Whatever fears Mill had in the thirties when he was writing "The Spirit of the Age" and "Civilization"—fears about the leveling effects of mass society upon intellectual life, the impulse to mediocrity and uniformity, the discouragement of originality and speculative boldness—were not borne out in the following decades. Certainly, the forties and fifties exhibited no slackening of intellectual productivity or creativity, no diminution either of the quality or of the quantity of ideas in circulation, no lessening of differences or weakening of dissent. The great Victorians can hardly be characterized in common, except by virtue of their distinctive greatness, their peculiar genius. Carlyle, Newman, Arnold, Macaulay, Ruskin, Darwin, Mill himself —each was unique, *sui generis*. (If novelists and poets are included, the roster becomes even more impressive; but then one expects "creative" writers to be highly individualistic.) In their religious (or irreligious) creeds, their political philosophies and social sympathies, their literary modes and styles of life, the great Victorians could not have been more diverse. And this heterogeneity communicated itself to the lesser thinkers of the age who may have been less distinguished in their own right but who were influential in the culture at large: Keble, Pusey, Maurice, Kingsley, Sterling, Bain, Lewes, Spencer, Lyell, Froude. In the decade or two following the publication of *On Liberty* other notables of equal distinction and distinctiveness entered the lists: Acton, Bagehot, Morley, Leslie Stephen, James Fitzjames Stephen, T. H. Huxley, Frederic Harrison, Lecky, Maine, T. H. Green.

The popular culture was no less varied and lively. This was true not only of the culture of the streets which Mayhew depicted so graphically, with its bawdy songs, ribald Punch and Judy shows, and melodramatic theatrical performances (the "penny gaffs"), but also of the culture of the more conventional working and lower middle classes. There were available, for their entertainment and edification, railway excursions to the seaside, the Crystal Palace, music halls, classical theater (the pit and gallery were cheap enough), free libraries and reading rooms, public lectures (which were often on surprisingly racy subjects), and, of course, books and newspapers. The abolition of the newspaper tax in 1855 reduced the cost of most popular dailies to a penny. (*The Times* remained at fourpence.) And the dailies and Sunday papers were as varied as they were numerous, both in London and in the provinces. Monthly magazines sold for a shilling, installments of novels for the same price, and cheap editions of books for as little as sixpence or ninepence—these ranged from scientific works and religious tracts to serious and trashy novels. All of this must be taken in conjunction with an extremely high literacy rate. By the late fifties (a decade before the passage of the Education Act), more than three quarters of the working classes could and evidently did read.

All of this is not to deny the persistence of a large measure of conformity and uniformity in English life, particularly in middle-class life—and particularly as compared with some periods in earlier and later centuries. But in the context of their times and values (values which Mill to a large extent shared), most Englishmen in the 1850s had a sense of relative ease and freedom, of greater, not fewer, opportunities, options, alternatives. Mrs. Grundy still existed, but she was visibly past her prime. Respectability was much sought after, by the lower as well as the middle classes; but eccentricity was possible and even had its own pretensions to respectability. Swinburne may not have published his pornographic poetry, but he was not deterred from writing it or from participating in the flourishing, if *sub rosa*, trade in pornography. And short of pornography there was much to amuse and titillate men of varied tastes and propensities.

Writing of the state of freedom in England in 1851, Herbert Spencer found more cause for satisfaction than alarm. As devoted to liberty as anyone of his generation (he was more rigorously laissez-fairist than Mill himself), he deplored the "occasional advocates" of the "repressive policy of the past." But he saw them as vestiges of the past resisting the dominant tendency of the present, and the latter was characterized by the "abatement of intolerance and the growth of free institutions." "A new Areopagitica," he reflected, "were it possible to write one, would surely be needless in our age of the world and in this country."[14]

14. Herbert Spencer, *Social Statics* (New York, 1965), p. 167. Spencer's only recorded opinion of *On Liberty* was in a letter acknowledging a gift of the book from Mill. Perhaps out of courtesy, Spencer praised Mill for defending "the claims of the individual *versus* those of society," suggesting only that he himself would have carried those claims even further than Mill. (*Life and Letters of Herbert Spencer* [London, 1908], p. 93 [HS to JSM, Feb. 17, 1859].) In his obituary notice of Mill in the *Examiner*, Spencer did not mention *On Liberty* at all. (Spencer, *Autobiography* [London, 1904], II, 506-08, appendix G.)

When that new Areopagitica was published, many readers were taken aback, not so much by the doctrine itself as by the description of the social "tyranny" which presumably inspired it. Macaulay accused Mill of "crying 'Fire!' in Noah's flood."

I went to the Athenaeum, and staid there two hours to read John Mill on Liberty and on Reform. Much that is good in both. What he says about individuality in the treatise on liberty is open, I think, to some criticism. What is meant by the complaint that there is no individuality now? Genius takes its own course, as it always did. Bolder invention was never known in science than in our time. The steam-ship, the steam-carriage, the electric telegraph, the gaslights, the new military engines, are instances. Geology is quite a new science. Phrenology is quite a new false one. Whatever may be thought of the theology, the metaphysics, the political theories of our time, boldness and novelty are not what they want. Comtism, Saint-Simonianism, Fourierism, are absurd enough, but surely they are not indications of a servile respect for usage and authority. Then the clairvoyance, the spirit-rapping, the table-turning, and all those other dotages and knaveries, indicate rather a restless impatience of the beaten paths than a stupid determination to plod on in those paths. Our lighter literature, so far as I know it, is spasmodic and eccentric. Every writer seems to aim at doing something odd—at defying all rules and canons of criticism. The metre must be queer; the diction queer. So great is the taste for oddity that men who have no recommendation but oddity hold a high place in vulgar estimation. I therefore do not at all like to see a man of Mill's excellent abilities recommending eccentricity as a thing almost good in itself—as tending to prevent us from sinking

*into that Chinese, that Byzantine, state which I should
agree with him in considering as a great calamity. He
is really crying "Fire!" in Noah's flood.*[15]

Most reviewers of *On Liberty* echoed one or another of
Macaulay's sentiments. Even Buckle, who was entirely
sympathetic to the doctrine itself, entered a small demurral
regarding the actual state of affairs in England. Expressing
the greatest reverence for Mill, he confessed that he did not
agree that individuality had diminished nor that it was likely
to do so in the future. On the contrary, he anticipated that
in this respect, as in most others, England would continue
on its inexorable course of progress.[16] James Fitzjames
Stephen, who is famous for his later book-length attack on
Mill, was at first well disposed to the thesis of *On Liberty*.
Reviewing the book in two successive editions of *The Saturday Review*, he devoted the first part to what amounted
to a eulogy of Mill for recalling Englishmen to the principle
of liberty—a principle which had been thought firmly
established until Mill proved that it was being undermined
by a powerful new tyranny.[17] The second part of the review, however, as if to gainsay the first, suggested that this
"melancholy" view of affairs (several reviewers used the
word "melancholy" in describing the tone or message of
On Liberty) was only part of the truth. Individuality was,
to be sure, as important as Mill said it was and intolerance as
abhorrent. But the conformity that society exacted was for
the most part of a limited and trivial kind. In the most
important areas of life, freedom was more available and
individuality more widespread than ever before. A person
might be obliged to wear a hat or coat of a particular cut,
to shave, and to observe certain conventions about what

15. G. O. Trevelyan, *Life and Letters of Lord Macaulay* (London, 1876), II, 456–57.
16. *Fraser's Magazine*, LIX (1859), 526–33.
17. *The Saturday Review*, VII (1859), 186.

could or could not be said in mixed company. But this was a small "quit-rent" for the privilege of reading what he pleased, thinking what he liked, educating his children in a manner of his choosing, and practicing any or no religious creed. In important matters such as these, "there probably never was a time when men who have any sort of originality or independence of character had it in their power to hold the world at arm's length so cheaply."[18]

This theme was repeated with interesting variations. *The National Review*, for example (in an essay possibly written by Bagehot), conceded that public opinion had become more "homogeneous," reflecting fewer conflicting modes of thought and fewer divergent social types. But so far from being a threat to liberty, this "moral monotony" was seen as the necessary and commendable result of liberty. What was disappearing, the *Review* claimed, were not individual varieties of character but sharply demarcated social types, the highly distinctive types associated with class, region, and sect; and they were disappearing precisely because individual freedom was increasing. Nothing had been more "exigeant and irritating in its despotism" than the sectarianism and provincialism of local groups. The decline of the various forms of local despotism, each with its own stringent code of opinion and custom, had indeed led to a greater similarity of thought and behavior, but this uniformity derived from a far larger social base than the old codes and was less oppressive in its effect upon the individual.[19]

Another critic insisted that any serious person could get a hearing for any idea on any subject however unconventional, in proof of which he observed that "a generation

18. *Ibid.*, p. 213. A fortnight later the *Review* revoked even this concession about the lack of individuality in the trivial matters of life. It then pointed out that beards were being flaunted, "unprotected females" were stalking across Europe, tobacco was breaking through the "decorum of heavy respectability," and in dozens of other ways eccentricity was becoming so commonplace it was "ceasing to be eccentric." (*Ibid.*, p. 270.)

19. *The National Review*, VIII (1859), 393-424.

which has produced and which has listened attentively to Mr. Carlyle, Mr. Froude and Mr. Buckle cannot be charged with shrinking blindly from independence of thought."[20] One reviewer cited the popularity of Mill himself as evidence of both the exercise of independence and the prevalent respect for it. For this reason he found the tone of Mill's book curiously out of keeping with its source: "It might almost indeed have come from the prison-cell of some persecuted thinker bent on making one last protest against the growing tyranny of the public mind, though conscious that his appeal will be in vain—instead of from the pen of a writer who has perhaps exercised more influence over the formation of the philosophical and social principles of cultivated Englishmen than any other man of his generation."[21]

There were, of course, other substantive and more serious objections to the doctrine of *On Liberty*. Some critics took issue with the absolute value attached to liberty and individuality. Others questioned whether a totally permissive policy was in fact the best way to produce strong and energetic characters, whether a repressive system, such as Calvinism, did not more often have that effect. Some even cited Mill's own writings on the necessity of a strong social bond for the creation of strong individual character. But it was the question of social and historical fact—whether England was in fact experiencing the kind of social tyranny Mill described—that was raised as often as any other single objection.

Some of Mill's own statements on this issue, reflecting on the actual state of affairs in England during this period, have already been quoted: the letter (written about the same time he was drafting his first essay on liberty) in which he observed that the "practical doctrines" of Comte had not

20. *Bentley's Quarterly Review*, XI (1860), 442.
21. *The National Review*, VIII (1859), 393.

made "the least headway" in England;[22] his *Autobiography* (written during the same years as *On Liberty*), referring to the freedom of opinion which then prevailed on all the "great subjects of thought";[23] and the bulk of his other writings, which give a very different impression of the "spirit of the age" from that of *On Liberty*. To these might be added some observations dating from the following decade—his statement, for example, to the House of Commons in 1867 in the course of the debate on the Reform Bill. Responding to the objection that woman suffrage was a "novelty," a strange and new idea, he pointed out that theirs was an age which rapidly assimilated strangeness and newness. "And as for novelty, we live in a world of novelties; the despotism of custom is on the wane; we are not now satisfied with knowing what a thing is, we ask whether it ought to be."[24]

More revealing is a passage of the *Autobiography* written about 1861, which has an obvious (although not explicit) bearing upon *On Liberty*. Mill was explaining why he had earlier been pessimistic about the immediate prospects of human improvement but had since become more optimistic. "More recently a spirit of free speculation has sprung up, giving a more encouraging prospect of the gradual mental emancipation of England"; together with the movement for political freedom in the rest of Europe, this gave "to the present condition of human affairs a more hopeful aspect."[25] Later still, in 1869, in the course of a rather ambiguous defense of *On Liberty*, he admitted that the "present facts" —the facts as they were when the essay had first appeared and as they continued to be a decade later—did not seem to warrant the fears of *On Liberty*:

22. Above, p. 90.
23. Above, p. 157.
24. *Parliamentary Debates*, 3rd Series, Hansard 187:819 (May 20, 1867).
25. *Autobiography*, p. 168.

Nothing can better show how deep are the foundations of this truth [the importance of liberty and variety], than the great impression made by the exposition of it at a time which, to superficial observation, did not seem to stand much in need of such a lesson. The fears we expressed, lest the inevitable growth of social equality and of the government of public opinion, should impose on mankind an oppressive yoke of uniformity in opinion and practise, might easily have appeared chimerical to those who looked more at present facts than at tendencies; for the gradual revolution that is taking place in society and institutions has, thus far, been decidedly favourable to the development of new opinions, and has procured for them a much more unprejudiced hearing than they previously met with.[26]

He went on, however, to explain that these "present facts" —the revolution in society which was proving favorable to the development of new opinions—represented a transitory period in history, a time when men were abandoning their old beliefs but had not yet acquired new ones. Before long, he predicted, a new body of doctrine would arise which would have all the popular support, institutional sanction, and social power of the old creed. "It is then that the teachings of the 'Liberty' will have their greatest value. And it is to be feared that they will retain that value a long time."[27]

Mill's defense of *On Liberty* consisted, in effect, in postdating *On Liberty*. If liberty and individuality were not then a problem—and he agreed they were not—they might become so in the future, when the social power of the masses would be exerted in favor of a new monolithic creed. But this strategy, whatever its other merits, leaves the

26. *Ibid.*, pp. 177–78.
27. *Ibid.*, p. 178. See below, pp. 269–70.

anomaly of *On Liberty* unresolved. It deprives us of the most plausible explanation of that anomaly: that Mill was responding, immediately and dramatically, to the circumstances of his time—the supposedly intolerable, coercive ethic associated with "Victorianism," an ethic which could be exposed and combated only by some such radical doctrine as he proposed. If, however, it was not his own time but some future time that worried him, a time when England might become homogenized and Americanized *à la* Tocqueville, then we are left with our original problem: Why did he not seek the remedy for that situation where he himself on other occasions—and Tocqueville as well—had sought it?

Why, in short, did Mill require the "one very simple principle" of *On Liberty*? If the problem was not excessively urgent, if the condition of England was not intolerable, why did he have recourse to such drastic solutions as "absolute" liberty and the "sovereign" individual? Why did he not rely, as the "other" Mill did, on a variety of social and historical forces to counteract the tyranny of the mass: a clerisy of intellectuals, the countervailing power of the landed class, a reformed and revitalized establishment, a liberty qualified and supplemented by other principles such as duty, morality, discipline, the public good, tradition, community, nationality, society? This "other" Mill was, admittedly, not as dramatic as the Mill of *On Liberty*. But in the absence of a dramatic problem, there would have been no need for a dramatic solution.

VII

THE ESSAYS ON WOMEN

THE QUESTION REMAINS, therefore, of what we are to make of a work which Mill himself, and posterity still more, took to be his *chef d'oeuvre* but which is so significantly at variance with the bulk of his *oeuvre*. Part of the answer may lie with a subject that is not ordinarily discussed in connection with *On Liberty* but that may have a large bearing upon it. This is the subject of women—the state of their "subjection," as Mill saw it, and the need for their "enfranchisement," enfranchisement in the largest social as well as political sense.

Until recently it would have been with some diffidence that one might have ventured to suggest this as even a partial explanation for *On Liberty*. The disparity between Mill's essays on women and his essay on liberty would have seemed so great that it would have been thought ludicrous to bring them together in this fashion. Causes, it was generally assumed, ought to be commensurate with their effects; and *On Liberty* was too momentous an event to be understood, however partially, in terms of the relatively minor subject of women. Today, however, that theory of historical causation no longer seems so compelling; momentous events, it has been demonstrated, can indeed have the most trivial causes. Moreover, the experiences of the past decade may incline us to take more seriously the subject of women both in itself and as it may shape an entire ideology.

Whatever Mill's own contemporaries or later generations may have thought of the matter, there is no doubt of the importance he himself attached to the subject that was then known as "the woman question." (Mill himself abhorred this expression, as he did others using the words "sex" or "female."[1]) His increasing preoccupation with this issue is evident in his correspondence, where it looms larger in each successive volume, until in the final two volumes it becomes a major, perhaps the dominant, theme of his letters and, it would seem, of his daily activities. References to it appear in most of his books: in the *Political Economy* he argued for the economic equality of women, in *Representative Government* for their political equality. His systematic treatment of the subject, however, was reserved for two essays. The first, "Enfranchisement of Women," originally appeared in the *Westminster Review* in 1851 and was reprinted in *Dissertations and Discussions*, where he attributed it to his wife. (It should perhaps more properly be considered a joint work.[2]) The second longer, more systematic essay, "The Subjection of Women," was written in 1860–61 and published as a pamphlet in 1869. The two essays differ in minor respects but are sufficiently similar, both in their fundamental thesis and in their mode of reasoning, to permit them to be considered together.

These essays have been generally read as pleas for sexual equality. James Fitzjames Stephen, in his critique of Mill, *Liberty, Equality, Fraternity*, took "The Subjection of

1. *Later Letters*, I, 66 (JSM to William E. Hickson, May 1851); *ibid.*, p. 177 (to Harriet Mill, Mar. 6, 1854); *ibid.*, p. 500 (to [?], after Nov. 9, 1855); *ibid.*, II, 510 (to George Holyoake, Sept. 21, 1856).

2. On the authorship of this essay, see the note appended to this chapter. For convenience, Mill will be spoken of here as the "author," on the understanding that he may well have been only co-author.

Women" as a primary illustration of the egalitarianism that, as he saw it, was one of Mill's fatal weaknesses. And when the essays were recently reissued, it was under the title of *Essays on Sex Equality*.[3] There is some warrant for this reading in the essays themselves. As Mill put it in the first essay, the point at issue was the admission of women, in law and in fact, to "equality in all rights, political, civil, and social, with the male citizens of the community."[4] And in his second essay he said that the principle presently governing the relations between the sexes, that of subordination, had to be replaced by a "principle of perfect equality, admitting no power or privilege on the one side, no disability on the other."[5] As the argument developed, however, the emphasis shifted from equality to liberty. In effect, equality was the means, liberty the end. It was for the sake of perfect freedom that perfect equality was required. The purpose of political, civil, and social equality was to establish the conditions under which individuals, men and women alike, could function more freely, develop their individuality more completely, cultivate without hindrance their intelligence, capacities, and character.

Equality in this sense was equality of opportunity—which is to say, freedom of opportunity, the freedom to compete freely and equally with men. Repeatedly in the two essays Mill insisted that he was seeking nothing more than what liberals had always sought and, in the case of men, had already achieved. Restrictions and monopolies on trade had been abolished, privileges of caste and birth reduced. In the marketplace and in law, in contractual and personal relations, the principles of free choice and free action had re-

3. John Stuart Mill and Harriet Taylor Mill, *Essays on Sex Equality*, ed. Alice S. Rossi (Chicago, 1970).

4. *Dissertations and Discussions*, II, 413.

5. "The Subjection of Women," in *On Liberty, Representative Government, The Subjection of Women*, ed. Millicent Garrett Fawcett (World's Classics edn.; London, 1969), p. 427. Referred to in subsequent footnotes as *Subjection*.

placed the older principles of social regulation and legislation.

> *It is not that all processes are supposed to be equally good, or all persons to be equally qualified for everything; but that freedom of individual choice is now known to be the only thing which procures the adoption of the best processes, and throws each operation into the hands of those who are best qualified for it. Nobody thinks it necessary to make a law that only a strong-armed man shall be a blacksmith. Freedom and competition suffice to make blacksmiths strong-armed men, because the weak-armed can earn more money by engaging in occupations for which they are more fit.*[6]

It was the "peculiar character" of the modern world that human beings were not born to their place in life nor confined to their place of birth, but were instead free to employ their faculties and opportunities to make of their lives what they could. Matters formerly prescribed by law and government were now left to the "unfettered choice of individuals."[7] The accomplishments had been considerable: "political liberty," "personal freedom of action," and "pecuniary independence" had already been established for men, as had "freedom of industry, freedom of conscience, freedom of the press."[8] What was necessary was to extend these liberties to the half of mankind which had so far been deprived of them. Women should not be subjected to restrictions that men no longer tolerated for themselves. They should not be consigned to a realm that others deemed appropriate to them. One sex could no more determine the proper limits of the other than any one individual could

6. *Ibid.*, p. 447.
7. *Ibid.*, p. 446.
8. *Dissertations*, II, 418, 420.

make that determination for another individual. "The proper sphere for all human beings is the largest and highest which they are able to attain to."[9] If occupations were open to women as well as men, without favor or impediment, different employments would naturally fall to individuals of different capabilities. All that was required was the largest exercise of freedom.

> *Each individual will prove his or her capacities, in the only way in which capacities can be proved—by trial; and the world will have the benefit of the best faculties of all its inhabitants.*[10]

> *There are no means of finding what either one person or many can do, but by trying—and no means by which any one else can discover for them what it is for their happiness to do or leave undone.*[11]

> *Every restraint on the freedom of conduct of any of their human fellow creatures, (otherwise than by making them responsible for any evil actually caused by it), dries up* pro tanto *the principal fountain of human happiness, and leaves the species less rich, to an inappreciable degree, in all that makes life valuable to the individual human being.*[12]

These passages, and others that might have been cited, suggest how close these essays are to *On Liberty* in conception and substance. The point needs to be made all the more clearly because it tends to be obscured by those who today profess the highest regard for them. In the canon of the women's liberation movement, the essays have long occupied a prominent and honorable place. But like all sacred texts,

9. *Ibid.*, p. 422.   10. *Ibid.*, p. 423.   11. *Subjection*, pp. 457–58. 12. *Ibid.*, p. 548.

they have been more often invoked than read. Most recently they have been used to lend credence and authority to what has become the dominant ideology of the women's movement, an ideology of equality—and a particular kind of equality at that, not so much the equality of opportunity as the equality of achievement, of results. It is this ideology that focuses attention on numbers, the number of women in particular trades and occupations and at particular grades and ranks, on the assumption that this is the visible test of equality. And when the results of this test prove unsatisfactory, it seeks to correct them by legislative decree or administrative fiat. This strategy is a far cry from Mill's insistence upon free choice and free competition. Indeed, it would seem to encourage a revival of precisely the kind of regulation which he deplored, the determination in advance of the "proper spheres" of men and women.

As the women's movement has currently chosen to emphasize equality rather than liberty, so it has also distracted attention from the individualistic nature of Mill's argument. For Mill the central problem was the individual: how to give to the individual woman the same degree of liberty enjoyed by the individual man, how to make more complete individuals of both women and men. While this may still be represented as the ultimate aim of the movement, the more immediate and urgent problem is taken to be the entire class, the collective body, of women. In part the emphasis upon class reflects the prevailing concern with numbers: numbers can only be a function of a class; they tell us nothing about individual cases. In part it reflects a concern with power, the collective power that presumably resides in a united class rather than in separate individuals. Whatever the cause, the effect is a radical redirection of effort. Where Mill sought to liberate women in order to release the greatest variety of individuality, the movement today emphasizes the search for a common identity, a shared "consciousness," a "sisterhood" which will promote the common cause against a common enemy. This is perhaps why the movement is willing to speak of "woman" in the singular while Mill always insisted upon the plurality of "women."

In one respect, however, Mill and the current women's liberation movement are entirely in accord. They are both concerned with liberation—in Mill's case, liberation from custom, tradition, history, and society. It is astonishing, at first reading, to find Mill devoting so much space to what is essentially a negative argument. One might have expected him to concentrate on the positive point, the simple right of every individual to live his life as fully and freely as possible. That positive argument, however, could not be made until the negative one had been disposed of. The most formidable obstacle to the liberation of women, Mill found, was the weight of received opinion and custom which had so long relegated women to a subordinate position. It was this body of opinion and custom that had first to be refuted. And not only did specific opinions and customs have to be challenged: the idea, for example, that women were physically inferior to men, that their distinctive mental qualities fitted them for certain occupations and not for others, or that the proper ordering of domestic life required them to complement rather than compete with men. Over and above all these was the force of opinion and custom as such, the general presumption that whatever had been decreed by time must have truth in its favor, that if women had for so long, indeed for all of recorded history, been placed in a position of inferiority, this must testify to the fact of their inferiority. "Universal practice," "universal opinion," "universal usage," all told powerfully against women;[13] when these happened also to coincide with the most intense and deeply rooted feelings of men, no amount of rational argument, no appeal to right or justice or reason could prevail.

13. *Dissertations*, II, 419; *Subjection*, p. 428; *ibid.*, p. 429.

What now made it possible, Mill hoped, for counterarguments to be heard was the spirit of modernity. Just as the abolition of traditional restrictions in trade and industry established a precedent for the abolition of similar restrictions in the case of women, so the new spirit of inquiry gave promise of releasing women from the bondage of custom. "This strongest of prejudices, the prejudice against what is new and unknown, has, indeed, in an age of changes like the present, lost much of its force; if it had not, there would be little hope of prevailing against it." Three fourths of the world still took "it has always been so" as sufficient argument against any innovation. But it was also the boast of modern men that they did and knew things their forefathers did not. This was the "most unquestionable point of superiority" of the present over the past. Habit was no longer the tyrant it had been; the worship of custom was becoming a "declining idolatry."[14]

Only in one respect did the spirit of modernity falter, and that was in the case of women. "The social subordination of women thus stands out an isolated fact in modern social institutions; a solitary breach of what has become their fundamental law; a single relic of an old world of thought and practice exploded in everything else."[15] It was the discrepancy between this one social fact and the entire "progressive movement" of history that raised a prima-facie presumption against this single anomaly. Now that Negro slavery had been abolished, the "law of servitude in marriage" constituted the only "monstrous contradiction" in the modern world: "Marriage is the only actual bondage known to our law. There remain no legal slaves, except the mistress of every house."[16]

14. *Dissertations*, II, 420.
15. *Subjection*, p. 449.
16. *Ibid.*, p. 522. The remark about the abolition of Negro slavery (evidently a reference to the American Civil War) must have been added when Mill prepared the essay for publication in 1869.

The case of women, in short, was the case of humanity *in extremis*. It was women who experienced, in its most fatal form, the social tyranny described in *On Liberty*, and it was their condition of servitude that would be most dramatically relieved by the adoption of the principle of liberty advocated in that work. They were the worst victims of the present system and they would be the chief beneficiaries of the new. When Mill commented upon the meeting of the Women's Convention in Massachusetts in 1850 (the same convention that was to be the point of departure for "Enfranchisement of Women"), he spoke optimistically of the changes that might come in his lifetime on this issue—this which was "of all practical subjects the most important."[17] In this sense, *On Liberty* may be taken as the generalized statement, the theoretical formulation, of this most important of all practical subjects. For what it did was to posit for all mankind the liberty that was most practically and urgently required for women.

Looked at from the perspective of women, *On Liberty* appears in a new light. For if the situation of women was the single "monstrous contradiction" to the general condition of mankind, then mankind, as distinct from womankind, was by no means in an intolerable state. If the conditions of men and women were as dramatically different as Mill made them out to be in the essays on women, if liberty did in fact prevail in the world in sufficient measure to permit men to develop their characters and potentialities in such notable contrast to women, if restrictions and regulations, the tyranny of custom and opinion, had been so effectively diminished for everyone except women, then the message of *On Liberty* seems gratuitous—except of course, for women. *On Liberty*, indeed, need never have been written; the essays on women would have sufficed to correct the one "monstrous contradiction" that remained.

17. *Later Letters*, I, 49 (to Harriet Taylor, after Oct. 29, 1850).

On Liberty, however, *was* written—possibly because Mill, in spite of his momentary optimism at the time of the Massachusetts Women's Convention, came to think that women alone would not be able to effect the necessary change and that men would not address themselves to the problem unless it was their problem as well. But to make it their problem, he had to redefine liberty, to give it an absolute character which put it beyond the present reach of men. By this tactic, men as well as women were made victims of the same social tyranny. Men, to be sure, were less monstrously tyrannized and victimized, but they were sufficiently so to give them a common stake in the battle for liberty. Absolute liberty eluded them, as much as it did women. And anything short of absolute liberty (except for the qualification about injury to others) was an infringement on each person's sovereignty, a denial of his individuality, an impediment to his full development as a human being, a "complete and consistent whole." By comparison with the condition of women, that of men might seem tolerable. But by comparison with the absolute standard set up in *On Liberty*, both sexes were in the same onerous situation, shared the same disabilities and deprivations.

Having given men and women a common stake in liberty, Mill also gave them a common enemy—in society, custom, popular opinion, and tradition. The question of a common enemy was as important as the common goal. For had Mill not made of society the enemy, men and women would have been put in a position of implacable enmity. If women were, as Mill repeatedly said, the "slaves" of men,[18] the implication would seem to follow that the slaves could liberate themselves only by turning against their masters and that their masters would have to protect their own interests by suppressing that insurrection. This,

18. *Subjection*, pp. 462, 463, 465, 522.

indeed, is the conclusion drawn by some of the more combative members of the women's liberation movement today; the war of the sexes plays the same part in their ideology as the class war did in Marx's. Mill went out of his way to avoid precisely this conclusion.

In his essays on women, Mill insisted that men had as much to gain as women from the liberation of women, that the interests of the two were identical. A marriage between unequals, he argued at some length, was equally degrading to both. A wife whose entire existence was circumscribed by the petty details of domestic life necessarily had a debasing effect upon a husband whose perspective was larger and whose aspirations might be higher. "Her conscious, and still more her unconscious influence will, except in rare cases, reduce to a secondary place in his mind, if not entirely extinguish, those interests which she cannot or does not share."[19] Unlike many who professed to be champions of women, Mill denied that women, in their present condition, had an elevating moral influence; more often, he said, their influence was for the bad. Concerned only with the immediate interests of their families, they were likely to distract or discourage their husbands from pursuing "public virtue," the "public good."[20] In the present situation, the better things were, the worse they were. The more kindly, benevolent, considerate the husband, the more responsive he was to his wife's feelings. And her feelings were entirely absorbed in her family. "She neither knows nor cares which is the right side in politics, but she knows what will bring in money or invitations, give her husband a title, her son a place, or her daughter a good marriage."[21] It was, therefore, in the best interests of men, for the best cultivation of their faculties and potentialities, that the liberation of women was required.

19. *Dissertations*, II, 436–37.
20. *Ibid.*, p. 442.
21. *Subjection*, p. 472.

But if men were not the enemy of women, then something or someone else had to be. And that something Mill located in the combined force of received opinion and established tradition, the whole "experience of mankind" which conspired to keep women in subjection.[22] In the course of his attack upon this universal experience, Mill implicitly took cognizance of a point he had made in his essay on Coleridge. He had then said that the important question to ask of any received tradition or opinion was not "Is it true?" but rather "What is the meaning of it?" —on the assumption that if it had persisted so long and persuaded so many, it must have some important meaning, some significant truth.[23] In "The Subjection of Women" Mill granted that "the generality of a practice is in some cases a strong presumption that it is, or at all events once was, conducive to laudable ends." But he immediately deflected the force of this argument by saying that this particular practice had never had the benefit of a "conscientious compromise between different modes of constituting the government of society," that it was not the result of "deliberation, or forethought, or any social ideas, or any notion whatever of what conduced to the benefit of humanity or the good order of society."[24] The present status of women, he insisted, was the result of nothing more than their physical inferiority and was a survival from a time when physical strength was the primary fact governing the relations among men.

Whatever the cogency of Mill's answer, it did not address itself to Coleridge's question, which never assumed that society engaged in conscientious experiments or conscious deliberations, but rather that it unconsciously and without forethought evolved modes of behavior which had

22. *Ibid.*, p. 450.
23. *Essays on Politics and Culture*, p. 121.
24. *Subjection*, p. 431.

meaning and truth. Mill could not confront that question because he could not risk granting any degree of legitimacy to a practice he found thoroughly abhorrent. All he could do was to reject the entire past and present experience of mankind, the whole body of history and tradition, of social conventions and institutions, which had supported that practice. He had, in short, to illegitimize the experience of mankind in order to legitimize the claims of women.

Reading *On Liberty* in conjunction with the essays on women, one is impressed by the way they complement and reinforce each other. The peculiarities of *On Liberty*, those aspects of it which are so out of keeping with most of Mill's other work—the absolute nature of the principle of liberty, the exaltation of individuality whatever its particular form, the animus against society, opinion, and tradition—become understandable when seen in the context of these essays. The essays on women were not, as might be thought, miniature versions of *On Liberty*, the application of *On Liberty* to a particular practical problem. Rather it would seem that *On Liberty* was the case of women writ large, the liberation of women magnified to the point where it became the liberation of all mankind.

THERE REMAINS one difficulty. If the doctrine of liberty was required for the liberation of women, if the subjection of women was the single "monstrous contradiction" to the principle of liberty, why did the issue of women not figure more prominently in *On Liberty*? The latter referred to women only occasionally, in connection with the Mormon practice of polygamy, the marriage contract as an example of contractual relationships, and the "almost despotic power of husbands over wives," about which, Mill added, there was no need to say more because it was so patent an infringement of liberty and because the remedy (equal rights under the law) was so obvious.[25] It is curious to find him dealing so fleetingly with this "most important" of all practical problems. Perhaps he did so because he had already published one essay on the subject and was thinking of writing another. Or perhaps, and more probably, he felt it would weaken his case if he allied liberty too closely to the cause of women.

Whereas Mill could, and did, expect *On Liberty* to be warmly received, he could not have had the same expectation of any work that made too much of the issue of women. He might well have thought it more prudent and more effective to take his examples from other areas—from religion, or trade, or the temperance movement—confident that if the general proposition were accepted, all the particulars, including women, would fall into place. Whether or not Mill consciously adopted this as a strategy, he could hardly have been unaware of the derision that was bound to greet anyone who associated himself with the cause of women. He was to experience this later in Parliament, when he proposed amending the suffrage bill to include women. And it may have been for the same reason, and in the hope that popular opinion on the subject would change, that he delayed publishing "The Subjection of Women" for eight years. When it was finally published, in 1869, it was received with varying degrees of dismay and hostility even by his own friends.

Whatever Mill's reasons for muting the issue of women in *On Liberty*, there is no doubt of the importance he himself attached to it. Nor can there be any question of the close connection between the arguments of *On Liberty* and those of the essays on women. Whole passages from the essays could have been transposed intact to *On Liberty*. And crucial themes of *On Liberty* are difficult to understand except in relation to the question of women. Indeed,

25. *On Liberty*, p. 160.

of all of Mill's writings, only the essays on women are entirely consonant with *On Liberty*.

"The Subjection of Women" was deplored by most of Mill's friends, by Alexander Bain as much as the others. But Bain saw what the rest did not. Mill's "strongest case" in *On Liberty*, he wrote, was the "relationship of the sexes" which was "little more than hinted at."[26] Bain did not elaborate upon this comment. But it may provide us with matter for thought.

Note on the Authorship of "Enfranchisement of Women"

THIS ESSAY IS generally credited to Mill in spite of his own insistence (not at the time of writing but some years later) that it was largely written by his wife. In a recent reprint it has been attributed to his wife alone. (The volume of which this essay is part, *Essays on Sex Equality*, edited by Alice S. Rossi, carries the names of John Stuart Mill and Harriet Taylor Mill as joint authors; but this particular essay is assigned to Harriet Mill alone.) The evidence, however, is more complicated than this would suggest.

Two years before the publication of "Enfranchisement of Women," Harriet Taylor had evidently started to write on this or a similar subject. In February 1849 Mill urged her to finish her "pamphlet" or, better yet, to convert it into a little book.[27] The following year he told the editor of the *Westminster Review* that he (Mill) was thinking of writing on that subject. The editor, William Hickson, misunderstood Mill to be proposing an article on divorce, whereupon Mill explained that he

26. Bain, p. 108.
27. *Later Letters*, I, 13 (Feb. 21, 1849).

wanted to write on the "entire position" of women as determined by custom and law.[28] In March 1851 (a month before his marriage), Mill wrote to Hickson offering him an article on the emancipation of women: "I have one nearly ready, which can be finished and sent to you within a week."[29] Two months later, in connection with another piece, Mill wrote again: "I will endeavour to write something besides the article on the women's subject."[30] Unless Mill was being deliberately deceptive, it would seem that he then thought of himself as the author of the article and that the editor accepted it as such. Since the essay, like all others in the *Review*, was published anonymously, there was no formal attribution of authorship at the time.

In 1854 the publisher John Chapman asked permission to reprint the article. Although Mill was offended by Chapman's "vulgarly" referring to it as "the article on Woman," he was pleased that the request had been addressed to his wife.[31] Discussing their decision not to have it republished, Mill reminded his wife that the essay would appear in any collection of articles that might be published during or after their lifetime. It would then, he told her, be "preceded by a preface which will show that much of all my later articles, and all the best of that one, were, as they were, my Darling's."[32]

In 1856 the essay was reprinted by George Holyoake. Rebuking Holyoake for not asking the permission of the author (and for his "vulgarity" and "sentimentality" in changing "women" in the text to "woman"), Mill spoke of it as "my

28. *Ibid.*, p. 47 (Mar. 19, 1850).

29. *Ibid.*, p. 56 (Mar. 3, 1851).

30. *Ibid.*, p. 65 (May 6, 1851).

31. *Ibid.*, p. 177 (Mar. 6, 1854). Mill speculated that Chapman may have been told of Mrs. Mill's part in the writing of the essay by either Harriet Martineau or Mrs. Gaskell. The latter, however, is unlikely. In her biography of Charlotte Brontë published three years later, Mrs. Gaskell quoted, without correction or comment, a letter by Brontë written soon after the article had appeared, in which Brontë explained that she had first assumed it to have been written by a woman but had then learned that it was by Mill himself. (See above, pp. 49–50.)

32. *Ibid.*, p. 190 (Mar. 20, 1854).

wife's article."[33] In his own autobiography, obviously forgetful of Mill's rebuke, Holyoake said he had obtained the permission of Mrs. Mill to distribute her article.[34]

After his wife's death, when the essay was reprinted in *Dissertations and Discussions*, Mill fulfilled his promise to her by including a prefatory note attributing it to her. All his recent essays, he explained, were "joint productions," but this was "hers in a peculiar sense, my share in it being little more than that of an editor and amanuensis." He added that its authorship was "known at the time, and publicly attributed to her."[35]

It is curious that Mill never mentioned this essay in any of the versions of his *Autobiography*—not in the *Early Draft*, where it would have made a fitting conclusion to the period of his life covered in that draft, nor in the final version where he referred to "The Subjection of Women" as based on her "teaching" but never alluded to the earlier essay.[36] Perhaps this is because, as he said in *Dissertations and Discussions*, he felt that the essay did not do justice to her: "Had she lived to write out all her thoughts on this great question, she would have produced something as far transcending in profundity the present Essay, as, had she not placed a rigid restraint on her feelings, she would have excelled it in fervid eloquence."[37] (But then, he added, nothing she could have written would have done her justice.)

Alice Rossi, in whose volume Harriet Mill figures as the "primary" author of "Enfranchisement of Women" (in the table of contents, she appears as the sole author), offers other evidence of Mrs. Mill's authorship. Rossi finds it significant that an early essay by Harriet Taylor agrees with "Enfranchisement of Women" in commending the employment of married women, whereas Mill's later essay, "The Subjection of Women," disapproved of such employment except in special cir-

33. *Ibid.*, II, 509–10 (Sept. 21, 1856).
34. George Holyoake, *Sixty Years of an Agitator's Life* (London, 1892), I, 225.
35. *Dissertations and Discussions*, II, 411.
36. *Autobiography*, p. 173.
37. *Dissertations and Discussions*, II, 412.

cumstances.[38] But in an edition of the *Political Economy* published shortly after the "Enfranchisement" essay, Mill did allow for the employment of married women on much the same grounds as the essay.[39] It may, of course, be argued that his wife was responsible for that passage in the *Political Economy* (although there is no specific evidence for this). Even if this were true, however, it provides evidence of her influence over Mill, not of her "primary," still less sole, authorship of this essay.

In any event, it is noteworthy that Mill's attribution of the essay to his wife became more pronounced over the course of the years and particularly after her death. If Harriet had really been the author, it is unlikely that Mill would have written to her, as he did in 1854, that "all the best" in it was by her. In view of his usual tone of unrestrained adulation, this seems markedly qualified. But more of this, and of the nature of their "collaboration" in general, in the following chapters.

38. *Essays on Sex Equality*, pp. 41–42.

39. Compare the several editions of the *Political Economy* (I, 394) in respect to the crucial passage on the employment of women. In 1852 the weight of the argument was in favor of their employment; after 1862 (the first edition to appear after his wife's death) it was heavily against it.

VIII

A PERSONAL AND PUBLIC AFFAIR

THE RELATIONSHIP BETWEEN *On Liberty* and the essays on women can be demonstrated by textual and intellectual analysis. But the compelling nature of Mill's concern with the question of women, the pressures that brought it into play and kept it in the forefront of his consciousness, can only be accounted for in emotional terms. Contemplating Mill's personal life, one may wonder less at the extent of his preoccupation with this issue than at his ability to resist an even greater obsession with it. It is not his writings on women that are surprising. What is surprising is the amount of intellectual and emotional energy he managed to expend on other issues. For the "woman question" was an intrusive and persistent fact of his personal life—and not only from the time when he became involved with Mrs. Taylor, but long before, from his earliest childhood. If Mrs. Taylor represented for him the emancipated woman, his mother was the archetype of the enslaved woman. The titles of his essays—the "enfranchisement" and "subjection" of women—were, perhaps not by accident, the existential realities of his life.

The reader of Mill's *Autobiography* cannot fail to note the omission of any mention of his mother, an omission that would be curious in any autobiography but is still more in this one, where his father and wife play so large a part. This omission may lend substance to a complaint sometimes made about the *Autobiography*: that it is an arid, impersonal work concerned only with things of the mind. His father and wife figured so largely in it, one might suppose, because they exercised so large an intellectual influence on him; his mother, having no such influence, was irrelevant and therefore unmentioned. Mill himself contributed to this impression of the *Autobiography* when he described it as a record of his "mental history,"[1] and when he gave currency to the popular image of the Benthamite—and of himself in the period of his discipleship—as a "mere reasoning machine."[2] But Mill did himself, and the book, an injustice. What is extraordinary about his "mental history" is the passion and drama with which it was infused, in part because it was so intimately related to his personal life. And "reasoning machines" do not suffer nervous breakdowns. One cannot, in fact, separate his "crisis" from his complicated emotional life. It was not a mere "father figure" from whom Mill so painfully liberated himself; it was his flesh-and-blood father —a fact that must impress even the least psychoanalytically minded reader.

If the presence of his father is so obtrusive in the *Autobiography*, the absence of his mother is no less so. But she had not always been absent. In the early drafts of the *Autobiography* she had made an appearance, if only briefly. But these brief references to her were so harsh that the reader can only judge it an act of compassion on Mill's part to have

1. *Autobiography*, p. 93.
2. *Ibid.*, p. 76. The *Early Draft* spoke of a "dry, hard, logical machine" (p. 101). Carlyle described the *Autobiography* as "the life of a logic-chopping engine, little more of human in it than if it had been done by a thing of mechanized iron," the "autobiography of a steam-engine." (*Thomas Carlyle: A History of His Life in London, 1834–1881*, ed. J. A. Froude [London, 1884], II, 420 [TC to John Carlyle, Nov. 5, 1873].)

later omitted them. (Some of the deletions were suggested by his wife, from motives, one may suspect on the basis of other evidence, that were not entirely kindly.[3]) The picture that emerges from those early drafts is of a mother who was as painfully submissive as the father was domineering. Yet Mill's animus was directed more against his mother than against his father. "My father's children," Mill wrote, "neither loved him, nor, with any warmth of affection, any one else." Like most English families, he added, his was totally lacking in genuine affection, and he grew up "in the absence of love and the presence of fear."[4] For all this he blamed not his father but his mother:

> *That rarity in England, a really warm hearted mother, would in the first place have made my father a totally different being, and in the second would have made the children grow up loving and being loved. But my mother with the very best intentions, only knew how to pass her life in drudging for them. Whatever she could do for them she did, and they liked her, because she was kind to them, but to make herself loved, looked up to, or even obeyed, required qualities which she unfortunately did not possess.*[5]

It was his "father's children" Mill described as unloved and unloving, but his mother whom he held responsible for those deficiencies. Looking back upon his childhood, he deplored his own "ill-breeding and impertinence," his arrogance and disputatiousness. He suspected that these qualities

3. Her letters show her to have been exceedingly suspicious of, even hostile to, his mother and sisters. If she deleted Mill's harsh comments, it was possibly because here, as in other changes she made in the *Autobiography*, she wanted to present Mill in the best light, and his remarks about his mother might have reflected more unfavorably upon Mill than upon his mother.

4. *Early Draft*, pp. 183–84.

5. *Ibid.*, p. 184.

came from his father's encouraging him to talk with adults on terms of equality. His father did not see these defects of character because in his presence his son was awed and subdued. His mother did occasionally rebuke him, "but for her remonstrances," Mill observed, "I never had the slightest regard."[6] The comment suggests distaste rather than guilt, a repugnance for the "offensive habit" of impertinence, rather than remorse for having treated his mother so shabbily. The implication was that it was her fault she was not respected, and her fault too, not his father's or his own, that his character suffered in the process.

These references to his mother were deleted in an early stage of the rewriting of the *Autobiography*. What remained in the *Early Draft* (the autobiography as it stood at the time of his wife's death) were only a few indirect allusions to his mother. In one sense these were even more invidious than the earlier comments since her existence was now acknowledged only in so far as it impinged upon his father. At one point Mill referred to his father's "ill assorted marriage" which lacked the "inducements of kindred intellect, tastes, or pursuits";[7] at another he deplored the fact that his father had never developed the capacities for feeling that Mill felt certain were within him: "In an atmosphere of tenderness and affection he would have been tender and affectionate; but his ill assorted marriage and his asperities of temper disabled him from making such an atmosphere."[8] Mill did not stop to wonder whether his mother's character, perhaps even intellect, might not have thrived in an atmosphere of tenderness and affection and in the absence of her husband's well-known "asperities of temper." Nor did he consider the fact that the marriage was as "ill-assorted" for his mother as for his father, and that it was at least as damaging to her as to him.

6. *Ibid.*, p. 56 n. This was deleted by his wife.
7. *Ibid.*, p. 36.
8. *Ibid.*, p. 66.

Even these oblique references were deleted from the final version of the *Autobiography*, so that no mention at all of his mother remained. When the *Autobiography* was published soon after his death, his sister, obviously hurt by the complete omission of herself as well as her mother, recorded in a private letter some of her own memories of their childhood. Without having read the early draft of the *Autobiography*, she confirmed one part of it although she put it in a quite different light. She too remembered her parents as "living as far apart under the same roof, as the north pole from the south." But this, she insisted, was from no fault of her mother. How could her mother be anything but a "German Hausfrau" when she had to care for a large family with very small means? If she failed as an intellectual companion to her father, "*his* great want," she recalled, "was 'temper,'" especially in the early years of their childhood. (This too she charitably attributed to "circumstances."[9])

His sister did not comment on Mill's relations with his parents, but two friends of his younger brother's did. They had known the family not in John's childhood but in his early manhood. One recalled a week-long visit in the summer of 1830. John then struck him as a "great favourite" with his family. He seemed to be "very fond of his mother and sisters, and they of him"; he displayed toward them an "affectionate playfulness," a "sunny brightness and gaiety of heart and behaviour."[10] Another friend of the same period carried away much the same impression of a young man "devotedly attached to his mother and exuberant in his playful tokens of affection"; only towards his father was he "deferential, never venturing to controvert him in

9. F. A. Hayek (ed.), *John Stuart Mill and Harriet Taylor: Their Friendship and Subsequent Marriage* (Chicago, 1951), p. 286, quoting a letter from Harriet I. Mill to the Rev. J. Crompton, Oct. 26, 1873.

10. *Ibid.*, p. 32, quoting H. Solly, *These Eighty Years* (London, 1893), I, 147, and *The Workman's Magazine* (1873), p. 385.

argument nor taking a prominent part in the conversation in his presence."[11] These two comments, made quite independently, are strikingly similar to each other—and strikingly dissimilar from Mill's own account.

Mill's memories of his childhood may well have been colored by his later experiences. The first draft of the *Autobiography* was written at a time when his relations with his mother and sisters were at their worst, his marriage having caused a considerable estrangement among them.[12] (His father had died long before, so that he was spared the resentment Mill came to feel toward the rest of the family.) Perhaps, too, Mill's lack of sympathy toward his mother had something to do, paradoxically, with his strong views about sexual equality. His mother was visible, painful evidence of the "subjection" he found so distressing. In his essays on women he was able to explain that unfortunate condition historically and socially; but in the case of his own mother he could not maintain that distance. He saw in her only a personal failure of character—and what was worse, a want of intelligence. That Mill should have been lacking in consistency and objectivity in a situation that was so highly charged comes as no surprise. Nor is it surprising that he gave no recognition of the emotional complexities and depths which gave rise to such anomalies.[13]

However one understands Mill's feelings, or however he himself understood them, there is no doubt that the example of his mother provided a dramatic personal illustration of the theme that was later to preoccupy him. When in his essays on women he insisted upon the blatant inequality of

11. *Ibid.*, p. 33, quoting Mss., King's College, Cambridge.

12. See below, p. 212.

13. Apart from the obvious psychoanalytic explanations, one must also take into account the example of his wife, who must have appeared to Mill as a standing rebuke to his mother. By her own strength of will and mind, and in notable contrast to his mother, she resisted the forces of subjection and asserted her superiority.

the sexes or upon the fact that men suffered as much as women from that inequality, he was testifying to what he knew from personal, painful experience.

THE IMPACT of Mill's father also made itself felt on a different level, that of women's "enfranchisement" in the narrow, electoral sense. In his "Essay on Government" James Mill had made it a fundamental principle of representative government that the interests of the governed be identical with those of the governing body. From this principle he deduced that the suffrage ought to be extended to everyone except those whose interests were "indisputably included" in those of others. In this special category were children, whose interests were those of their parents, and women, "the interest of almost all of whom is involved either in that of their fathers or in that of their husbands."[14] The exception made in the case of women was one of the points raised by Macaulay in his critique of this essay. (Not that Macaulay himself favored the enfranchisement of women; his quarrel was with the principle of identity of interests, which could only be applied, he argued, in this inconsistent fashion.)

In his *Autobiography* Mill confronted this objection in his usual ambivalent manner. He defended his father against Macaulay's criticism (without identifying Macaulay by name), while dissociating himself from the position taken by his father. His father, he argued, had not meant to say that women *should* be excluded from the franchise—only that this was the only ground on which they or any other group *might* be excluded. The question remained, however, of whether a woman's interests could properly be identified with those of her husband or father. And here Mill unequivocally dissented from his father's view. He thought then, he said, as he thought since, that there was no such

14. James Mill, *An Essay on Government* (Library of Liberal Arts edn.; New York, 1955), pp. 73–74.

identity of interests. The interest of women was no more "involved" in that of men than the interest of subjects in that of kings, and "every reason which exists for giving the suffrage to anybody, imperatively requires that it be given to women." On this "most important point," he added, he and all his friends agreed with Bentham rather than with James Mill.[15]

One might suspect that Mill was reading back into his youth opinions that developed later in life. But here there is reason to think that he was in fact faithfully reflecting his early views. Two years before the appearance of James Mill's essay, Bentham had published a *Plan of Parliamentary Reform* advocating universal suffrage—not manhood suffrage, which was the common proposal of most radical reformers, but universal suffrage. Bentham's *Plan* became something like the platform of the Philosophic Radicals. Even those radicals, like James Mill, who thought Bentham impolitic in proposing measures that went against the grain of the time, did not venture to disagree with him in principle. The idea of women's suffrage, therefore, was familiar enough in the circle of the young Mill during the early 1820s; indeed, in that heretical group it was the prevailing orthodoxy. Moreover, it was entirely in keeping with whatever else is known about John Mill at this time—his criticism of his father for being excessively prudent (in matters of religion, for example) and his own imprudence in distributing the birth-control tracts.

At this time too, a year after the birth-control incident, John Mill wrote his first article for the *Westminster Review*.[16] The article was a continuation of a critique, begun

15. *Early Draft*, pp. 98–99. (This is somewhat differently worded in the final version; see *Autobiography*, p. 73.)

16. In the final version of the *Autobiography* (p. 66), Mill spoke slightingly, and only in a footnote, of his first contribution to the *Westminster Review*. It is interesting to compare this with the *Early Draft* (p. 93), not for the light it throws on the question of women (he did not, in fact, refer to this aspect

by his father in the preceding issue, of the *Edinburgh Review*. One of the points in the son's—not the father's—indictment of the *Edinburgh Review* was its perpetuation of the stereotype of the female character and female virtues. Like most of their contemporaries, the *Edinburgh* writers, Mill said, supported a double standard of morality. They commended independence and courage in a man while admiring exactly the opposite traits in a woman. They professed to esteem such strong-minded women as Mme. de Staël and Miss Edgeworth at the same time that they praised Shakespeare for portraying, as the "very perfection of the feminine character," the type of woman who existed only for others and was supported largely on the "strength of affections."[17] In these respects, Mill said, the *Edinburgh* reviewers were like those men who pretended to admire well-educated women while deliberating choosing for themselves wives who were so ignorant and helpless that they would never presume to subject their husbands to criticism or even comparison.

IN 1830 MILL BECAME a habitué of another circle in which feminism was an even livelier issue than it was among the Philosophic Radicals. This was the group with which Harriet Taylor was then much involved and which had as its

---

of it), but rather for what it tells us about the editing of the *Autobiography*. Mill's first draft explained in detail how he had written and rewritten the article under the close supervision of his father. (He was at the time, as he pointed out, not quite eighteen.) In the several edited versions, his wife toned down or eliminated one after another of his self-depreciating remarks, until finally the lengthy paragraph was reduced to a one-sentence footnote.

In the course of all this rewriting, Mill confused the date of his own article with that of the first issue of the *Westminster Review*. Thus, in the *Autobiography*, the first number of the journal is incorrectly given as April 1824 rather than January 1824.

17. "Edinburgh Review," *Westminster Review*, I (1824), 525–26.

leading spirit the famous Unitarian minister William Fox. Mill had met Fox earlier, perhaps as early as 1824 when Fox contributed to the first issue of the *Westminster Review*. But it was only after his friendship with Mrs. Taylor that Mill became closely associated with this group and began to write for Fox's journal, *The Monthly Repository*.

The magazine had recently achieved some small notoriety because of its "advanced" views of marriage and divorce, the status of women, and the relation of the sexes. In the issue immediately preceding that in which Mill's first article appeared, Fox himself had written a piece urging a higher level of education for women and commenting on the anomaly that women should be deprived of the suffrage while a princess was preparing to become the reigning sovereign of England.[18] The following year Fox wrote a more provocative article under the somewhat disingenuous title, "The Dissenting Marriage Question."[19] Taking as his point of departure a proposal many Dissenters had made, that the marriage contract be a purely civil transaction and that any religious ceremony be completely voluntary, he went on to a much more radical suggestion that went far beyond the intention of these Dissenters. If the marriage contract were a purely civil matter, Fox reasoned, the dissolution of the contract should also be purely contractual dependent only upon the will of both parties. Since it was the supposedly sacramental nature of marriage that had made dissolution difficult, the secularization of marriage would enormously facilitate divorce.

Mill did not comment on this article, but he did complain to Fox when another contributor recommended improved educational and occupational opportunities for women but

18. William Fox, "A Political and Social Anomaly," *The Monthly Repository*, VI (1832), 637–42.
19. Fox, "The Dissenting Marriage Question," *ibid.*, VII (1833), 136–42.

in such a manner as would have reenforced the conventional female roles.[20] Nor was he sparing in criticism of other friends whose treatment of women, collectively or individually, might be thought disparaging. Carlyle, for example, was no believer in equality, female or male. When he once said in praise of Mme. Roland that she was almost more a man than a woman, Mill rebuked him. Was there really, he asked, any distinction between the "highest masculine and the highest feminine character"? He assured Carlyle that the women he knew who had the highest measure of what were generally considered feminine qualities also had more of the highest masculine qualities than he had ever seen save in one or two men—"and those one or two men were also in every respects almost women." The second-rate of both sexes, he granted, probably did conform to the conventional distinctions, but the first-rate were alike in the "highest" qualities.[21]

WITH COMTE, MILL pursued the issue more systematically because it played so prominent a part in the Positivist system. Today Comte's views on women are generally associated with the later development of his thought, the period following his impassioned affair with Mme. Clothilde de Vaux and his apotheosization of her, after her death, in the symbol of the Virgin Mother. In his *System of Positive Polity* and *Catechism of Positive Religion* this female deity stood at the pinnacle of his religion, outranking even the High Priest of Humanity. The Virgin Mother, representing the entire species of women, was to serve as the guardian of the new morality. And since morality was ultimately

20. *Earlier Letters*, I, 160 (July 4, 1833). Mill was referring to the article "On Female Education and Occupations," *The Monthly Repository*, VII (1833).

21. *Earlier Letters*, I, 184 (Oct. 5, 1833).

to supersede even sociology in the hierarchy of knowledge —and therefore in the hierarchy of power—Comte might seem to have given women a most exalted position. But even here, Mill recognized, the exaltation of women was achieved at the expense of their human and civic equality. Thus to preserve their purity and sanctity, Comte imposed restrictions on marriage even stricter than those of the Catholic Church, prohibiting not only divorce but also the remarriage of widows.

That, however, was the later Comte, with whom Mill had ample cause to quarrel on these and other grounds. It was the earlier Comte who had initially attracted him—the sociologist who in the *Course of Positive Philosophy* had tried to systematize the study of mankind and create a science of society. This enterprise Mill continued to defend even after he was repelled by the excesses, as he thought them, of Comte's later work. But one part of Comte's earlier work seriously troubled Mill at the time. This was his view of women as a distinct species with distinctive—and inferior, as it happened—physical, intellectual, and moral qualities. (Even later, when Comte emphasized the moral superiority of women, he retained his original conviction of their physical and intellectual inferiority.) In the *Course* he cited the findings of phrenology as evidence of this inferiority; the brains of women, he said, were demonstrably smaller and less complex than those of men.

Mill took issue not with Comte's facts but with his conclusions. He admitted to Comte that the physiological evidence was as Comte had presented it: the muscular, nervous, and even "very probably" the cerebral structure of women resembled that of children rather than that of adult men. But he went on to suggest that this might prove to be the result of insufficient exercise rather than of innate anatomical differences. He also argued that the recent history of women, the considerable advance in their position in the past half century, was presumptive evidence that their condition was socially rather than bio-logically determined.[22] After a lengthy correspondence he finally brought the discussion to a close, late in 1843, by assuring Comte that he had not arrived at his opinion lightly and would not give it up easily. "There are few questions I have thought about more, and while in general I am known for not remaining fixed in opinions once they have been proved ill founded, this one has resisted every attempt to dispute it."[23]

Mill carefully preserved this correspondence. It was not his usual habit to keep drafts of his own letters but he did so in this case, and he even went to the trouble of having them bound together with the relevant parts of Comte's letters. He then presented the volume to Harriet Taylor, apparently anticipating her approval. Instead she frankly confessed her displeasure even with his part of the ex-change. She had not expected better of Comte; he was "essentially *French*," therefore on such matters less than admirable. "This dry sort of man," she told Mill, "is not a worthy coadjutor and scarcely a worthy opponent." But she was disappointed that Mill had not stood up to him more firmly:

> *I am surprised in your letters to find your opinion undetermined where I had thought it made up—I am disappointed at a tone more than half-apologetic with which you state your opinions. And I am charmed with the exceeding nicety elegance and fineness of your last letter. Do not think that I wish you had said* more *on the subject, I only wish that what was said was in the tone of conviction, not of suggestion.*[24]

She was all the more dissatisfied, she added, because intellect-

22. *Ibid.,* II, 592 (Aug. 30, 1843).
23. *Ibid.,* p. 611 (Oct. 30, 1843).
24. Hayek, p. 114 (n.d.).

ually and morally Mill was far in advance not only of
Comte but of his entire age. No one else had his "perfect
impartiality," his "fixed love of justice," his "gift of intellect." No one was more competent than he to speak on
the question of women.

To Mill, acutely sensitive to the least hint of criticism
on her part, her effusive praise only underlined her dis-
approval. Regretting what he now saw as "concessions"
to Comte, he determined never to show the correspondence to any one else[25] (nor, of course, to publish it, which
may have been his original intention). Two years later,
when he reopened the subject with Comte, he was much
more aggressive in stating his own views, less deferential
toward Comte's supposedly superior scientific knowledge.
To one friend he complained of Comte's habit of reducing
sociological differences, including the differences between
men and women, to biological ones. He then made an
interesting connection between the case of women and of
liberty. If Comte's principles were ever put into practice,
he said, they would be the "most contrary to human liberty
of any now taught or professed; for it seems to me that he
would make everybody's way of life (or at all events after
one choice) as inexorably closed against all change of
destination or purpose, as he would make the marriage-
contract."[26]

If Comte proved so unsatisfactory, Mill found much to
praise in the writings of other socialists; indeed, it was
their position on women that especially attracted him. In
the *Political Economy*, the question of women's equality
came up in two contexts: the economic arguments in its
favor and the position of socialists in relation to it. Even
in the first edition of this work, when Mill was most critical
of socialism, he conceded its superiority on this score. Un-

25. Bain, p. 74.
26. *Earlier Letters*, II, 739 (JSM to John Pringle Nichol, Sept.
30, 1848).

like the present system, which ensured the "entire domestic subjection of one half the species," Owenism and other forms of socialism had the virtue of advocating the complete equality of women.[27] It was partly for this reason that Mill was moved to take a more kindly view of socialism in later editions of the *Political Economy*. He intimated as much in a letter to Harriet Taylor written at the very time he was preparing the revised edition of that work. Praising the Fourierists for their unequivocal stand on the equality of women and their unorthodox views of marriage, he admitted that this predisposed him in their favor: "This strengthens one exceedingly in one's wish to prôner [boost] the Fourierists besides that their scheme of association seems to me much nearer to being practicable at present than Communism."[28] The Saint-Simonians were admirable for the same reason: "In proclaiming the perfect equality of men and women, and an entirely new order of things in regard to their relations with one another, the Saint-Simonians in common with Owen and Fourier have entitled themselves to the grateful remembrance of all future generations."[29]

THE CAUSE OF "perfect equality" served Mill as a touchstone in the most varied situations: American equality was pronounced defective so long as it excluded an entire sex and an entire race;[30] the Chartists were commended for including women in their proposals for political reform;[31] novels were praised for no other apparent reason than that they took a progressive stand on "marriage, divorce, and the position of women."[32] To one French novelist whose book had been unfavorably reviewed in the British press, Mill

27. *Political Economy*, II, 979.
28. *Later Letters*, I, 10 (Feb. 19, 1849).
29. *Early Draft*, p. 140.
30. *Essays on Politics and Culture*, p. 182.
31. *Earlier Letters*, II, 727 (JSM to J. F. Mollett, Dec. 1847).
32. *Later Letters*, I, 298 (JSM to HM, Jan. 19, 1855).

wrote that he himself entirely shared his views on marriage and sexual equality and that he was profoundly convinced that such opinions were at the heart of "liberty, democracy, fraternity . . . and the future of social and moral progress."[33]

In smaller ways Mill's sensitivity to the issue—a growing sensitivity with the passage of years—may be charted. He became uncomfortable, for example, with the use of "man" and "men" as generic terms. In the editions of the 1850s—the *Logic*, *Political Economy*, and *Dissertations and Discussions*—"man" was often changed to "one," and "men" to "people" or "persons." *On Liberty* was almost consistent in this respect, "human beings," "persons," or "individuals" being used where "men" might have been the more natural and graceful form. (Mill did, however, retain "him" and "his" as neutral pronouns.) That this usage was intentional is evident from his later strategy when he raised the question of woman suffrage in Parliament. During the debate on the Reform Bill of 1867, Mill moved that the word "man" in that bill be replaced by "person."[34] It was on this simple amendment that the issue of woman suffrage was debated and voted upon for the first time in the House of Commons.

In introducing his amendment, Mill took the opportunity to repeat many of the arguments he had used in "The Subjection of Women." (Although published later, the essay had been written several years earlier.) The exclusion of women, he said, was the single example of a disability suffered by an entire group for an entirely capricious reason. It was a gross injustice to women and a great detriment to men. So long as women were excluded from

33. *Earlier Letters*, II, 736 (JSM to Eugène Sue, May 1848). Mill also wrote a letter to the editor of the *Examiner* protesting the review. Without mentioning the question of women specifically, he praised Sue for portraying "principles of conduct and ideas of moral and social improvement, decidedly in advance of the age." (*Examiner*, Dec. 11, 1847, p. 787.)

34. 3 Hansard 187:817 ff. (May 20, 1867).

politics, they would concern themselves with personalities; they would care more for their husbands' personal interest than their public duty. "Unless women are raised to the level of men," Mill warned, "men will be pulled down to theirs."[35] He disposed of the common objections to woman suffrage: that the interests of women were represented by the male members of the family, that their influence could more effectively be exercised in non-political ways, that their proper duties and sphere of activities were domestic. And he showed how the extension of the suffrage was related to other necessary reforms in education and employment. In summing up the debate, Mill observed that he was not then arguing for universal suffrage—that motion was not before the House. All he was arguing for was that women should be admitted to the suffrage (and to educational and occupational opportunities) on the same terms and with the same qualifications as men.

When the amendment was voted on, Mill was pleased to receive as many votes as he did: seventy-three, which was over one quarter of those voting. Emboldened by this result, he joined with his stepdaughter and others in organizing a Society for the Representation of Women. He also lent his support (and upon his death a considerable legacy) to institutions of higher education for women. (He drew up the first examinations in political economy for Girton College, Cambridge.[36]) A few months before his death he was even prepared, for the sake of the cause, to abandon the political allegiance of a lifetime. Throughout his life he had been a Radical or Liberal or some combination of the two. And throughout, even in that period when he was most Coleridgean, most appreciative of conservatism as a philosophy—what he then called "speculative Toryism"—

35. *Ibid.*, p. 822.
36. Professors (and students) of economics might be interested in the examination paper Mill set for the course in political economy at Girton. It is reprinted in *Letters*, ed. Elliot, II. 336–37.

he was consistently and profoundly contemptuous of "practical Toryism," Conservatism as a party, the "stupidest party," as he once referred to it.[37] Yet when, for a short while in November 1872, it appeared that the Conservatives might support a woman's franchise bill, Mill urged that Conservative candidates likely to vote for such a bill be favored over Liberals.

> *The time, moreover, is, I think now come when, at parliamentary elections, a Conservative who will vote for women's suffrage should be, in general, preferred to a professed Liberal who will not. Of course there may be reasons in particular cases for not acting on this rule; but the bare fact of supporting Mr. Gladstone in office, certainly does not now give a man a claim to preference over one who will vote for the most important of all political improvements under public discussion.*[38]

"The most important of all political improvements"—it is almost an exact echo of Mill's remark, almost a quarter of a century earlier, that women's equality was "of all practical subjects the most important."[39] Throughout these years Mill repeatedly gave it that unique and exalted distinction. Occasionally he permitted another cause to share its honors, as when he cited the "two great issues of the future: emancipation of women and cooperative produc-

37. *Earlier Letters*, I, 83 (JSM to John Sterling, Oct. 20–22, 1831); "Coleridge," *Essays on Politics and Culture*, p. 155; *Representative Government*, in *Utilitarianism, Liberty, and Representative Government* (Everyman edn.; London, 1940), p. 261. During the parliamentary debate of May 31, 1866, Mill was called upon to explain his reference to the "stupidest party." (3 Hansard 183:1592.)

38. *Later Letters*, IV, 1917 (JSM to G. C. Robertson, Nov. 5, 1872).

39. *Ibid.*, I, 49 (JSM to HT, after Oct. 29, 1850).

tion."[40] But more often it stood alone as "the most vitally important political and social question of the future."[41]

FROM A LATER PERSPECTIVE, looking back upon the great body of work produced by Mill on a formidable variety of subjects, one is inclined to lose sight of the essays on women —unless, like the women's liberation movement, one has a professional interest in that subject. In a sense, Mill himself had a professional interest in it. To be sure, his interpretation of "liberation" was different, in important respects, from that of the movement as we now know it, many of its latter-day disciples being more concerned with equality of results than with freedom of opportunity, with "woman" as a collective entity than with "women" as individuals, with sexual matters than with social or political ones. But one cannot doubt Mill's profound and enduring commitment to women's liberation as he understood it.

After considering his essays and letters, his public and private activities, one may be prepared to take seriously a suggestion that otherwise may seem bizarre: that the woman question did have a profound effect upon Mill's conception of liberty. The suggestion would not be made, the occasion for it would not have arisen, if *On Liberty* itself were unproblematical—if it were consistent within itself and within the entire corpus of Mill's work. But because it is problematical, it does require explanation. And it is in seeking such an explanation that one may be impressed by the fact that *On Liberty* has a philosophical affinity with the essays on women which it does not have with any of Mill's other writings. If one also finds, in the evidence of his daily life, a large preoccupation with the subject of women, the connection becomes eminently plausible as well as logical.

40. *Ibid.*, IV, 1535 (JSM to P. Godwin, Jan. 1, 1869).
41. *Ibid.*, p. 1830 (JSM to J. Giles, Aug. 24, 1871).

One question remains. If Mill did have an abiding concern with this issue, why was it not reflected in all his work? Why were not all his writings of a piece, all in the vein of *On Liberty*? The answer lies partly with the nature of his writings, partly with their timing. The subject of women's liberation is obviously more directly and immediately related to the subject of liberty than to such other matters as the distribution of wealth, the logic of the social sciences, the nature of representative government, the utilitarian foundations of ethics, the problems of democracy in America, or the relative merits of Bentham and Coleridge. To be sure, if in the course of these other subjects, the question of women arose, Mill made his position quite clear. But for the rest it did not impinge upon those subjects and did not, therefore, affect the discussion of the larger issues. The case of liberty, however, was very different, for that did have, most immediately and obviously, a bearing upon the condition of women.[42]

In addition, there is the matter of chronology. Mill always maintained, and quite rightly, that he was not a late convert to the cause of women, that he had held to the principle of sexual equality from his youth. But it is also true that his dedication to the cause became more pronounced over the years. If his wife did not convert him, she did, as Mill admitted, give him a more acute sense of the problem and of its urgency.

But that perception of the vast practical bearings of women's disabilities which found expression in the book on the "Subjection of Women" was acquired mainly through her teaching. But for her rare knowl-

42. This may also account for the inconsistencies between *On Liberty* and other of his writings dating from the same period. Where the case of women—and therefore the case for absolute liberty—was not directly implicated, Mill was able to assume his more customary mode of thought.

*edge of human nature and comprehension of moral
and social influences, though I should doubtless have
held my present opinions, I should have had a very
insufficient perception of the mode in which the consequences of the inferior position of women intertwine
themselves with all the evils of existing society and
with all the difficulties of human improvement.*[43]

It is surely significant that when Mill came to discuss
"The Subjection of Women" in his *Autobiography*, he
should have done so in the context of a discussion of his
wife's influence; just as, in the first draft of the *Autobiography*, he should have interjected the subject of
women's equality in the middle of the eulogy of his wife.
The very dating of the two essays is suggestive. "Enfranchisement of Women" was started just before their
marriage and completed, appropriately, on their honey-
moon, and "The Subjection of Women" was the first
extensive piece of writing he undertook after his wife's
death. It is not surprising, therefore, that the question of
women should have intruded upon his thought more per-
sistently and profoundly during the period of their marriage
—which was also the period when Mill was writing and
rewriting *On Liberty*.

43. *Autobiography*, p. 173.

IX

THE "PERFECT FRIENDSHIP"

THE FIGURE OF Harriet Taylor Mill has hovered behind much of this account. If she has not been brought to the forefront earlier, it is because her presence might have overshadowed the entire subject, precluding any serious consideration of ideas and texts. Mill himself was aware of this possibility, so that even as he was praising her most generously, he was careful not to allow his praise to detract from the ideas at issue. Thus, in his *Autobiography* he made it clear that while his wife's influence was decisive in some stages and aspects of his thought, his concern with women's equality long predated his acquaintance with her. He made this point not to belittle her influence; on the contrary, he wanted to be certain that his readers would not belittle her by assuming that only in this area did she exercise any real influence. He also wanted to ensure that the issue itself would not be denigrated by its identification with her, its reduction to what might be regarded as a woman's natural, perhaps self-serving interest. In testifying to his own prior and independent commitment to it, he gave it the dignity of a serious philosophical and social problem.

In the case of *On Liberty*, Mill did not have to be so

cautious, did not have to prove his own interest or role in it. He could attribute to his wife a large share in its conception and composition, knowing that that attribution, however often and explicitly stated, would be largely discounted by his readers. It is tempting to assume, as many of his contemporaries did, that Mill understated her influence on the subject of women and overstated it in regard to *On Liberty*. The evidence, however, suggests that she had an important effect upon both matters and that it made itself felt in complicated and unexpected ways.

The history of their relationship goes back to 1830. Mill was twenty-four and Harriet Taylor twenty-three when they first met.[1] It was as if he had willed her into existence. Only the year before, he had complained of his acute sense of loneliness, the lack of a "perfect friendship" to sustain him in "all the great objects of life."[2] Shortly afterwards he found the perfect friend in the improbable person of Mrs. Taylor, wife of a prosperous merchant and the mother of two children (a third child was born the following year). In spite of the flat statement in his *Autobiography*, "It was years after my introduction to Mrs. Taylor before my acquaintance with her became at all intimate or confidential,"[3] it is apparent that their acquaintance became intimate and confidential almost immediately. As early as 1831 a "reconciliation" had to be effected between Mill and her husband.[4] And a love letter written by Mill to her the following summer contained every cliché of that genre, including its being written in French.[5]

1. "Harriet" was also the name of his mother and sister (and maternal grandmother). Whatever the psychological significance of this, it should be kept in mind when consulting the indexes of biographies of Mill, where "Harriet Mill" may refer to his mother, sister, or wife.

2. *Earlier Letters*, I, 30 (JSM to John Sterling, Apr. 15, 1829).

3. *Autobiography*, p. 129.

4. Hayek, p. 37 (B. E. Desainteville to John Taylor, early 1831 [?]).

5. *Earlier Letters*, I, 114 (Aug. [?], 1832).

For almost twenty years Harriet Taylor remained his "incomparable friend,"[6] while being married to and continuing for the most part to live with her husband. Mill frequently dined in her London house, he paid extended visits to her in the country (where her husband rarely joined her), and he took trips abroad with her, sometimes accompanied by one of her children. They made little secret among their friends of their love for each other. But they also insisted that they were intimate in every sense but the sexual. Later Harriet gave a German friend to understand that during the whole of this time she had been nothing more than a *"Seelenfreundin."*[7] When Mill was writing his *Autobiography*, she advised him to describe their premarital relationship as one of "strong affection, intimacy of friendship, and no impropriety." It would provide an "edifying picture," she added, for "those poor wretches who cannot conceive friendship but in sex—nor believe that expediency and the consideration for feelings of others can conquer sensuality."[8]

Although the historian has no reason to doubt her word, some of their friends and relatives apparently did, or at the very least questioned the propriety of a *Seelenfreundschaft* that so brazenly flouted convention.[9] When his father taxed him with being in love with another man's wife, Mill

---

6. *Autobiography*, p. 160.

7. Theodor Gomperz, *Briefe und Aufzeichnungen*, ed. Heinrich Gomperz (Vienna, 1936), I, 233. Gomperz had the impression that during this time she was only a *Seelenfreundin* to her husband as well.

8. Hayek, p. 196 (Feb. 14–15, 1854).

9. Carlyle was one of those who fully accepted their protestations of innocence, perhaps because he well knew what it meant to be celibate. Yet even he could not resist derisive references to Harriet Taylor as "Platonica." (J. A. Froude, *Thomas Carlyle: A History of the First Forty Years of His Life* [London, 1882], II, 448 [TC to John Carlyle, Aug. 15, 1834].) Speculating about the affair after Mill's death, Carlyle reaffirmed his conviction that it was "entirely innocent." (*Letters of Charles Eliot Norton*, ed. Sara Norton [Boston, 1913], 498.)

replied that "he had no other feelings towards her, than he would have towards an equally able man."[10] The reply did not satisfy his father but it did discourage him from pursuing the subject. Their situation was hardly improved when their good friends William Fox and Eliza Flower chose to set up house together in spite of Fox's marriage.[11] It was about this time too that Mill's father became seriously ill. The guilt generated by this conjunction of events may well have played some part in the mysterious illness which beset Mill in the winter of 1836 shortly before his father's death —an illness which left him prematurely bald, with tics and twitches that disfigured him for the rest of his life.[12]

The relationship continued in this unsatisfactory manner, with Mill living at home with his mother and sisters while contriving to spend as many weekends as possible in the country with Mrs. Taylor. Her husband uneasily, and with only occasional apologetic protests, acquiesced in this arrangement, their friends gossiped about it, and Mrs. Taylor felt ill-used by everyone, including Mill when he was insufficiently sensitive to what she took to be slights and offenses. By the mid-forties the situation had deteriorated to the point where Mill discouraged or actually broke off relations with some of his oldest friends; the Carlyles, Austins, and Grotes were almost entirely dropped, while Bain, Roebuck, d'Eichthal, and others were barely tolerated. Mr. Taylor died in 1849. But it was not until almost two years later, after observing a more than respectable period of mourning, that Mill and Harriet Taylor were finally married.

Perhaps to compensate for their unorthodox relationship before, Mill was overly anxious about the legal niceties of

---

10. Bain, p. 163.

11. One of the many curiosities about this affair is the fact that Fox's wife was also named Eliza.

12. J. A. Froude, *Thomas Carlyle: A History of His Life in London, 1834-1881*, I, 74; Bain, p. 42; Hayek, pp. 100-1.

the marriage ceremony. A year after their marriage he wrote a formal letter to his wife requesting that they go through another ceremony, this time in a church to dispel any question of its legality. It appears that in signing the register the first time, he did so in his customary manner, "J. S. Mill," and after being told that the full name was required, he filled in "John Stuart" in the little space left him, so that the signature had an "unusual appearance." He was writing her about this not because she did not know it but in order to have a formal explanation of it lest there be any doubt, "either to our own or to any other minds," of the legality of their marriage.[13] There does not appear to have been a second ceremony, but the letter itself is extraordinary testimony to a tortured sensibility.

If his marriage eased some of the difficulties of his life, it exacerbated others. It embittered his relations not only with most of his friends but with his family as well. He never forgave his mother and sisters for being tardy in paying their respects to his wife (it was, in fact, not discourtesy but timidity and fear that kept them back, Mill having earlier discouraged any overtures on their part); and having neglected to inform his brother of his marriage, he charged him with insolence when his brother later presumed to mention it. Taking a house in Blackheath, a suburb of London, the Mills removed themselves, geographically as well as spiritually, from the center of intellectual and social life. During the seven years of their marriage, they seldom (if ever) dined out and rarely entertained at home, their few guests being generally visitors from abroad. Mill maintained no regular connection with any journal or political group (he broke with the *Edinburgh Review* when a nephew of Mrs. Austin became the editor), attended no meetings except for an occasional session of the Political Economy Club, met few people apart from his colleagues at the India

13. *Later Letters*, I, 96 (July 13, 1852).

Office and some of his more venturesome friends who occasionally visited him there. The domestic household included Mrs. Mill's daughter, Helen, who assumed housekeeping responsibilities, and for a while her son, with both of whom there was some friction.

Their insulation was completed when they both came down with tuberculosis. Convinced that they had only a short while to live, they resented more than ever any intrusions from without. Their invalidism, to be sure, did not interfere with trips abroad; indeed, it was for reasons of health that they traveled, together or separately—separately when their illnesses did not coincide or when Mill's job prevented him from accompanying her. In October 1858, when Mill retired from the India Office, they embarked upon an extended stay abroad, their health better than it had been for some time. Within a week Mrs. Mill was taken ill. On November 3 she died at Avignon and was buried there. Mill purchased a small house within sight of the graveyard and installed in it the furniture from the hotel room in which she had died. In later years it was to that house that he periodically retreated, as to a shrine.

"It is doubtful if I shall ever be fit for anything public or private, again," Mill wrote in the throes of his grief. "The spring of my life is broken."[14] In fact, the spring of his life mended so well that he recovered, both in his private and public life, some of his lost vigor. Although he continued to live at Blackheath with his stepdaughter Helen, who took over a good deal of the management of never as complete as his wife's.[15] He became reconciled his professional as well as domestic affairs, her control was

14. *Ibid.*, II, 574 (JSM to William Thornton, Nov. 9, 1858).

15. In his later years many of his letters were written by Helen, some evidently dictated by him but others composed by her (perhaps after consultation with him, but this is not clear). Some friends were disturbed by what they took to be his excessive deference to her. (See, for example, *Letters of Norton*, I, 330, 400.)

with the surviving members of his family, gradually resumed his old friendships, and cultivated numerous new ones. In 1851 he had refused the offer of a seat in Commons; in 1865 he accepted it and served for three years until the general election, when he stood again but failed to be returned. He wrote, published, lectured, served on committees, became involved in good works and good causes, kept up an enormous correspondence, dined out, weekended, and—an even larger departure from his earlier routine—gave weekly dinner parties at Blackheath and entertained house guests at Avignon. When the lease ran out on the house in Blackheath, he moved back to London. He and his stepdaughter lived there only a little more than two months when they left for their annual vacation in France. It was near Avignon, on one of his customary botanical expeditions after a fifteen-mile walk (on other occasions he was known to walk for thirty miles), that Mill was suddenly stricken with erysipelas. He died a few days later, on May 7, 1873, at the age of sixty-seven, and was buried next to his wife.

This sketch of Mill's life may help demonstrate what might not otherwise be evident—how central his wife was in all his affairs, how decisively she had affected his activities and shaped his life. The period after her death confirms this, for then, when he was released from her immediate influence, he entered upon a quite different mode of existence. Mill often protested that his marriage was not like that of others. We may do well to take him at his word.

We would also do well to attend more carefully to Mill's claims about his wife's intellectual influence. It is tempting to dismiss these as pieties, eulogies, the effusions of a uxorious husband. But if some of his statements are evidently excessive, others can be shown to contain a surprising amount of truth.

There is no reason to doubt his assertion, in the early draft of the *Autobiography*, that in the first years of their acquaintance he had been most impressed by the "poetic elements of her character," that because of her he had become "more attuned to the beautiful and elevated," "more capable of vibrating in unison" with human feeling and character.[16] Those were the years when he was reacting against the hard, narrow rationality of Benthamism, when he was seeking a new "poetic culture" in Wordsworth, Coleridge, and Goethe. But he was not yet comfortable in that culture, was still guilty about abandoning the old and feeling lonely and ill at ease in the new, when he found in Harriet Taylor the sensibility he so much admired but had not himself achieved.

It was a sensibility that convention decreed to be feminine—and that Mill himself for a time evidently thought of as such. In the first draft of the *Autobiography*, he described Harriet Taylor in those early years: "Her education, her personal habits and tastes were all peculiarly feminine."[17] This sentence was finally deleted, but only after an intermediate stage when it was amended (upon her suggestion) to make her education masculine while her habits and tastes were feminine. What remained in the final version of the *Autobiography* was a testimonial to a "rich and powerful nature" which until that time (the time of their meeting) had "chiefly unfolded itself according to the received type of feminine genius." But this was prefaced by a tribute to her passion for "self-improvement" and was followed by a description of the unfolding of her nature to the point where it finally encompassed all qualities and virtues.[18]

If Mill had been satisfied to praise her "poetic" nature, to judge her the superior in this respect not only of himself

16. *Early Draft*, p. 154.
17. *Ibid.*, p. 197.
18. *Autobiography*, p. 130.

but of everyone he had ever known, the reader might have had some reservations about his objectivity but none about the depth of his convictions. A passage in the first draft of the *Autobiography* has the ring of sincerity even in the extravagance of its praise:

I had always wished for a friend whom I could admire wholly, without reservation and restriction, and I had now found one. To render this possible, it was necessary that the object of my admiration should be of a type very different from my own; should be a character preeminently of feeling, combined however as I had not in any other instance known it to be, with a vigorous and bold speculative intellect. Hers was not only all this but the perfection of a poetic and artistic nature. With how eminent a practical capacity these endowments were combined, I only understood by degrees; but the rest was enough without this to make me feel that in any true classification of human beings such as I are only fit to be the subjects and ministers of such as hers; and that the best thing I, in particular, could do for the world would be to serve as a sort of prose interpreter of her poetry, giving a logical exposition to those who have more understanding than feeling, of the reasonableness of that which she either knew by the experience or divined by the intuition of one of the richest and strongest of natures guided by the most unselfish and high-minded of characters.[19]

In successive drafts of the *Autobiography*, these and similar passages were amended or deleted so that less was made of the "poetic" aspect of her nature, her capacity for "feeling" and "intuition," and more of the intellectual and

19. *Early Draft*, p. 199.

practical aspect. Her poetic sensibility remained but was encased in an intellect so powerful that it effectively dispelled any aura of conventional femininity. Moreover, the intellectual qualities he attributed to her were precisely those one might have associated with Mill himself. Again and again he insisted that her superiority to him resided in those areas where he was commonly thought to be strongest: the realms of the philosophical and of the practical. She excelled, he said, in the two most important regions of thought: that of "ultimate aims . . . the highest realizable ideal of human life," and that of the "immediately useful and practically attainable." Her mind was the "same perfect instrument" in penetrating into the "highest regions of speculation" and into the "smallest practical concerns of daily life." It was as "preeminently practical in its judgments and perceptions of things present, as it was high and bold in its anticipations for a remote futurity." In both respects she was his master. His own strength lay in a subordinate area, the "uncertain and slippery intermediate region" of theory, of moral or political science. And even here her influence was important in preserving him from undue dogmatism, keeping his mind open to "clearer perceptions and better evidence."[20]

Had Mill rested his case here, with the assertion of his wife's superiority over him—and in those areas where he himself might have been supposed to be superior—the reader might still have been tolerant if skeptical. What finally strains both credulity and tolerance was his abasement not only of himself but of everyone else as well, his insistence upon her superiority over everyone in every respect. He did, to be sure, delete from the first draft of his *Autobiography* the statement that he had "never known any intellect in man or woman which, taken for all in all, could be compared to hers," that "all other intellects when

20. *Autobiography*, pp. 131-33.

looked at beside hers seem to be but special talents, a peculiar knack acquired by study and practice of dealing with some one particular thing."[21] But he might just as well have let this sentence stand, since the rest of the *Autobiography* was imbued with the same sentiments and tone.

In the early years of their acquaintance, he recalled, he had often compared her with Shelley in spiritual and temperamental quality, but she soon left the poet far behind: "In thought and intellect, Shelley, so far as his powers were developed in his short life, was but a child compared with what she ultimately became."[22] He himself could not presume to pass judgment on Carlyle "until he was interpreted to me by one greatly the superior to us both—who was more a poet than he, and more a thinker than I—whose own mind and nature included his, and infinitely more."[23] In the case of all the other intellectual influences that had acted upon him—the Coleridgeans and the German poets and philosophers—he had had to separate the truth from the error; in her alone "I could not, as I had done in those others, detect any mixture of error."[24] His father, whom he acclaimed as the Voltaire of the English radical movement, had no equal among men "and but one among women."[25] Mill did not have to specify which woman he had in mind since he had earlier endowed his wife with qualities that not even Voltaire, let alone James Mill, could have aspired to: the mind and imagination of a "consummate artist," the soul and eloquence of a "great orator," the discernment and sagacity of the most "eminent among the rulers of mankind."[26]

And so the eulogy continued, each virtue balanced by another, lest it be thought that she had the one and not the

---

21. *Early Draft*, p. 194.   22. *Autobiography*, p. 131.
23. *Ibid.*, p. 124.   24. *Ibid.*, pp. 172–73.
25. *Ibid.*, p. 144.
26. *Ibid.*, p. 131.

other; and each ascribed to her in the superlative degree. Her unexcelled intellectual gifts ministered to a moral character "at once the noblest and the best balanced which I have ever met with in life." Her "passion of justice" might be supposed to have been her strongest feeling, had that quality not been rivaled by her "boundless generosity" and "lovingness." She combined "the most genuine modesty" with the "loftiest pride," a "simplicity and sincerity which were absolute" with an "utmost scorn" for the mean and cowardly and a "burning indignation" at the brutal and tyrannical.[27]

This litany of virtues was repeated, with variations, in the preface to "Enfranchisement of Women" when that essay was reprinted in *Dissertations and Discussions*. In attributing its authorship to her, Mill explained that it reflected only the faintest image of a "mind and heart which in their union of the rarest, and what are deemed the most conflicting excellencies, were unparalleled in any human being that I have known or read of." All those "excellencies" which existed singly and separately in others were united in her: gracefulness and seriousness, a healthy and yet tender conscience, generosity and a sense of justice, a loving heart and profound intellect. In the "intellectual department" as well she exhibited the same amalgam of opposites: "a vigour and truth of imagination, a delicacy of perception, an accuracy and nicety of observation, only equalled by her profundity of speculative thought, and by a practical judgment and discernment next to infallible." So manifold and elevated were these faculties that the "highest poetry, philosophy, oratory, or art, seemed trivial by the side of her, and equal only to expressing some small part of her mind." In any one of these disciplines she could easily have taken the "highest rank"; instead she was content to be the "inspirer, prompter, and

27. *Ibid.*

unavowed coadjutor of others." If mankind continued to improve, Mill concluded, "their spiritual history for ages to come will be the progressive working out of her thoughts, and realization of her conceptions."[28]

Nor was it only in public that Mill was so effusive. His private letters to her were adulatory to the point of obsequiousness. He generally addressed her in the third person, in the manner of royalty. He was solicitous beyond measure, wary of any nuance that might seem to be critical or slighting, deferential to her every wish, respectful of her every opinion, quick to reverse himself on any issue, tirelessly confessing his own failings and praising her superior judgments and talents. His obeisance was very nearly complete—and all the more remarkable because it was sustained over so long a period of time. After her death Mill was grieved by the thought that they had been married for only seven and a half short years, but their relationship had been maintained on this level for over a quarter of a century.

IT IS INTERESTING to read Freud's comments on this relationship. There is nothing particularly "Freudian" about those comments; he was a very young man when he delivered himself of them. But they are perhaps all the more interesting for that because they anticipate some of the issues later raised by the women's liberation movement.

In 1880, when he was only twenty-four and still a medical student, Freud translated, purely by chance and for money, a volume of essays for the German edition of Mill's works. One of the essays was "Enfranchisement of Women."[29]

28. *Dissertations and Discussions*, II, 411-12.

29. In the letter quoted below, Freud spoke of it as a translation of Mill's "last work." (*Letters of Sigmund Freud*, ed. Ernst Freud [New York, 1960], p. 75 [SF to Martha Bernays, Nov. 15, 1883].) This has led some of Freud's commentators to assume that he had translated "The Subjection of Women" (e.g., Philip Rieff, *Freud: The Mind of the Moralist* [New York, 1959], p.

Three years later he discussed it in a letter to his fiancée. He praised Mill for being freer than any of his contemporaries from the "domination of the usual prejudices." But the result of that freedom was, as often happened, a lack of a "sense of the absurd." In Mill's case the lack manifested itself in his treatment of women, which Freud found so unrealistic as to appear not "quite human." Mill had argued for example, that a married woman could earn as much as her husband,[30] as if the management of a household and family did not "claim the whole person and practically rule out any profession." All this Mill forgot, "just as he omitted all relations connected with sex." His *Autobiography* too —Freud was evidently sufficiently interested in Mill to follow up the essays with the reading of other of his works —was "prudish" and "unearthy." One would never suspect from it that "humanity is divided between men and women, and that this difference is the most important one, . . . that the woman is different from the man, which is not to say that she is something less, if anything the opposite." This "inhuman" quality was also reflected in Mill's relations with his wife, in the fact that he married late in life, that he had no children, and that he never mentioned love "as we know it."[31] It was generally doubted, Freud added, that his wife was as wonderful as he had made her out to be. That Freud himself shared these doubts is evident from the fact that he

---

167). What Freud had translated was the early essay, "Enfranchisement of Women," translated under the title "Ueber Frauenemancipation." This essay appeared in the final volume of the German edition—hence the confusion about the "last work."

30. Freud's memory was faulty here. Mill did not claim that a married woman could earn as much as her husband. He only made the point that the joint income of husband and wife would not necessarily be reduced, as was commonly thought, to the sum previously earned by the husband alone. He added that even if a woman's labor did somewhat diminish the value of a man's, that loss would still be worthwhile if it led to some measure of independence for the woman.

31. *Letters of Freud*, pp. 75–76.

completely disregarded Mill's attribution of the essay to her.

As interesting as the letter itself was the occasion for the writing of it. It was Freud's fiancée who had raised the subject of Mill and his wife. Freud took the opportunity to correct any misconceptions she may have had of the proper relations of husband and wife. He reminded her of what he had had to tell her once before, that he himself could not think of his "delicate, sweet girl" as a competitor and that he had every intention of getting her "out of the competitive role into the quiet, undisturbed activity of my home." It was possible, he conceded, that a different kind of education would succeed in suppressing a woman's "delicate qualities" and permit her to earn her living like a man; in that case, one might have to become reconciled to the disappearance of "the most lovely thing the world has to offer us: our ideal of womanhood." But Freud doubted that such a state of affairs would ever arise.

> . . . I believe that all reforming activity, legislation and education, will founder on the fact that long before the age at which a profession can be established in our society, nature will have appointed woman by her beauty, charm, and goodness, to do something else.
>
> No, in this respect I adhere to the old ways, to my longing for my Martha as she is, and she herself will not want it different; legislation and custom have to grant to women many rights kept from them, but the position of woman cannot be other than what it is: to be an adored sweetheart in youth, and a beloved wife in maturity.[32]

It was on the basis of a much more sophisticated and complicated system of thought that Freud eventually worked out the implications of the biological, psycholog-

32. *Ibid.*, p. 76.

ical, and cultural differentiation of the sexes. But it is interesting to find that determinism appears, however primitively,
so early in his career. For the Mill biographer, it is especially
interesting to find it expressed in a confrontation with Mill,
to see in Freud all those attitudes (including the habit of
speaking of "woman" in the singular) that were so abhorrent to Mill, to watch Freud making the inevitable connection between Mill's writing about women and his personal
relations with his wife, and to observe Freud's skepticism
about the claims made by Mill on behalf of his wife. One
can only regret that Freud did not have available to him the
early draft of Mill's *Autobiography* with its intriguing
references to his mother.

MILL's EULOGY of his wife provoked Freud, as it has many
readers of the *Autobiography*, to question his judgment
of women in general. But it raises the more serious question of her influence on his other work—whether her role
was as great as Mill represented it and what the implications of that might be. It is for this reason that the subject
has been discussed at such length here (and yet not nearly
the length to which Mill himself went). If we cannot credit
Mill's claim that she transcended the highest reaches of any
known poetry, philosophy, oratory, or art, how can we
credit his claim that his writings of this period were really
"joint productions"?

As if to anticipate such questions, Mill went to some
pains to specify the nature of her influence. Their ideas,
he explained, were held "so completely in common," they
had so thoroughly discussed together "all subjects of intellectual or moral interests," that it was irrelevant which of
them "holds the pen." The one who "contributes least
to the composition may contribute most to the thought";
and it was she, he went on to suggest, who contributed most

to the thought. In their joint productions he represented her
as the senior partner.

> *Over and above the general influence which her mind
> had over mine, the most valuable ideas and features in
> these joint productions—those which have been most
> fruitful of important results, and have contributed most
> to the success and reputation of the works themselves
> —originated with her, were emanations from her mind,
> my part in them being no greater than in any of the
> thoughts which I found in previous writers, and made
> my own only by incorporating them with my own
> system of thought. During the greater part of my
> literary life I have performed the office in relation to
> her, which from a rather early period I had considered
> as the most useful part that I was qualified to take in
> the domain of thought, that of an interpreter of orig-
> inal thinkers, and mediator between them and the
> public.*[33]

Most of Mill's biographers have tacitly assumed that this
account was part of his eulogy and no more credible than
the rest. And most of his friends were agreed, in spite of
his own protestations, that his wife's influence was decisive
on the subject of women's rights—and only on that subject.
Some attributed his "extraordinary hallucination" to her
habit of imbibing his opinions and then delivering them back
as her own, transformed by her impassioned manner.[34] One
friend disputed this; her talent, he thought, lay not in
mimicry—Mill would not have appreciated that, and in any

---

33. *Autobiography*, pp. 171–72.

34. Bain, pp. 171–72. Harold Laski attributed to Bain the theory
that Harriet "repeated to him in the morning what he had said
to her the night before and astounded him by the depth of her
grasp." (*Holmes-Laski Letters*, ed. M. D. Howe [Cambridge,
Mass., 1953], I, 471.) In fact, Bain described this as the opinion
of some of Mill's other friends, which he himself did not share.

case she was intellectually incapable of reproducing his arguments—but rather in disputation, in controverting his views.[35] Still others could only suppose that Mill was so besottedly in love with her as to mistake her intellectual pretensions for intellectual distinction. Carlyle remembered her as "full of unwise intellect, asking and re-asking stupid questions"; when she was not actually saying provocative things, she managed to look as if she were thinking them— "those great dark eyes, that were flashing unutterable things while he was discoursin' the utterable concerning all sorts o' high topics."[36]

Mill's friend and biographer Alexander Bain expressed the opinion of most of his friends at the time and of most biographers since when he said that Mill's work (with the notable exception of the essays on women) was generally so much beyond the capacity of his wife as to be "entirely withdrawn from possible bias on her account."[37] But this is to confuse two distinct issues: her intellectual ability and her intellectual influence. Although Mill made the highest claims for her in both respects, the two questions can be separated and judged independently. Fortunately there is some objective evidence bearing on each: a few of her early writings and about fifty letters. Other of her letters were destroyed at her suggestion, but some clues to them can be found in Mill's replies, most of which, fortunately, have survived.[38]

The impression that emerges is of a sharp mind, personal and intuitive, quick to generalize and pronounce judgment, confident in the correctness of her opinions and

35. Bain, pp. 172–73.

36. David A. Wilson, *Life of Thomas Carlyle* (London, 1924), II, 378; *Letters of Norton*, I, 497.

37. Bain, p. 172.

38. Her instructions to destroy her letters were referred to in *Later Letters*, I, 140 (JSM to HM, Jan. 26, 1854). Mill kept only one letter from this period, probably so that he might consult it while writing the *Autobiography*. (Hayek, pp. 195–96; see above, p. 210.)

not at all diffident in advancing them. In the inevitable comparison with Jane Carlyle, Harriet Mill makes a rather poor showing. Both were overshadowed but not the least overawed by their famous husbands; both were strong-minded, assertive, and acerbic; both were consumed by personal and intellectual frustrations. Mrs. Carlyle, however, had the saving grace of humor, so that even when she was most bitter she could be witty and amusing, and in the throes of her misery—and she had at least as much cause for grievance as Mrs. Mill—she could see herself with some objectivity. And Mrs. Carlyle was not only strong-minded; she had a genuinely strong mind. In reading her letters one regrets her failure to use her talents to better avail; one wishes she had applied her acumen to ideas as well as persons or commented on public affairs as shrewdly as she did on private affairs. Whether she could have sustained more serious intellectual efforts had she been encouraged to do so is problematic; what is certain is that Carlyle did not encourage such efforts; indeed, he would probably not have tolerated them. Mill, on the other hand, gave his wife every encouragement, every opportunity, which she consistently evaded. And it must be said that the opinions she voiced and her mode of expressing them do not inspire confidence. Perhaps she was wiser than Mill in resisting his importunities, in refusing to put herself to the test. In any event, the effect of her letters is to cast doubt on her genius and on his judgment. One can only suppose that he assumed her strength of mind to be commensurate with the strength of her convictions, her intelligence equal to her passion.

Yet the same letters, which give little evidence of intellectual distinction, give abundant evidence of her considerable intellectual influence on Mill. Interspersed with complaints about the servants' consumption of meat and the tradesmen's bills, recriminations against neighbors, friends, and relatives, and shrewd advice about financial investments and publishers' contracts, were a host of suggestions to

Mill about his work. She told him what subjects he ought to write about, the order in which he ought to write them, and the points he should stress; and she proposed innumerable and important revisions for new editions of his works. If the reader of these letters finds her tone somewhat peremptory, he may be even more taken aback by Mill's docile acquiescence.[39]

UNFORTUNATELY, there are few letters that throw light on the writing of *On Liberty*. But there are many about the *Political Economy*, the first of his works, Mill said, in which "her share was conspicuous."[40] Since this was a lesser claim than he made for her in the case of *On Liberty*, the evidence of her influence in the earlier book may be at least presumptive evidence of a similar influence in the later one. Moreover, the letters bear out to a significant extent the nature of her influence as Mill described it in the *Autobiography*.

One important chapter of the *Political Economy*, "On the Probable Futurity of the Labouring Classes," was "entirely due to her," he said: "She pointed out the need of such a chapter, and the extreme imperfection of the book without it: she was the cause of my writing it; and the more general part of the chapter . . . was wholly an exposition of her thoughts, often in words taken from her own lips." Of the rest of the work, he supplied the "purely

39. A recent editor of Mill points out that Hayek published only a selection of her letters, that those he found too trivial to print reenforce the impression of a vain, mean-spirited, domineering woman. (*Early Draft*, p. 25.)

40. *Autobiography*, p. 173. Mill was here speaking of her contribution to his books. She had earlier collaborated with him in the writing of half a dozen brief articles for the *Morning Chronicle* in 1846. In the bibliography he himself compiled, he noted next to these titles some variant of "a joint production, very little of which was mine." (*Bibliography of the Published Writings of John Stuart Mill*, ed. N. MacMinn, J. R. Hainds, and J. M. McCrimmon [Evanston, Ill., 1944], pp. 59–66.)

scientific" part, she the "general tone" which distinguished it from similar scientific treatises.[41] Its main theme was the separation of production and distribution, production being governed by scientific, deterministic laws of nature, and distribution by social arrangements that were the product of human will and effort. This distinction, Mill admitted, he had originally learned from the Saint-Simonians. But it was Harriet Taylor who made it the animating principle of the book. And it was she who urged upon him a more sympathetic consideration of the various socialist schemes. Her contribution to this work illustrated, he said, the character of her influence in general: "What was abstract and purely scientific was generally mine; the properly human element came from her: in all that concerned the application of philosophy to the exigencies of human society and progress, I was her pupil, alike in boldness of speculation and cautiousness of practical judgment."[42]

Since the letters concerning the *Political Economy* date from the period immediately following the publication of the first edition, they do not throw any light on his assertion that it was she who was entirely responsible for the chapter on the laboring classes. But they do reveal her responsibility for a good many of the crucial revisions in later editions. They demonstrate his manner of coping with her suggestions—a mild demurral followed by a dutiful submission. And perhaps most important, they illustrate the gravity of the issues that were being decided in so personal a fashion.

In the first letter, for example, Mill pointed out that one paragraph which she objected to "so strongly and totally" had always seemed to him to be "the strongest part of the argument." To omit it now would imply a change of opinion. It was, therefore, necessary to see "whether the opinion has changed or not." (Note "the" opinion, not "my" opinion.) Hers, he wrote, evidently had, the original pas-

41. *Autobiography*, p. 174.   42. *Ibid.*, p. 175.

sage having been "inserted on your proposition and very nearly in your words." "This is probably," he continued, "only the progress we have been always making and by thinking sufficiently I should probably come to think the same—as is almost always the case, I believe *always* when we think long enough."[43] Of another sentence which he

43. *Later Letters*, I, 8–9 (Feb. 19, 1849); italics in original. The deleted passage was a strongly worded argument against socialism:

> *Those who have never known freedom from anxiety as to the means of subsistence, are apt to overrate what is gained for positive enjoyment by the mere absence of that uncertainty. The necessaries of life, when they have always been secure for the whole of life, are scarcely more a subject of consciousness or a source of happiness than the elements. There is little attractive in a monotonous routine, without vicissitudes, but without excitement; a life spent in the enforced observance of an external rule, and performance of a prescribed task: in which labour would be devoid of its chief sweetener, the thought that every effort tells perceptibly on the labourer's own interests or those of some one with whom he identifies himself; in which no one could by his own exertions improve his condition, or that of the objects of his private affections; in which no one's way of life, occupations, or movements, would depend on choice, but each would be the slave of all: a social system in which identity of education and pursuits would impress on all the same unvarying type of character, to the destruction of that multiform development of human nature, those manifold unlikenesses, that diversity of tastes and talents, and variety of intellectual points of view, which by presenting to each innumerable notions that he could not have conceived of himself, are the great stimulus to intellect and the mainspring of mental and moral progression. [Political Economy, II, 978.]*

In the second edition the whole of the above passage was replaced by the following:

> *On the Communistic scheme, supposing it to be successful, there would be an end to all anxiety concerning the means of subsistence; and this would be much gained for human happiness. But it is perfectly possible to realize this same advantage in a society grounded on private property; and to this point the tendencies of political speculation are rapidly converging. Supposing this attained, it is surely a vast advantage on the side of the individual system, that it is compatible with a far greater degree of personal liberty. [Ibid.]*

In later editions, this latter passage was also eliminated, phrases of it appearing in other contexts.

had wanted to add to the new edition and she had vetoed, he feebly protested that it was a "favourite of mine": "I cannot help thinking that something like what I meant by the sentence ought to be said though I can imagine good reasons for your disliking the way in which it is put."[44] And of still another deleted sentence, he said that if that were untenable, "then all the two or three pages of argument which precede and of which this is but the summary, are false, and there is nothing to be said against Communism at all—one would only have to turn round and advocate it—which if done would be better in a separate treatise."[45] In view of the fundamental changes she was proposing, he suggested that the new edition be put off for several months so that they might consider the issues more carefully after her return.

Yet his very next letter, written two days later, conceded all the changes she had requested, altering or deleting each of the "objectionable passages." He asked her to judge whether his amended statement about Communism was sufficiently moderate, "and altogether whether any objection can be maintained to Communism." He himself thought his reservations about the present applicability of Fourierism to be valid; "but if *you* do not think so, I certainly will not print it, even if there were no other reason than the certainty I feel that I never should long continue of an opinion different from yours on a subject which you have fully con-

44. *Later Letters*, I, 9 (Feb. 19, 1849). The deleted sentence read: "It is probable that this will finally depend upon considerations not to be measured by the coarse standard which in the present state of human improvement is the only one that can be applied to it." (*Political Economy*, II, 980.)

45. *Later Letters*, I, 9 (Feb. 19, 1849). The deleted sentence read: "I believe that the majority would not exert themselves for any thing beyond this [a reduction of the hours of labor and a considerable variety of the kind of it], and that unless they did, nobody else would; and that on this basis human life would settle itself into one invariable round." (*Political Economy*, II, 980.)

sidered."[46] A month later, he was pleased to report: "I have followed to the letter every recommendation. The sentence which you objected to in toto of course has come quite out."[47]

Mill's praise of Harriet Taylor for her practical as well as speculative brilliance was meant to apply to political and social affairs. But he was equally impressed by her practical talents in more mundane matters. When there was some question of getting the correct type face for the second edition of the *Political Economy*, he was much agitated because a decision had to be made in her absence: "It is as disagreeable as a thing of that sort can possibly be—because it is necessary that something should be decided immediately without waiting for the decision of my only guide and oracle"; the wrong type face, moreover, might make the book "an unpleasant object to the only eyes I wish it to please."[48] After she had insisted that he renegotiate his contract with his publisher, exacting much better terms than those he had earlier agreed to, he decided that on this score, as well as her revisions, she had a "redoubled title" to the "joint ownership" of the book.[49]

Five years later, Harriet Mill, as she then was, played the same dual role—editorial and practical—when one of the chapters of the *Political Economy* was to be reprinted separately. But now there were no demurrals on Mill's part, however apologetic or fleeting, no substantive discussion of issues at all, only assurances of complete acquiescence both in regard to the contract and to revisions in the text: "I will answer Furnivall [the publisher] as you say"; "I wrote to Furnivall in the manner you wished"; "I shall not attempt any alterations till I hear from you"; "I think I agree in all

46. *Later Letters*, I, 11 (Feb. 21, 1849).
47. *Ibid.*, pp. 18–19 (Mar. 21, 1849).
48. *Ibid.*, p. 15 (Mar. 14, 1849).
49. *Ibid.*, p. 17 (Mar. 17, 1849).

your remarks; and have adopted them almost all."[50] It was in the same spirit that he registered his submission in personal affairs. When his mother died, his own inclination, in view of their embittered relations, was to refuse the small inheritance left to him. His wife sharply rebuked him for the vanity of behaving like a "man of fortune," to which he promptly replied: "Of course as your feeling is so directly contrary, mine is wrong, and I give it up entirely."[51]

The "boldness of speculation" he attributed to her is also evident in these letters—if by boldness is meant a zeal for simple, clearcut, dramatic solutions, an impatience with the kinds of complexities and difficulties that came more naturally, as he intimated, to himself. At one point, for example, having already agreed to all her changes, he confessed he was still troubled by one problem. Even if the "more obvious and coarser" objections to communism—the objections he had voiced in the first edition—were to diminish or cease to exist in the course of time, would not others arise, less obvious and coarse, which could not now be anticipated but which might eventually prove troublesome? He did not mean to imply, he hastily added, that "*you* cannot realize and judge of these things—but if you, and perhaps Shelley and one or two others in a generation can, I am convinced that to do so requires both great genius and great experience," and these qualities were lacking in the "present race of mankind." He then went on to quote her in a manner that suggested that she had not, in fact, anticipated, let alone solved, the problems. Against his argument, that men could not rise to the selfless heights required of them under communism, she had replied that "in 'ten years' the children of

50. *Ibid.*, pp. 159, 162, 166, 185 (Feb. 13, 18, 20, and Mar. 14, 1854). The qualification "almost" in the last sentence referred to changes proposed by her which were unclear to Mill (her syntax was notably erratic) or which did not fit the text where she had inserted them. There is some excuse for his docility in this case, since the proposed reprint was of the chapter she had inspired.

51. *Ibid.*, p. 223 (July 4, 1854).

the community might by teaching be made 'perfect.' " (The single quotation marks represent her words as quoted by Mill.) Mill had then pointed out that this supposed that there were "perfect people to teach them," to which she had countered: "If there were a desire on the part of the cleverer people to make them perfect it would be easy." Mill posed the obvious objections: How was that desire to be produced? Even if they themselves were granted "absolute power," they might improve people but could they perfect them? They might produce people with good intentions, but could they change their character, eliminate all those vices— self-flattery, vanity, irritability—which beset the cleverest people? Finally, as if embarrassed to have to raise such questions, he suggested postponing the discussion until her return.[52]

If this is at all typical of her mode of reasoning—and from her letters on other subjects it would seem to be—one can begin to understand what Mill meant by her "boldness of speculation," although one might find it hard to share his admiration for that boldness. Compared with him, she did indeed rise to the heights of speculative fantasy, being satisfied with nothing less than "perfect" human beings. Her "practicality" also told her how to go about creating those perfect human beings—within "ten years." In fact her speculativeness and practicality were of a piece. She was practical as only genuine utopians are. Convinced that perfection was entirely practicable, she thought it could be brought about by social engineering. Like most utopians, she believed that the highest reaches of the spirit could be achieved by a proper ordering of social institutions. And like most utopians, she also believed that all that was required for these exalted aims was the exercise of will. The idea that human beings or social institutions might prove recalcitrant, might resist the attempt to perfect them, that perfection itself might, in the realization, prove less than perfect, she dismissed as sympto-

52. *Ibid.*, p. 19 (Mar. 21, 1849).

matic of a failure of character, a form of moral and intellectual cowardice.

Her boldness and practicality exhibited themselves in other ways—in her response, for example, to the dramatic events of 1848. It was the revolutions on the Continent which fired her romantic imagination, inspiring her conversion to socialism and thus the revision of the *Political Economy*. The "labour" question, she decided, was second only to the "condition of women question" as the great issue of the time, and it would continue to have that prominence until "the hydra-headed selfishness of the idle classes is crushed by the demands of the lower."[53] Rejoicing in the "noble spectacle of France," she was delighted when the revolution seemed to spread to Ireland and was annoyed with Mill for taking a dim view of the prospects for a successful Irish uprising. How could he know, she objected, that such a rising would not succeed? Besides, she insisted, with the logic and fervor of all revolutionaries: "If it did not succeed it might do good if it were a serious one, by exasperating and giving fire to the spirit of the people. The Irish would I should hope not be frightened but urged on by some loss of life." She hastened to add that she was not recommending that Mill say this publicly (he was then writing occasional pieces for the *Daily News*): "This is entre nous and is not the thing to say to these dowdies—the more that it might not prove true."[54] Perhaps this last bit of advice is what Mill meant when he praised her "cautiousness of practical judgment."[55] Or perhaps that practical cautiousness is better typified by a letter written by her to her husband during the height of her enthusiasm for revolution and socialism. At a time when she was accusing her old friends of "tame and stupid servility" because they did not share her revolutionary zeal, she was also explaining to her husband

53. Hayek, p. 124 (HT to Fox, May 12, 1848).
54. *Ibid.*, p. 125 (HT to JSM, July 25, 1848).
55. *Autobiography*, p. 175.

that she was obliged to give up her "nice little house" in the country because its appearance was spoiled by the building of "poor people's poor little places opposite."[56]

Mill saw his modest talents as complementing her considerable ones. Her genius was to initiate and create, his to qualify, discriminate, and formulate. To this differentiation of roles she gracefully assented. Indeed, one might suspect that this idea, like so many others with which Mill credited her, had been "inspired" by her. Very early in their relationship, she had anticipated some such division of labor. The opening sentence of her brief statement on marriage and divorce, written in 1832, is typical of her later letters, in which her most effusive praise of him somehow redounded to her own credit: "If I could be Providence for the world for a time, for the express purpose of raising the condition of women, I should come to you to know the *means*—the *purpose* would be to remove all interference with affection. . . ."[57] It was characteristic of her to take upon herself the role of Providence while casting him in that of mediator charged with devising the means to carry out her end.

If she did not inspire this idea of their proper "division of labour," as Mill described their joint efforts,[58] she certainly acquiesced in it. She made no objections, for example, to Mill's proposal to dedicate the *Political Economy* to her. Nor did she quarrel with the substance of that dedication: "To Mrs. John Taylor, as the most eminently qualified of all persons known to the author either to originate or to appreciate speculations on social improvement, this attempt to explain and diffuse ideas many of which were first learned from herself, is with the highest respect and regard dedicated."[59]

Ten days before publication, she wrote to her husband, ostensibly to ask his advice about accepting the dedication

56. Hayek, p. 129 (HT to John Taylor, Sept. 20, 1848).

57. *Ibid.*, p. 75; italics in original. For a discussion of this essay, see below, p. 262.

58. *Later Letters*, I, 43 (1850[?]).

59. Hayek, p. 122.

but actually to explain why she intended to do so: "Dedications are not unusual, even of grave books, to women, and I think it calculated to do good if short and judicious." At that moment, she told him, she had in her hand a volume by Sismondi on political economy dedicated to Mme. de Sismondi. What did he recommend? "On the whole," she concluded, "I am inclined to think it desirable."[60] With great delicacy and diffidence Mr. Taylor replied that he thought all dedications in bad taste, and this one, "under our circumstances," wanting in both taste and tact. He rejoiced in the "justice and honour" accorded to her but urged her to forego a tribute that could only stimulate gossip and cause him much unpleasantness.[61] Unmoved by his appeal, she decided to accept the dedication. Perhaps out of deference to him, however, it was inserted only in the gift copies distributed by Mill and Mrs. Taylor.[62] Whatever qualms she may have had about the propriety of the dedication, she seems to have had none about its substance. Mill's description of her as the person "most eminently qualified . . . to originate or to appreciate speculations on social improvement" seemed to satisfy her criteria of a good dedication: "short and judicious."

Nor did she cavil at the tributes paid to her in the early draft of the *Autobiography*, which she herself read, edited, and approved. She did, to be sure, suggest some small changes. To the passage extolling her superiority in the two

---

60. *Ibid.*, p. 120 (Mar. 31, 1848). As Hayek points out, the reference to Mme. Sismondi is disingenuous. It was the translator who dedicated the English edition to the widow of the author—a rather different matter from a lover (however platonic) dedicating his work to the wife of another man.

61. *Ibid.*, p. 121 (Apr. 3, 1848).

62. The dedication appeared in gift copies of the first and second editions. It was removed from the third (published in 1853, after their marriage), because, she explained to her brother, "it would have been no longer appropriate." (Hayek, p. 297.) This is not entirely clear. "To Mrs. John Taylor" would have been obviously inappropriate. But why could that not have been changed to "my wife" or "Mrs. John Mill"?

most important regions, that of the highest ideals and that of practical aims, Mill had initially added: "in both of which her intellect is supreme and her judgment infallible." She first proposed to replace "infallible" with "unerring"; only later did she strike out the whole phrase, leaving the rest of the statement intact[63]—and leaving intact, too, the tribute to her "most genuine modesty," the favorable comparison of her to Shelley, Carlyle, and James Mill, and all the rest of the eulogy. What changes she made had to do with the wording; with the substance she had no quarrel.[64]

The same differentiation of roles appears again and again, in public and private, from the earliest years of their friendship to the last years of Mill's life. He was her "pupil" and "subject," her "interpreter" and "mediator," her "editor" and "amanuensis"; she was the "inspirer" and "prompter," the "author" and "originating mind."[65] He once wrote to her: "I should like everyone to know that I am the Dumont and you the originating mind, the Bentham, bless her!"[66] It was, if unwittingly, a somewhat equivocal tribute. Dumont was Bentham's editor, and there was no doubt who was the intellectual superior of the two. But no one knew better than Mill (because he himself had edited one of Bentham's books) how much work Dumont had to do to make Bentham's writings publishable, to extract some intelligent order out of the chaos of his manuscripts, to render his tortured prose and clotted neologisms into something that would pass as English.

One need not accept at face value the Bentham-Dumont analogy to find it extremely revealing. Even if one cannot credit the idea that Harriet Taylor had an "originating

63. *Early Draft*, pp. 195, 153; *Autobiography*, p. 132.

64. Some minor changes reveal small, conventional vanities. For example, "married at an early age" became, at her suggestion, "married at a very early age." (*Early Draft*, p. 193.)

65. *Autobiography*, pp. 124, 130, 171–72, 175; *Dissertations and Discussions*, II, 411–12; *On Liberty*, p. 63.

66. *Later Letters*, I, 112 (Aug. 30, 1853).

mind" in the same sense as Bentham did, one may find it easier to understand how Mill might see it in this light, how he could interpret her comments as the expression of a profound if inchoate genius. In some ways she did resemble Bentham. They were both intolerant of intellectual differences and demanding in their personal relationships. They were both given to large generalizations and gross simplifications—Bentham, to be sure, in accord with a grand scheme and system, Harriet Mill more often in response to some whim or passion. They both prided themselves on being bold, unconventional, radical. They were both "free spirits" defying an oppressive establishment. But above all, they both had the inner conviction of a genius which never fully emerged into public view or received adequate recognition. In Bentham's case the genius was stifled in a torrent of words, a multitude of schemes and ideas which were never completed or realized; in Harriet Mill's case, mundane language was inadequate to convey the profundity of her thought. Each required an editor of extraordinary abilities, unlimited patience, and a genuine faith in the genius to which he was ministering.

We may suspect that the tasks of editor, interpreter, secretary, and mediator were far more formidable for Mill than for Dumont, that the raw materials Mill had to work with were more raw and the finished products much more his own creation than was the case with Dumont. Yet we must also credit his wife with giving an impulse and direction to some of his work which it might not otherwise have had. It is evident that without her the revised edition of the *Political Economy* would have been, in important respects, a different work. And the *Political Economy*, after all, had been written and revised before their marriage. In his *Autobiography* Mill described that work as the beginning of their serious collaboration. It was during the period of their marriage—which was also when *On Liberty* was composed—that their collaboration reached its height.

A "JOINT PRODUCTION"

THE CLOSER ANY COLLABORATION, the less evidence of it there is likely to be. And a marital collaboration is, of course, the hardest to document. In the case of the Mills, the nature of their life together adds to the difficulty. There were no dinner guests to record their table talk, no acquaintances to gossip about them, no chatty letters to friends or relatives. Fortunately—for the historian, not for them—there were bouts of ill health which occasionally separated them. And at those times they wrote letters to each other which were more revealing than they could have known.

During their first separation, for example, a period lasting little more than a week in August 1853, Mill wrote his wife daily (apart from the one day there was no post). In addition to keeping her abreast of housekeeping details, the state of his health, the books he read when he returned from the office, and the other events of the day, he informed her of every change he had made in a review he had written (the changes were largely verbal, "greatest" altered to "most distinguished" and the like), forwarded to her the letters he had received, and submitted for her approval drafts of his replies—these on professional as well as domestic matters. (One such reply, on the subject of India, he proposed sending "when dearest one has made it right."[1]) If during her absence he went to such lengths to keep her advised and to solicit her advice, one may imagine how close their collaboration was when she was present.

It was at this time that he alluded to a project which they had evidently discussed before—a series of essays on crucial subjects to be published together in a single volume. He was eager to get on with this work.

> *We must finish the best we have got to say, and not only that, but publish it while we are alive—I do not see what living depositary there is likely to be of our thoughts, or who in this weak generation that is growing up will even be capable of thoroughly mastering and assimilating your ideas, much less of reoriginating them—so we must write them and print them, and then they can wait till there are again thinkers. But I shall never be satisfied unless you allow our best book, the book which is to come, to have our two names in the title page. It ought to be so with everything I publish, for the better half of it all is yours, but the book which will contain our best thoughts, if it has only one name to it, that should be yours.*[2]

Another series of letters resulted from a more prolonged separation in the winter of 1853–54, when she was recovering on the Continent from a severe hemorrhage which nearly took her life, and he was bearing up under a somewhat milder attack of tuberculosis at home. Again he consulted her about all the problems that beset him: Should he see another doctor? Put in a fresh supply of candles? Review Harriet Martineau's edition of Comte? (His reluctance

---

1. *Later Letters*, I, 109 (Aug. 27, 1853).

2. *Ibid.*, p. 112 (Aug. 30, 1853). It was this letter that concluded with the remark about his being the Dumont to her Bentham; see above, p. 237.

came from the difficulty of speaking frankly about Comte's atheism, hers from her distrust of Harriet Martineau; the review was not written.) Pay a bill of one shilling, three-pence for a washing-tub hoop? Acknowledge a letter from Mrs. Grote? (Mrs. Grote's letter caused Mill much anguish: she was clearly unworthy of a reply, but if Mr. Grote wrote, something would have to be said; but this meant disobeying Harriet's instructions to burn all of her—Harriet's—letters, since her letter suggesting the terms of reply would have to be kept so that Mill might refer to it in composing his letter to Grote. . . .)

Beleaguered by these time-consuming trivia, and with constant intimations of mortality, Mill became increasingly anxious that the *Autobiography* be completed. The first draft had been started before her departure, and during her absence he had reached that point in his intellectual history "when your influence over it began."[3] He had also written a description of her, but this still awaited her revision, and "until revised by you it is little better than unwritten." Of their relationship, however, he had not yet ventured to say anything beyond the fact that it had been an "intimate friendship for many years"; he left it for her to decide what more should be said to "stop the mouths of enemies here-after."[4]

This delicate subject preoccupied them more than any other. Mill was torn between impulses of candor and pru-dence. If the autobiography were not to be published for a hundred years, he would be inclined to say everything "simply and without reserve." But since it was desirable to publish it soon after their deaths, to preempt the subject lest others misrepresent it, it had to be done carefully, so as "not to put arms into the hands of the enemy." No one, whether writing his own life or the life of another, undertakes to "tell everything"; perhaps, he suggested, they might add a

3. *Ibid.*, pp. 165–66 (Feb. 20, 1854).
4. *Ibid.*, p. 138 (Jan. 23, 1854).

note to this effect.[5] In his diary he took comfort from the example of Goethe, whose autobiography "tells just as much about himself as he liked to be known" and was judiciously entitled, *Aus meinem Leben, Dichtung und Wahrheit.* "The *Aus*," Mill observed, "even without the *Dichtung* saves his veracity."[6] But even with some such private or public reservation, Mill wanted more guidance from his wife than she had yet given him. She had already suggested the tone he should take and the impression he should convey: the assurance that there had been affection and intimacy but no "impropriety." But he begged her to write for him the dozen or so lines which would definitively describe their relationship.[7]

At the same time that he was urging the completion of the *Autobiography*, he was also becoming increasingly anxious about the collection of essays which was to contain their "best thoughts."[8] In view of the "shortness and uncertainty of life," it was more than ever vital that they get on with this most important work.

Two years, well employed, would enable us I think to

5. *Ibid.*, p. 154 (Feb. 10, 1854).

6. *Letters*, Elliot edn., II, 373 (Diary, Feb. 19, 1854).

7. *Later Letters*, I, 166 (Feb. 20, 1854). Her earlier suggestions had been rather vague:

> *Should there not be a summary of our relationship from its commencement in 1830—I mean in a dozen lines—so as to preclude other and different versions of our lives at Kis [Kingston] and Wal [Walton]—our summer excursions, etc. This ought to be done in its genuine truth and simplicity—strong affection, intimacy of friendship, and no impropriety. It seems to me an edifying picture for those poor wretches who cannot conceive friendship but in sex—nor believe that expediency and the consideration for the feelings of others can conquer sensuality. But of course this is not my reason for wishing it done. It is that every ground should be occupied by ourselves on our own subject.* [Hayek, p. 196 (Feb. 14-15, 1854).]

8. See above, p. 240. The project should not be confused with the reprinting of Mill's earlier essays, which were eventually published as *Dissertations and Discussions*.

get the most of it into a fit state for printing—if not
in the best form for popular effect, yet in the state of
concentrated thought—a sort of mental pemican,
which thinkers, when there are any after us, may
nourish themselves with and then dilute for other
people.[9]

This image of a "mental pemican" is truly extraordinary.
Like the American Indian pounding into a paste the meats,
nuts, and fruits that made up his basic staples, so Mill and
his wife set about the preparation of a concentrated essence
of wisdom for the sustenance of later generations—intellectuals (if there were any after them) to take their nourishment straight and ordinary people in diluted form. The
image is all the more remarkable coming from Mill, who
in other circumstances was remarkably modest. But he was
not now talking about himself. It was the thought of his
wife's death that made him so anxious, and about her he
was not at all modest. Their work had to be completed so
that her ideas, as only he could transcribe them, would be
preserved and immortalized.

The fact that they were both ill, and of the same disease,
prompted them to speculate about who would be the sur-
vivor. She suspected it would be he, and he could only
hope they would both live long enough to "write together
'all we wish to leave written.'" (This last phrase, including
the plural pronoun, was evidently a quotation from her
letter.) For most of what remained to be written, he assured
her, "your living is quite as essential as mine, for even if the
wreck I should be could work on with undiminished faculties, my faculties at the best are not adequate to the highest
subjects and have already done almost the best they are
adequate to." If he happened to survive her, he promised
to do all that he could to make their unfinished work "such
as you would wish, for my only rule of life *then* would be

9. *Later Letters*, I, 141–42 (Jan. 29, 1854).

what I thought you would wish as it now is what you tell me you wish." In any event, he emphasized, "I *am not fit* to write on anything but the outskirts of the great questions of feeling and life without you to prompt me as well as to keep me right."[10]

THEY HAD EARLIER drawn up a list of the "highest subjects" which would go into the making of the pemican. One of these, the essay "Nature," was already written, at least in its preliminary draft. He reminded her of the others in the arbitrary order in which they had put them down: "Differences of character (nation, race, age, sex, temperament). Love. Education of tastes. Religion de l'Avenir. Plato. Slander. Foundation of Morals. Utility of religion. Socialism. Liberty. Doctrine that causation is will." To these he added two more that she had proposed in a recent letter: "Family, and Conventional."[11]

The first subject, "Differences of character," he thought he could do most with on his own.[12] But in spite of this clear expression of preference, and the fact that the subject had long fascinated him (it had come up repeatedly in his correspondence with Comte, and in the *Logic* he had coined the term "ethology" to signify what he took to be the most important social science of the future, the study of the formation of character), she countered with the suggestion that he first address himself to "Utility of Religion." She even drew up a kind of prospectus for that essay:

> *About the Essays dear, would not religion, the Utility of Religion, be one of the subjects you would have most to say on—there is [therein?] to account for the existence nearly universal of some religion (superstition) by the instincts of fear, hope and mystery etc.,*

10. *Ibid.,* p. 168 (Feb. 24, 1854). Italics in original.
11. *Ibid.,* p. 152 (Feb. 7, 1854).   12. *Ibid.*

and throwing over all doctrines and theories, called religion, and devices for power, to show how religion and poetry fill the same want, the craving after higher objects, the consolation of suffering, the hope of heaven for the selfish, love of God for the tender and grateful —how all this must be superseded by morality deriving its power from sympathies and benevolence and its reward from the approbation of those we respect.[13]

Mill's first reaction to this suggestion was less than enthusiastic. Her "programme" was "beautiful," but it would take her to fulfill it; he could try, but a few paragraphs would exhaust all he had to say on the subject. Within two weeks he was able to report that he had "fairly set to" the theme after thinking about it for many days. A fortnight later he was diligently working away at it, although he had still not reached that part of the subject "which you so beautifully sketched," having started on a more "commonplace" aspect of it, religion as a sanction for morality. At the same time, he reminded her that all he had written was nothing more than "mere raw material," to be worked up by both of them into a finished product. Another fortnight saw the essay completed—"such a one as I can write though very far inferior to what she could." Two days later he awaited further instructions: "I want my angel to tell me what should be the next essay written. I have done all I can for the subject she last gave me."[14]

The record of the genesis and evolution of "Utility of Religion" is hardly as complete as the historian would like. Yet such as it is, it is suggestive of the pattern of work, the mode of intellectual cooperation, which characterized this period of Mill's life. We do not know what his wife contributed to the revision of the essay; the manuscript has not

13. Hayek, pp. 195–96 (Feb. 14–15, 1854).
14. *Later Letters*, I, 165, 178, 190, 195, 197 (Feb. 20, Mar. 6, 20, Apr. 3, 5, 1854).

survived, and since the work of revision was done while they were together at Blackheath, there are no letters bearing on it. (They took, in fact, no extended vacations away from each other after the spring of 1855—a fact of some inconvenience to their biographers.) But even if the final version of the essay were essentially the same as the first draft, her influence must be judged to be considerable. Not, to be sure, in the actual composition of the essay; his twenty-five pages of polished prose and reasoned discourse can hardly be reduced to the shorthand jottings of her initial proposal. But it would also be unfair to limit the evidence of her influence to the passages which reflect her literal words or specific suggestions. Nor could one say that in proposing this topic she was merely repeating what Mill himself had said on earlier occasions; his first reaction to her letter makes it clear that he had not previously given the matter much thought, that it was probably she who had originally put it on their list. Without her initiative an essay on that subject would probably not have been written—or if written, may have been very different in substance and tone. One can only conclude that in this instance at least Mill had characterized her role correctly when he described her as the "inspirer" and "prompter," the "originating mind."

At the same time, one is driven to reflect on the nature of the ideas she had inspired. It may be significant that the only essays dating from this period which Mill chose not to publish during his lifetime were on the subject of religion: "Nature" and the "Utility of Religion." (The first, if not initiated by his wife, was certainly written and revised under her close supervision; at one point Mill told her he was incorporating into it three of her sentences "verbatim."[15]) It may also be significant that toward the end of his life, he wrote yet another essay on the subject under the title of "Theism." And that final essay was considerably more

15. *Ibid.*, p. 144 (Jan. 30, 1854).

sympathetic to orthodoxy than the earlier ones, especially on the subject of the "utility" of religion.[16]

IN THE ORIGINAL LIST of eleven essays that were to make up the pemican, "Liberty" came next to last. Although Mill had said that the subjects were not ranked in the order of their importance or in the order in which they proposed writing them, the list must to some extent have reflected the concerns that were uppermost in their minds. Liberty—as a subject to be treated abstractly, on its own, rather than, say, in the context of economic policy or the question of women —did not then seem to be of the greatest urgency. "Nature" was written first (both in its preliminary and final forms), and only then did they cast about for their next assignment, he proposing "Differences of character" and she "Utility of religion." Neither opted for "Liberty."

It may be that this neglect of "Liberty" reflected less their sense of priority than their notion of what Mill could best do on his own. (They were, it must be remembered, separated at the time.) Mill might have shied away from

16. It may be argued that Mill's attitude toward religion changed toward the end of his life. But this would not account for his failure to publish these early essays in 1859 or the early sixties, when he was releasing all the other work he had done during the period of his marriage. In the introduction to the posthumous volume, edited by his stepdaughter, Helen Taylor maintained that Mill thought his early essays on religion "fundamentally consistent" with his last one, as evidence of which she cited his intention, shortly before his death, of publishing "Nature" as well as "Theism." (*Three Essays on Religion* [London, 1874], p. viii.) But Mill did not, evidently, intend to publish "Utility of Religion." Most of his friends—secularists like John Morley and Alexander Bain—were distressed by "Theism" because it defended not only the social utility of religion but also the logical "possibility" of the existence of God and the special mission of Christ. In a private letter written about the same time as "Theism," Mill went so far as to suggest that the effect of prayer could not be proved to be an entirely natural phenomenon and that he would not exclude the possibility of some "supernatural influence." (*Later Letters*, III, 1414 [JSM to Henry Jones, June 13, 1868].)

the subject because he thought it could better be done while they were together. He had explained his choice of "Differences of character" by saying that it was "the one I could do most to by myself, at least of those equally important"[17]—from which one might infer that he felt "Liberty" to be too important to do on his own or that he felt inadequate to do it. And she may have bypassed it for the same reasons, because she wanted to be more actively engaged in it. Whatever their motives, the fact is that "Liberty" was probably the only essay of this period that was entirely written, both in its original and revised versions, while they were together.

Shortly after writing the first draft of the essay on liberty, Mill left England, in December 1854, hoping to get some relief on the Continent from the tubercular condition that had become acute. For over six months he traveled through Italy. It is curious to read the letters he wrote on this trip; they were composed in equal parts of details about the state of his health (the coughing of blood, loss of weight, indigestion, perspiration, rheumatic pains, and a variety of other infirmities), the ardors of traveling (seasickness, drafty trains, indigestible foods, flea-ridden inns), and a regimen of sightseeing which would have taxed the energy of the most robust man (exhaustive tours of the museums and ruins, seven-hour walking trips—a one- or two-hour walk he took as testimony of his debility). And all of this was capped by a daily thousand-word letter to his wife. (One might be suspicious of his invalidism, were it not that so many of his contemporaries enjoyed their ill health in the same vigorous fashion.) Interspersed among descriptions of paintings, sights, and symptoms were plans for their life work. It was now, for the first time, that the subject of liberty emerged into prominence. Instead of including the essay on liberty, written a few months earlier, in the

17. *Later Letters*, I, 152 (Feb. 7, 1854).

pemican volume, he now proposed to expand it and issue it as a separate book.

His *Autobiography* slightly dramatized the event in suggesting that the idea for the book had first come to him while he was "mounting the steps of the Capitol"[18]—perhaps an unconscious echo of Gibbon who was inspired to write *The Decline and Fall of the Roman Empire* as he sat "musing amidst the ruins of the Capitol while the barefooted friars were singing vespers in the Temple of Jupiter."[19] In fact, Mill first mentioned the idea in a letter to his wife written the day after his arrival in Rome before he had yet visited the Capitol. If he was slightly deceived about the exact timing of that event, he may also have been wrong in thinking, as he implied in the *Autobiography*, that the idea for the volume had originated with him alone. Again, from the letter written to his wife at the time, it would appear that they had entertained the idea before, perhaps while they were working on the essay itself. Whatever these small failings of memory, there is no doubt of the importance he now attached to the project.

> *On my way here cogitating thereon I came back to an idea we have talked about and thought that the best thing to write and publish at present would be a volume on Liberty. So many things might be brought into it and nothing seems to me more needed—it is a growing need too, for opinion tends to encroach more on liberty, and almost all the projects of social reformers in these days are really liberticide—Comte, particularly so. I wish I had brought with me here the paper on Liberty that I wrote for our volume of Essays—perhaps my dearest will kindly read it through and tell me whether it will do as the foundation of one part*

18. *Autobiography*, p. 170.
19. Edward Gibbon, *Autobiography*, ed. Lord Sheffield (World's Classics edn.; London, 1950), p. 160.

of the volume in question—if she thinks so I will try to write and publish it in 1856 if my health permits as I hope it will.[20]

The idea took the familiar course. A few days after his initial letter, he broached the matter again. His health was improving and with it his mental energy, and he felt that he could write a "very good volume on Liberty, if we decide that is to be the subject." In due course he was able to report that he could now start seriously thinking about it "since my darling approves of the subject."[21] His enthusiasm grew, not only because of the opportunity it would give them to say what needed saying but also because it was a subject that would attract much attention.

We have got a power of which we must try to make a good use during the next few years of life we have left. The more I think of the plan of a volume on Liberty, the more likely it seems to me that it will be read and make a sensation. The title itself with any known name to it would sell an edition. We must cram into it as much as possible of what we wish not to leave unsaid.[22]

Like the pemican, the volume on liberty would help them realize their intellectual ambitions. Painfully aware of the possibility of death, Mill was eager to see, while he was still alive, the fruits of their labors. From the beginning he had set a timetable for the preparation of the pemican: two years, he had thought, would see it finished. And from the beginning he had insisted upon the need to release this distillation of wisdom during their lifetime. His letters in the years of their marriage were full of publication plans—

20. *Later Letters*, I, 294 (Jan. 15, 1855).
21. *Ibid.*, pp. 300, 320 (Jan. 19, Feb. 9, 1855).
22. *Ibid.*, p. 332 (Feb. 17, 1855).

for the pemican, for the reprinting of his earlier essays, and, of course, for *On Liberty*. He even tried to anticipate the spacing of these books so that they would appear at suitable intervals. The reprinted essays, for example, should be issued directly after his return from the Italian trip, lest it coincide with the liberty book; nor should it be delayed until after the publication of the liberty book, because by that time they would have ready a volume of new essays. He had a host of other good reasons for the immediate publication of the earlier essays: if they themselves saw to it, they could select what they wanted to preserve instead of leaving it to others to reprint the "trash" they would prefer to disown; his reputation was then at its height and the sale of such a volume was likely to be good; volumes of essays tended to be widely reviewed because everyone thought himself competent to review a miscellany of essays whereas few would venture to review a work of political economy or logic; and above all there was the question of timing, the hope of publishing a volume annually for the next several years. He concluded this lengthy plan with his usual solicitation: "Will my dearest one think about this and tell me what her judgment and also what her feeling is."[23]

Her judgment and feeling could not have been very favorable, because in spite of his importunities and in spite of the fact that he could easily have met that timetable, Mill published nothing of importance, not even a single review, during the remaining three and a half years of his marriage; nor did he have anything in the process of publication at the time of her death. His bibliography during this period consisted of slightly revised editions of the *Logic* and *Political Economy*, botanical notes contributed to the *Phytologist*, dispatches to India written in his official capacity, and a single anonymous letter to the *Daily News*. (For the entire period of his marriage, his only publications of any conse-

23. *Ibid.*, p. 348 (Feb. 25, 1855).

quence, apart from the revised editions, were three review-essays.) To those few people who had been told of his plans —his correspondence during this time was almost as sparse as his publications—he never explained why the promised volumes did not appear; toward the end he simply ceased mentioning them at all. That they did not appear was clearly his wife's doing. Apart from the evidence of his own wishes, amounting almost to entreaties, there is the fact that within months of her death both *On Liberty* and *Dissertations and Discussions* were published, and that thereafter most of the writings dating from this time were released in one form or another.

It is probable that Mrs. Mill did not expressly forbid publication, that her tactic was rather to procrastinate, to find one or another reason for putting off one after another project. This would account for Mill's continuing to hope for almost a year that *On Liberty* would be published imminently. But there must have been some general disposition on her part, and some recognition of it on his, to account for a delay so systematic that it amounted to a virtual prohibition of publication. And this disposition may be related to the peculiar circumstances of their life, which were also largely of her making—their deliberate withdrawal from society, the cultivation of their own relationship to the exclusion of everyone else. For the same reasons that she discouraged Mill's associations with the outside world, she may also have discouraged the publication of his writings. It is as if she kept his writings to themselves, as she kept him to herself. To have published them would have been to part with them, to share them with an alien world, and to permit that world to impinge upon their privacy. Under the pretext of wanting to perfect the writings (Mill, at least, was professional enough to know that they were as good as they would ever be—neither before nor after this period did he exhibit the same compulsion about perfection), they wrote and rewrote, taking them out again and again to change a word or alter a nuance of thought, or perhaps just to savor and admire. It was the ultimate in intellectual narcissism.

Their letters give the same impression of two beleaguered souls, the only remnants of virtue and wisdom in a corrupt and philistine world. This image is reenforced by the idea of the pemican, with its arrogant assumption that they alone were capable of genuine thought, that the most others could do was to take nourishment from the cake of wisdom and pass it on in diluted form to still others who were incapable of ingesting it in its purity. It would be an extraordinary assumption at any time, but still more at this, when most men were marveling, as we still marvel, at the giants of the age: Newman and Arnold, Carlyle and Macaulay, Tennyson and Browning, Dickens and Eliot, Gladstone and Disraeli—to say nothing of the giants abroad: Tocqueville and Comte, old and young Hegelians, post- and neo-Kantians, the schools of higher biblical criticism and of German historical scholarship. On his own, Mill would hardly have ignored the abundant evidence of intellectual vitality, still less would he have arrogated to himself a position of solitary eminence. But then, as has been said, it was not his eminence he was asserting but hers. And she, for her part, never tired of telling him how superior he was to all his countrymen, how he alone had the mind and heart to appreciate the great issues of the day (and, by implication, to appreciate, as no one else did, her superlative qualities). In their mutual admiration and congratulation, they stood together, apart from and above the rest of the sullied world.

THE HABITS that governed their personal lives spilled over into their intellectual lives, shaping their attitudes to men, society, morality, the life of the mind, and the world of affairs. And it was in *On Liberty* above all that these attitudes were revealed. In their original prospectus for the pemican, the subject of liberty may not have been given pride of place. But after the first draft of the essay was written, it became evident that of all the subjects they planned to write about, this was the most ambitious, the subject likely to attract the largest reading public. It must also have touched a deep chord in them. The themes developed there were so closely related to their own lives that even if they had not initially intended to go so far as they did in pressing the claims of liberty, they might have been incited to do so by the very act of writing.

Later John Morley was to characterize *On Liberty* as "one of the most aristocratic books ever written."[24] And so it was, emanating as it did from the most aristocratic— intellectually aristocratic, that is—of all couples. In a sense it was the philosophical expression of their existential situation. Cherishing their privacy and shunning society, they generalized their own condition, making of it an ideal for all mankind. They exalted in *On Liberty* all the qualities they valued in themselves: an individuality that was the prerequisite of genius, a hostility to the society they felt to be hostile to them, a contempt for the conventions they had been compelled to flout, and an overwhelming solicitude for the liberty that permitted them to cultivate their tastes and talents in defiance of the pressures toward conformity and mediocrity.

One reviewer complained that *On Liberty* sounded as if it had issued from the "prison cell of some persecuted thinker," rather than from the study of the most influential and respected writer of his generation.[25] This comment was not as far removed from Morley's as might be thought. The tone of the book is at the same time aristocratic and somewhat paranoid. Not only is the individual portrayed as

---

24. "Mr. Mill's Doctrine of Liberty," *Fortnightly Review,* XX (1873); reprinted in John Morley, *Nineteenth-Century Essays,* ed. Peter Stansky (Chicago, 1970), p. 125.
25. *National Review,* VIII (1859), 393. See above, p. 165.

innately superior to the mediocre mass; the mass is represented as always pressing against him, threatening to violate
his individuality and deny his superiority. It was in similar
terms that the Mills conceived of their personal situation. In
a section of his *Autobiography* written about the same
time as *On Liberty* and dealing with the same period of his
life, Mill explained why someone of "really high class of
intellect" would choose to have such minimal relations with
"society" as to be "almost considered as retiring from it
altogether." Society, he wrote, was "insipid"; it discouraged
serious discussion; it was useful only to those who hoped to
climb higher, while those already at the top could do no
more than comply with the customs and demands of their
station. And most of all, it was debasing to the intellectual,
whose feelings, opinions, and principles could only be lowered by contact with it.

> *A person of high intellect should never go into unin-
> tellectual society unless he can enter it as an apostle;
> yet he is the only person with high objects who can
> safely enter it at all. Persons even of intellectual aspira-
> tions had much better, if they can, make their habitual
> associates of at least their equals, and, as far as possible,
> their superiors, in knowledge, intellect, and elevation of
> sentiment. Moreover, if the character is formed, and
> the mind made up, on the few cardinal points of
> human opinion, agreement of conviction and feeling
> on these, has been felt in all times to be an essential
> requisite of anything worthy the name of friendship, in
> a really earnest mind.*[26]

Mill did not explain how aspiring intellectuals could hope
to associate with their superiors if their superiors would not
stoop to associate with their own inferiors. Nor did he reconcile the "essential requisite" of like-mindedness—the

26. *Autobiography*, pp. 159–60.

natural preference of intellectuals for friendships based on "agreement of conviction and feeling"—with the "collisions of opinions" which in *On Liberty* he took to be the requisite of intellectual vitality. But he made it clear from his remark that it was his own situation he was describing: "All these circumstances united, made the number very small of those whose society, and still more whose intimacy, I now voluntarily sought."[27]

Mill was here speaking of "society" in the narrow sense, the society of friends and acquaintances, of dinner parties and literary salons. But the same strictures applied to "society" writ large. The latter, as depicted in *On Liberty*, was as inimical to high thoughts and feelings, as conducive to mediocrity and mindless conformity, as the small talk of the dinner party. "Those who would either make their lives useful to noble ends, or maintain any elevation of character within themselves, must in these days have little to do with what is called society."[28] Mill was apologizing to Mazzini for venturing to invite him to visit Blackheath—one of the few such invitations extended during the life of his wife. But he could as well have been declaiming, as he did in *On Liberty*, against the "despotism of society," the "tyranny of opinion," the "collective mediocrity" of the "sovereign Many."[29]

That this attitude toward society—in both senses—was distinctively his wife's rather than his own is suggested by the marked change in his mode of life soon after her death. He spent most of 1859 in the house near Avignon, but almost immediately upon his return to England early in 1860, he was obliged to explain to his stepdaughter, only slightly apologetically, why he was accepting invitations from some people and making overtures to others. He still, he assured her, detested "society for society's sake," but when he could further a good cause by seeing people, he did not at all

27. *Ibid.*, p. 160.
28. *Later Letters*, II, 548 (JSM to Mazzini, Feb. 21, 1858).
29. *On Liberty*, pp. 76, 124.

dislike it; to be with some people, he discovered, was almost as pleasurable as a meeting of the *Political Economy Club*.[30] And it was with some relief that he received her approval of a letter he had written to Mrs. Austin, the first such letter in over ten years. By 1861 he was actually accepting a weekend invitation from Mrs. Grote—the same Mrs. Grote whose letter some years earlier he had refused to acknowledge. And so it went with one after another of his former friends. Relationships that had been suspended for over a decade were renewed in an easy, warm manner.

His correspondence provided a dramatic measure of this change, not only in the resumption of letters to old friends and in the vastly increased quantity of letters, but also in a distinct change of tone. Previously his communications had been full of grievances. He complained to publishers, curtly declined requests for personal information or photographs, was critical in commenting on articles and books, and was wary of solicitations from organizations. Later his letters became good-natured almost to a fault. He wrote warmly to fledgling authors, apologized for not promptly acknowledging an unsolicited manuscript and then managed to find something to praise in it, accepted gratefully the proposals of publishers, put up amiably with the delays of translators and invariably professed satisfaction with their work, was barely ruffled when several of his private letters were published without his permission, refused to blame anyone and harbored no resentment for his defeat in the election of 1868, and in general displayed none of the sensitivity and suspicion that had been so conspicuous during the years of his marriage.

IF THE MANNER of their life together was reflected in the tone and substance of *On Liberty*, so was a mode of thought that

---

30. *Later Letters*, II, 675 (Feb. 11, 1860).

was peculiarly his wife's. In the dedication to *On Liberty*, Mill described his wife as "the inspirer, and in part the author, of all that is best in my writings." This book in particular "belongs as much to her as to me"; if it was not better, it was because it lacked her final revisions, he himself being incapable of conveying so much as half of her "great thoughts and noble feelings," her "unrivalled wisdom."[31] These sentiments may be taken as the kind of pieties one expects in a dedication, all the more since it was written only weeks after his wife's death. What cannot be so easily discounted, however, is the portion of his *Autobiography* written almost a decade later, in which he made more precise and even larger claims regarding her part in *On Liberty*.

> *The "Liberty" was more directly and literally our joint production than anything else which bears my name, for there was not a sentence of it that was not several times gone through by us together, turned over in many ways, and carefully weeded of any faults, either in thought or expression, that we detected in it. It is in consequence of this that, although it never underwent her final revision, it far surpasses, as a mere specimen of composition, anything which has proceeded from me either before or since. With regard to the thoughts, it is difficult to identify any particular part or element as being more hers than all the rest. The whole mode of thinking of which the book was the expression, was emphatically hers. But I also was so thoroughly imbued with it, that the same thoughts naturally occurred to us both. That I was thus penetrated with it, however, I owe in a great degree to her.*[32]

> *The "Liberty" is likely to survive longer than anything else that I have written (with the possible exception of*

---

31. *On Liberty*, p. 63.   32. *Autobiography*, pp. 176–77.

the "Logic"), because the conjunction of her mind with mine has rendered it a kind of philosophic textbook of a single truth, which the changes progressively taking place in modern society tend to bring out into ever stronger relief: the importance, to man and society, of a large variety in types of character, and of giving full freedom to human nature to expand itself in innumerable and conflicting directions.[33]

After my irreparable loss, one of my earliest cares was to print and publish the treatise, so much of which was the work of her whom I had lost, and consecrate it to her memory. I have made no alteration or addition to it, nor shall I ever. Though it wants the last touch of her hand, no substitute for that touch shall ever be attempted by mine.[34]

These passages are especially revealing because they bear upon one of the most troublesome aspects of *On Liberty*—the "whole mode of thinking" which is so difficult to reconcile with Mill's other works. It was not his habit to be so absolutistic and simplistic, to try to reduce so complex a problem as the relations of the individual and society to a simple, single principle. That this was, however, his wife's distinctive mode of thought may be inferred from the kinds of suggestions she urged upon him in connection with his other writings, as well as from the kinds of tributes he paid to her—her "boldness of speculation," her preeminence in that region of thought concerned with "ultimate aims," her

33. *Ibid.*, p. 177.
34. *Ibid.*, p. 180. In a conversation with Lady Amberley (Bertrand Russell's mother), and in the presence of Mill, Helen Taylor said that in *On Liberty* were to be found her mother's "mind and thoughts for they were mostly hers." (*The Amberley Papers*, ed. Bertrand and Patricia Russell (London, 1937), I, 372–73.) Helen Taylor may have been only echoing the dedication to *On Liberty* or the *Autobiography* (which she probably read in manuscript)—or she may have been repeating what she had heard at home.

ability to pierce to the "very heart and marrow" of every problem, "always seizing the essential idea or principle."[35]

That Mill should single out this particular quality of *On Liberty*, its "mode of thinking," as "emphatically hers" confirms not only the nature and extent of her influence but also the fact that *On Liberty* itself represented a distinctive mode of thought. If Mill regarded it as distinctive, we can do no less. And when he went on to describe the "conjunction" of their minds as issuing in "a kind of philosophic text-book of a single truth," we may assume, from his description elsewhere of their respective roles and of her genius in "seizing the essential idea or principle," that it was she who provided the "single truth" which he then converted into a "philosophic text-book."

IF THIS PENCHANT for a "single truth," an "essential idea or principle," was his wife's characteristic mode of thought, the particular truth and principle of *On Liberty* was also characteristically hers. Here Mill's testimony may be supplemented by the few sustained pieces of writing we have by her. The first is a short essay probably written about 1832. Although it was not published during her lifetime, it was preserved among her effects, suggesting that either she or Mill or both attached some importance to it. Its theme was the "spirit of conformity" that threatened to undermine "individual character."

> ... *Whether it would be Religious conformity, Political conformity, Moral conformity or Social conformity, no matter which the species, the spirit is the same: all kinds agree in this one point, of hostility to individual character, and individual character if it exists at all, can rarely declare itself openly while there is, on all topics of importance a standard of conformity raised by the*

35. *Autobiography*, pp. 175, 132, 131.

indolent minded many and guarded by a [?] of opinion which, though composed individually of the weakest twigs, yet makes up collectively a mass which is not to be resisted with impunity.

What is called the opinion of Society is a phantom power, yet as is often the case with phantoms, of more force over the minds of the unthinking than all the flesh and blood arguments which can be brought to bear against it. It is a combination of the many weak, against the few strong; an association of the mentally listless to punish any manifestation of mental independence. . . .

. . . If by principle is intended the only useful meaning of the word, accordance of the individual's conduct with the individual's self-formed opinion . . . then eccentricity should be prima facie evidence for the existence of principle. . . .

. . . We would have the Truth, and if possible all the Truth, certainly nothing but the Truth said and acted universally. But we would never lose sight of the important fact that what is truth to one mind is often not truth to another. . . . In this view we comprehend that
All thoughts, all creeds, all dreams are true
All visions wild and strange—

. . . The capability of even serious error, proves the capacity for proportionate good. For if anything may be called a principle of nature this seems to be one, that force of any kind has an intuitive tendency towards good.

. . . Society abhors individual character. It asks the sacrifice of body heart and mind.[36]

Whether this manuscript prompted the inclusion of "liberty" in the pemican, whether it was actually consulted

36. Hayek, pp. 275–79.

by Mill when he wrote his first essay on that subject, or whether it merely represented a mode of thought that was naturally congenial to his wife, its resemblance to *On Liberty* is striking. And not only in its general theme—the value of individuality, the distrust of society, and the contempt for conformity—but also in many of its details: eccentricity raised to the level of principle, the relativity of truth, the connection between good and error, and the idea that force itself is conducive to the good. Above all, it resembles *On Liberty* in its posture—that of the romantic rebel standing alone against the overwhelming pressures of society, deriving his strength from his inner resources, and confident of his intellectual and moral (although not physical) superiority.

Some of the same characteristics are evident in another of her compositions dating from about the same time. This was a brief essay on marriage and divorce which was part of an exchange she and Mill had on that subject. Like the later essays on women, this one illustrates the close connection between the themes of sexual equality and liberty. It opened with a plea to Mill to provide the "means" for the achievement of her "purpose," which was the liberty of affection; and it continued with her own proposal of means—the abolition of all laws relating to marriage.

> *If I could be Providence for the world for a time, for the express purpose of raising the condition of women, I should come to you to know the* means—*the purpose would be to remove all interference with affection, or with anything which is, or which even might be supposed to be, demonstrative of affection. . . . I should think that 500 years hence none of the follies of their ancestors will so excite wonder and contempt as the fact of legislative restraints as to matter of feeling—or rather in the expression of feeling. When once the law undertakes to say which demonstration of feeling shall be given to which, it seems quite consistent not [?] to*

legislate for all, *and to say how many shall be seen and how many heard, and what kind and degree of feeling allows of shaking hands. The Turks' is the only consistent mode. I have no doubt that when the whole community is really educated, tho' the present laws of marriage were to continue they would be perfectly disregarded, because no one would marry.*

. . . . .

Love in its true and finest meaning, seems to be the way in which is manifested all that is highest best and beautiful in the nature of human beings—none but poets have approached to the perception of the beauty of the material world—still less of the spiritual—and hence never yet existed a poet, except by inspiration of that feeling which is the perception of beauty in all forms and by all means which are given us, as well as by sight. *Are we not born with the five senses, merely as a foundation for others which we may make by them—and who extends and refines those material senses to the highest—into infinity—best fulfills the end of creation—that is only saying,* who enjoys most is most *virtuous. It is for* you—*the most worthy to be the apostle of all the highest virtues to reach such as may be taught, that the higher the* kind *of enjoyment, the* greater *the* degree, *perhaps there is but one class to whom this* can *be taught—the poetic nature struggling with superstition: you are fitted to be the saviour of such.*[37]

In these somewhat inchoate sentiments may be found the familiar ingredients of romanticism: the glorification of feeling and the desire to be liberated from law, the identification of love with all that was "highest best and beautiful," the spiritualization of sensory pleasure, the paean to the

37. *Ibid.*, pp. 75–78.

"poetic nature" who alone was capable of realizing the "highest virtues," and the invocation of an "apostle" or "saviour" to teach those virtues to "such as may be taught." And here too may be seen the typical mode of reasoning of the romantic, the tendency to carry out ideas to their extreme. Thus, to legislate upon any "demonstration of feeling" was to legislate upon all demonstrations of feeling, including the conditions upon which people would be permitted to shake hands—or perhaps, as with the Turks, forbidden to do so. Similarly, a community that was "really educated" would disregard all laws of marriage to the point where "no one would marry."

This statement by Harriet Taylor becomes even more revealing when it is contrasted with Mill's part of the exchange. Indeed, Mill's essay reads as if it had been written in response to hers. Ostensibly endorsing her lofty ideals, he managed to inject into them a hearty dose of social reality. How easy it would be, he observed, for them to resolve for themselves alone such matters as the relations of men and women. The difficulty was to find solutions for "mankind at large." What was wanted was a "popular morality" which could effect the conciliations and compromises required for the mass of "conflicting natures," persuading them to renounce some desires in order to attain others and forestalling the state of war that would ensue if there were no such renunciation. This popular morality ought to be such as to cause least sacrifice to those "higher natures" who had the greatest capacity for happiness and who would suffer most by compromising or renouncing their desires. If all persons were of this higher order, there would be no moral problems, for then morality and inclination would be one: "If all resembled you, my lovely friend, it would be idle to prescribe rules for them: By following their own impulses under the guidance of their own judgment, they would find more happiness, and would confer more, than by obeying any moral principles or maxims whatever." But most people were not of this order. "Inferior natures" had genuine moral problems; it was for them that law and opinion set limits on marriage and divorce, on the "unbounded freedom of uniting and separating." For these people in the present state of civilization the bonds of marriage were not an unmitigated evil but a mitigated good. And while there should be freedom to dissolve an intolerable marriage, it was "highly desirable that the first choice should be, even if not compulsorily, yet very generally, persevered in." The alternative to an absolute prohibition of divorce was not an absolute "facility of divorce" in which the parties could separate "on the most passing feeling of dissatisfaction," but rather a provision for divorce that would limit it to extreme cases and discourage it in others.[38]

It is not as contributions to the "woman question" or even the question of divorce that the essays are cited here, but rather as they reflect upon *On Liberty*. For in *On Liberty* Mill cast aside the moderating, pragmatic considerations he had earlier urged and posed precisely the kinds of extreme and ideal alternatives he had earlier rejected. In the essay on marriage and divorce, he had warned against legislating for "higher natures," insisting rather upon a sound "popular morality" that could accommodate the needs of "lower natures"—the need to restrain and renounce desire and passion, to compromise among "conflicting natures"—without, to be sure, exacting too high a price from the higher natures. In *On Liberty* he implicitly denied the validity of such a conception of popular morality which would mediate among conflicting natures. Instead, he proposed a single ethic based upon a single type of nature. And this was an ethic of gratification and liberation rather than renunciation and restraint, an ethic appropriate to those for whom, as he had earlier put it, "morality and inclination would coincide," who could be trusted to follow "their own

38. *Ibid.*, pp. 58–73. For Mill's later views on divorce, see the note appended to this chapter.

impulses under the guidance of their own judgment." In *On Liberty*, it would seem, Mill discharged the mission Harriet Taylor had assigned him, that of apostle and savior of poetic natures—of those exceptional individuals who were the primary beneficiaries and the most worthy practitioners of liberty.

It might be objected that these early writings by Mrs. Taylor should not be taken so seriously, that they were youthful aberrations, the effusions and affectations of a romantic young woman. There was, in fact, something of this romantic, precious spirit among William Fox and his followers, some of whom clearly thought themselves a finer breed than the common bourgeois around them. One senses this even in Mill's polite description of Mr. Taylor: ". . . a most upright, brave, and honorable man, of liberal opinions and good education, but without the intellectual or artistic tastes which would have made him a companion to her."[39] And it emerges in the unconventional behavior of two of the most prominent couples in this circle, Mill and Harriet Taylor and Fox and Eliza Flower. But Mrs. Taylor's bohemian pretensions, if they were that, did not completely disappear with age, nor with her subsequent eminently respectable marriage to Mill. On the contrary, the bitter experiences of those early years, the long period during which she endured the aspersions, or fancied aspersions, of Mrs. Grote, Mrs. Carlyle, Miss Martineau, and the others, gave her a stake in unconventionality, a lasting commitment to it. The stance of the rebel provided a vindication not only of her past but also of her present, of that peculiarly withdrawn and isolated life they led together.

This is not to say that her "poetic" temper, as Mill called it,[40] her animus against society and bourgeois conventions, her idealization of individuality and nonconformity, were

39. *Early Draft*, p. 152.   40. See above, p. 216.

merely emotional responses to a personal situation. On the contrary, these attitudes clearly predated that situation, indeed made it possible for the situation to develop as it did. But once it did develop in that way, it may well have re-enforced the mode of thought and behavior that came naturally to her.

Nor does this suggest that Mrs. Mill was the "real" author of *On Liberty*, imposing her views upon a reluctant and unwilling collaborator. Mill was probably telling the literal truth when he wrote that the "whole mode of thinking . . . was emphatically hers," that he was, however, "so thoroughly imbued with it that the same thoughts naturally occurred to us both," but that he would not have been so "penetrated with it" had it not been for her.[41] There is an effort at precision here that must be respected. If *On Liberty* was a "joint production"—and there is every reason to think that, in a more important sense than the mere writing of it, it was just that—Mill, no less than his wife, was responsible for it. It does not diminish his responsibility to acknowledge her inspiration and influence, to recognize the extent to which he was, at that time and on that subject, "thoroughly imbued" with a mode of thought that was "emphatically hers."

MILL NEVER explicitly stated what might be inferred from these remarks and even more from his writings as a whole—that if *On Liberty* was most thoroughly imbued with his wife's mode of thought, his other works (including his later ones) were less thoroughly, in some cases not at all, imbued with it. In his *Autobiography* he distinguished only three periods in his life, the third being the whole of his life after her influence had become predominant. The period after her death he treated as an epilogue, as if history had come to an end, the "spring" of his life had been broken.

41. See above, p. 258.

and only the mechanics of living remained. Yet it was, as we have seen, a most eventful and productive time for him. And it had a distinctive intellectual as well as personal character.

It is as if, in releasing *On Liberty* and publicly giving his wife credit for a large part of it, he was free to go his own way. Memorials, as is well known, have a liberating effect upon the bereaved, relieving them not only of the guilt of survival but also of the weight of memories and responsibilities, the reproachful presence of the dead. And *On Liberty* was as much a memorial to his wife as the shrine at Avignon. The dedication that was nothing less than a eulogy, the issuance of the book in the precise form in which she left it, the public resolution never to alter a word were all conscious acts of piety and commemoration. Once they were performed, Mill went on to other matters.

It is curious how little attention he paid to this book after it was published—the book they had kept so obsessively to themselves, every word and sentence of which they had gone over again and again, the book that was to say all that most urgently needed saying and that would create a sensation. Apart from the usual proprieties and business chores—acknowledging compliments and reviews, arranging for translations and new editions—his correspondence is remarkably sparse on the subject of *On Liberty*, or indeed on the subject of liberty in general. Except for one occasion when he was attacked for contributing to the campaign of the celebrated atheist Charles Bradlaugh and cited *On Liberty* in his defense (the right of a political person to be judged by his political actions rather than by his religious opinions), the only other allusions to the book were in support not of liberty but of restrictions on liberty: the right of the government to prohibit marriage and to limit the employment of children.[42]

42. *Later Letters*, III, 1492 (JSM to Mrs. E. Lambert, Nov. 28, 1868); *ibid.*, p. 1124 (to Dr. H. MacCormac, Dec. 4, 1865); *ibid.*, IV, 1736 (to Charles de Beaulieu, June 21, 1870).

Even in the period immediately following the publication of *On Liberty*, Mill was much more taken up with the subjects raised in another essay published by him about the same time, an essay on parliamentary reform. Plural voting, proportional representation, and the question of the ballot occupied him much more than the problem of liberty. And some of these other issues involved a quite different mode of thought from that of *On Liberty*. His justification for open voting as against a secret ballot is revealing: "There will never be honest or self-restraining government unless each individual participant feels himself a trustee for all his fellow citizens and for posterity. Certainly no Athenian voter thought otherwise."[43] The idea that the individual should act, not freely, privately, in his own interests, but rather with self-restraint, on behalf of the public and of posterity, comes strangely from the author of *On Liberty*—almost as strangely as his appeal to the ancients.

This lack of concern with the subject of liberty, either in its specific application or in its general theory, may have derived from Mill's admission in the *Autobiography* (in the last part added in 1869 or 1870), that the present tendency of the time, so far from imposing an "oppressive yoke of uniformity in opinion and practice," seemed to be having precisely the opposite effect of encouraging the "development of new opinions." He hastened to add that this was a transitory state of affairs, and that once a new body of opinion became solidified, as must inevitably happen, the teachings of *On Liberty* would unfortunately acquire their "greatest value."[44] But in a private letter written shortly before this passage, Mill took an optimistic view of the destruction of the "old fetters." So far from anticipating a new

43. *Ibid.*, II, 608 (JSM to G. C. Lewis, Mar. 20, 1859). In the *Autobiography* Mill attributed to his wife the initiative in changing their views on the ballot (p. 180). He did not say on what grounds this conversion took place.
44. See above, p. 167.

oppressive uniformity, he looked forward to a "much better settlement" than had ever existed before.

> *The changes in the opinions and feelings of large bodies of Englishmen and Englishwomen even within the last few years, are as striking to me as they are to you. The old fetters of prejudice and routine seem to be giving way on all sides, and what is wanted now is clear and well considered positive opinions. All the great subjects, political, social, and religious, are brought into question; and there is a preparation going on in England, as there is in the United States, for a much better settlement of them than the world has yet had: but, naturally, the evidences of this are not as obvious on the surface as are those of the breaking up of old doctrines.*[45]

A few months later Mill commented on other social problems and tendencies in a manner that was even more alien to *On Liberty*. The "great questions of the future," he wrote, were the emancipation of women and cooperative production; these were the two great changes which would "regenerate society." But though the latter might come about without the help of "Parliaments and Congresses," the former could not. America had always been thought to be a country that "needs very little governing"; it was this that led its best minds to abstain from political life. But that period was over. "The present is surely a time in which, even in America, the action of legislation and administration is of transcendent importance; and in the old and complicated societies of Europe the need of political action is always, more or less, what exceptional circumstances make it in America at present." It was partly for this

---

45. *Later Letters*, III, 1434 (JSM to Charles Eliot Norton, Sept. 11, 1868).

reason, he explained, that he himself had gone into Parliament, and on this most important subject, the political enfranchisement of women, the results had far exceeded his expectations.[46]

This is a most revealing letter, first in its specification of the two most important issues of the time—neither of which was liberty; then in its admission that for the resolution of at least one of these issues, "legislation and administration" were of "transcendant importance"—which was hardly the message of On Liberty. (One may also note the optimistic assumption that the political enfranchisement of women was then well on its way to achievement, a miscalculation of half a century.[47]) Nor is this letter unique in these respects. In the last years of his life Mill repeatedly gave priority, in the present and foreseeable future, to the questions of women's equality and some form of social cooperation. And in respect to both issues Mill was far more dependent upon social action, more hopeful of social progress, less antagonistic toward society and public opinion, than in On Liberty.[48]

46. Ibid., IV, 1535 (JSM to Parke Godwin, Jan. 1, 1869).

47. Over half a century, if equality of franchise is considered. In 1918 Parliament gave the vote to women but only at the age of thirty, whereas the voting age for men was twenty-one. It took another ten years for the two to become equalized. In America women were enfranchised on the same terms as men in 1920.

48. Although Mill believed the "social question" to be one of the most urgent areas for reform and therefore considerably modified his earlier laissez-faire position, he did not become more of a socialist in his last years. On the contrary, his unfinished Chapters on Socialism was more critical of socialism than his Political Economy. On the question of socialism (as on liberty) his wife had evidently urged upon him a more extreme position than he would have taken on his own. The inconsistency in her views of socialism and of liberty may be explained in part by the fact that her sympathy for socialism had been aroused initially by the revolutions of 1848. By the late fifties, when On Liberty was written, that issue was no longer in the forefront of her consciousness.

This is not to say that Mill was no longer concerned with liberty; liberty as such was not the issue. After *On Liberty* as before, he had the liveliest appreciation of the value of liberty. What he did not have, before or afterwards, was a commitment to liberty in the form and degree he gave it in *On Liberty*. It was the absolute value of liberty, the absolute sovereignty of the individual, that distinguished this work from Mill's other writings and from the liberalism of his contemporaries. And it was this absolutistic doctrine that the influence of his wife and the circumstances of his life help account for. It took only a shift in the weight of the argument to convert the balanced, modulated, complicated view that was distinctively his into the simple and extreme view that was distinctively hers. That shift may not have seemed so drastic to Mill at the time. But in the history of social thought it has been momentous. For it marks the transition from a Whiggish mode of liberalism, in which liberty was one of several values making for a good society, to the contemporary mode, in which it is the supreme, indeed the only value.

After all that has been said in explanation of *On Liberty* —the impetus given to the doctrine by the "women question" or by the role of his wife—the discussion must finally return to *On Liberty* itself. Once that doctrine entered the public domain, whatever influences may have gone into its making recede in importance. It is ironic to have to make this point in connection with this of all books, in which fortuitous and personal circumstances played so large a part. But the irony may serve to reenforce the point: that ideas do have a life and force of their own independent of their creators. The historian or critic may understand *On Liberty* better for knowing as much as he can about its genesis. But he must also know when to put aside this knowledge and read *On Liberty* as generations of readers have read it— to read it in and for itself.

Note on Mill's Views on Divorce

IT IS CURIOUS that the brief essay of 1832 should have been Mill's only systematic discussion of divorce. But there are intimations of his changing views over the years, and they provide an interesting insight into his "mental history."

It is evident that in the first decade of his friendship with Harriet Taylor, she did not decisively influence his thinking—on this question or, probably, others. Thus in 1842–43, although he took issue with Comte on the subject of women in general, he professed to be "undecided" on the question of divorce; Mrs. Taylor was probably referring to this when she said she was disappointed to "find your opinion undetermined where I had thought it made up."[49] By 1848, however, when the *Political Economy* was published (the first book in which, as he said, "her share was conspicuous"), he had nothing but praise for those socialists who had unorthodox views on marriage and divorce.[50]

It was probably the appointment of the Divorce Commission in 1850 that prompted the editor of the *Westminster Review* to ask Mill for an article on divorce. Refusing to write on divorce per se, Mill explained that he preferred to put the subject in the larger context of the legal and social status of women. The resulting essay, "Enfranchisement of Women," did not mention divorce as such but did urge legal and social equality in all matters relating to men and women. The Commission issued its report in 1853, and a bill was introduced in 1854 which would have facilitated divorce without quite equalizing the conditions for men and women. Although this bill was withdrawn in the same session, it was evident that some measure of reform would be passed. It was in this atmosphere that Mill stated, in a private letter in 1855, his own position on divorce: "My opinion on Divorce is that though any relaxation of the irrevocability of

49. *Earlier Letters*, II, 546, 587 (Sept. 10, 1842; June 15, 1843); see above, p. 199.

50. See above, pp. 200–01.

marriage would be an improvement, nothing ought to be ultimately rested in, short of entire freedom on both sides to dissolve this like any other partnership. The only thing requiring legal regulation would be the maintenance of the children when the parents could not arrange it amicably—and in that I do not see any considerable difficulty."[51]

The Divorce Act of 1857 brought about, as Mill had anticipated, a considerable "relaxation" of the law. Divorce no longer required a special act of Parliament but was made an ordinary civil action, thus bringing it within the means of the middle class and even the poor. While the legal grounds for divorce were not exactly the same for women as for men, women could now initiate suits on terms of greater equality. The law also permitted (but did not absolutely require) clergymen to preside over the marriage of divorced persons.

The act was a far call from the "entire freedom" or complete legal equality Mill had urged only two years before. Yet he did not publicly comment on it. In *On Liberty* he expressed himself very cautiously on the subject, rebuking Humboldt for advocating exactly what he himself had done in 1855: putting marriage on a simple contractual basis to be dissolved like any other partnership.[52]

In "The Subjection of Women," as in his earlier essay, Mill refused to be drawn into a discussion of divorce, this time explaining that such questions could not be properly determined "until women have an equal voice in determining them, nor until there has been experience of the marriage relation as it would exist between equals." That his inclinations were very far from those of 1855, however, may be inferred from his final remark: "Until then I should not like to commit myself to more than the general principle of relief from the contract in extreme cases.[53]

When one woman, not personally known to him, sought his sympathy (perhaps also his assistance) in getting a divorce from a husband whose "ways of thinking and feeling," as she put it,

51. *Later Letters*, I, 500 (to [?], after Nov. 9, 1855).

52. See above, pp. 115–16.

53. *Later Letters*, IV, 1634 (to John Nichol, Aug. 18, 1869); see also *ibid.*, p. 1751 (to H. K. Rusden, July 22, 1870).

were different from hers, Mill tried to dissuade her. A divorce on those grounds, he said, would be a "long and difficult business to define." He himself advised her, on moral as well as legal grounds, and in view of the fact that her husband did not maltreat her and continued to have affection for her, to give up the idea of separation and cultivate instead a "mutual toleration" that would make their union bearable.[54]

In his uncompleted *Chapters on Socialism* Mill qualified not only his earlier enthusiasm for socialism but also for the socialists' views on marriage and divorce which he had once found so attractive. Fourier, for example, had believed that marriage should be completely unregulated by law, entirely a matter of individual agreement. Whereas Mill had earlier been so taken by this idea that he had wanted to "boost" the Fourierists on its account, he now found it so "peculiar" that he urged that it not be thought to reflect upon Fourier's economic principles.[55]

Thus, except for one short period in the mid-fifties, Mill's attitude toward divorce, like his attitude toward liberty, was liberal without being doctrinaire. He favored a relaxation and liberalization of the law, but not to the point of allowing for an absolute freedom which would make the individual totally sovereign, free to enter or leave the marital state without hindrance.

54. *Ibid.*, p. 1715 (May 1, 1870).
55. See above, p. 201; *Essays on Economics and Society*, ed. Lord Robbins and J. M. Robson (vols. IV–V of *Collected Works*; Toronto, 1967), II, 748.

PART THREE

The Legacy of an Idea

THE MORAL CAPITAL OF THE
VICTORIANS

I DEAS," LORD ACTON ONCE WROTE, "have a radiation and
development, an ancestry and posterity of their own, in
which men play the part of godfathers and godmothers
more than that of legitimate parents."[1] The idea of *On
Liberty*—not of liberty itself but of the particular idea of
liberty put forward by Mill—has had as complicated a history as anything Acton could have envisaged. Yet for all its
complications, for all its unanticipated consequences and
curious, even paradoxical turns, its genesis can hardly be in
doubt. Looking at the present state of the idea, one may be
tempted to assign to Mill the part of godfather rather than
that of father. But godfathers, it should be remembered, in
Mill's time as in Acton's, had a closer relationship to their
godchildren than many a father has today to his flesh-and-
blood progeny. When Acton used that image, it was not at
all to absolve the godfather of responsibility for his charges;
on the contrary, it was to suggest that however wayward
they might appear to be, he could not entirely disown them.

Today we are apt to lose sight of the distinctiveness of
On Liberty. Inured by long familiarity with it, we tend to

1. *Letters of Lord Acton to Mary Gladstone*, ed. Herbert Paul
(1st edn.; New York, 1905), p. 99 (Mar. 15, 1880).

assimilate its particular idea of liberty with any idea of liberty, with liberty per se. Thus the origin of liberty has been variously attributed to the philosophers of antiquity,[2] the "forests of Germany," Renaissance humanists, and seventeenth-century social-contract theorists. Even within modernity we find Mill's progenitors in a variety of thinkers as disparate as Milton, Locke, and Spinoza, Smith and Paine, Jefferson and Madison.

Milton above all we take to be the noblest of Mill's ancestors, perhaps because he is the most quotable. No discussion of *On Liberty* is complete without a tribute to the *Areopagitica*. Yet Mill himself did not mention that work, and perhaps for good reason. Milton was a passionate defender of freedom of thought, but within well-defined boundaries, his freedom extending only to "neighbouring differences, or rather indifferences." Opinions that diverged widely from the prevailing ones, that were not a matter of indifference—"popery and open superstition," or beliefs

2. When Acton and others praised the idea of liberty in antiquity, it was a very different kind of liberty from that which Mill had in mind. The ancients were not unfamiliar with the modern idea of liberty; they were wary and fearful of it. The democratic city, as Socrates described it, had the chief characteristics of Mill's liberal society—liberty, individuality, and variety; but there they appeared as spurious virtues.

> *In the first place, then, aren't they [men in a democratic regime] free? And isn't the city full of freedom and free speech? And isn't there license in it to do whatever one wants?*
>
> . . . . .
>
> *And where there's license, it's plain that each man would organize his life in it privately just as it pleases him.*
>
> . . . . .
>
> *Then I suppose that in this regime especially, all sorts of human beings come to be.*
>
> . . . . .
>
> *It is probably the fairest of all regimes. . . . Just like a many-colored cloak decorated in all hues, this regime, decorated with all dispositions, would also look fairest, and many perhaps . . . like boys and women looking at many-colored things, would judge this to be the fairest regime.* [*The Republic of Plato*, trans. Allan Bloom (New York, 1968), p. 235 (bk. VIII, 557 b, c).]

which were "impious or evil absolutely either against faith or manners"—he did not propose to tolerate. On the contrary, he advised that they be "extirpated" on the grounds that they were subversive of all religion, law, and "civil supremacies."[3]

And so it was with the other moderns who are generally invoked as the forefathers of liberty. Each fell short of the degree of liberty Mill insisted upon. The concluding chapter of Spinoza's *Tractatus Theologicus Politicus* has a strikingly modern title: "That in a free state every man may think what he pleases, and say what he thinks." But that freedom, Spinoza made clear, applied only to thought and speech and not to action. And it was limited even in respect to thought and speech; it was a right of man only "as long as he does no more than express or communicate his opinion, and only defends it out of honest rational conviction, and not out of anger, hatred, or a desire to introduce any change in the state on his own authority."[4] Moreover, freedom, for Spinoza, was a condition of reason. Only a man governed by his reason was free; to the extent to which he was not rational, he was in bondage.

Locke had a less exalted view of freedom than Spinoza. Indeed, in his state of nature he allowed for a degree of liberty that came close to Mill's. In that state men were presumed to have a "perfect freedom to order their actions and dispose of their possessions and persons as they think fit, within the bounds of the law of nature." And that law of nature (again in anticipation of Mill) provided that "no one ought to harm another in his life, health, liberty, or possessions."[5] But that was the state of nature. And men left

3. John Milton, *Complete Prose Works*, ed. Don M. Wolfe (New Haven, 1959), II, 565. (I have modernized the spelling and punctuation in the quotations from Milton and Locke.)

4. Benedict de Spinoza, *The Political Works*, trans. A. G. Wernham (Oxford, 1958), p. 231.

5. John Locke, *Two Treatises on Government*, ed. Peter Laslett (Cambridge, Eng., 1967), pp. 287, 289 (*Second Treatise*, chap. II, pars. 4, 6).

that state to enter civil society precisely because the law of nature, even with its guarantee against harm, was an inadequate basis for "life, health, liberty, or possessions." In civil society men committed themselves to a variety of laws and institutions limited only by the principle of consent. Law then became the precondition of liberty. Liberty did not start where law ended; on the contrary, "wherever law ends, tyranny begins."[6] Even the liberty of opinion was restricted in civil society. For Locke, as for Milton, "no opinions contrary to human society, or to those moral rules which are necessary to the preservation of civil society, are to be tolerated by the magistrate." Thus, toleration was not to be extended to adherents of a church subordinate to a foreign power or to those who denied the existence of God, in the latter case because "promises, covenants, and oaths, which are the bonds of human society, can have no hold upon an atheist."[7]

Even in more recent times and on the part of its more zealous advocates, liberty had a more restricted meaning than Mill gave it. Both Jefferson and Paine, while suspicious of government as an actual or potential enemy of liberty, had entire confidence in the people and in society as the bulwarks of liberty. Jefferson once reflected upon the fortunate situation of the Indians who managed without government; there "public opinion is in the place of law and restrains morals as powerfully as laws ever did anywhere."[8] And Paine, for whom government was, at best, a "necessary evil," looked upon society as nothing less than a "blessing."[9] Moreover, those who were willing to give the largest ex-

6. *Ibid.*, p. 418 (chap. XVIII, par. 202).

7. Locke, *A Letter Concerning Toleration*, ed. Patrick Romanell (New York, 1955), pp. 50, 52.

8. *Writings of Thomas Jefferson*, ed. H. A. Washington (New York, 1861), II, 99–100 (Jefferson to Col. Edward Carrington, Jan. 16, 1787).

9. Thomas Paine, *Common Sense and the Crisis* (New York, 1960), p. 13. See also *The Rights of Man* (Penguin edn.; London, 1969), pp. 185 ff. (part II, chap. I).

tension to liberty of speech conceded that liberty of action fell under different principles and had a more limited range. And to the extent to which liberty of action was thought desirable, it presupposed a voluntary structure of controls. Whatever their other differences, the Founding Fathers were agreed that self-control and self-restraint would have to make up for the want of external constraints, that free men more than others required a strong sense of discipline, a firm rein on their passions, impulses, private interests, and desires. They were as impressed as Montesquieu with the importance of *vertu* in a republic. And like Montesquieu they believed that "the natural place of virtue is near to liberty; but it is not nearer to excessive liberty than to servitude."[10]

Confronted with these and all the other differences that one can point to between Mill and his "forefathers," the modern liberal is apt to respond with suspicion and impatience—suspicion of the scholar who dwells pedantically upon distinctions that seem to be only of historical interest, and impatience with thinkers who could not rise above their historical limitations, who had not the rigor of mind or strength of character to carry out their ideas to their logical

---

10. Baron de Montesquieu, *The Spirit of the Laws*, trans. Thomas Nugent (New York, 1949), p. 111 (bk. VIII, sect. 3). The idea of self-restraint—the mastery of the passions—as a necessary condition of freedom was implicitly or explicitly held by most thinkers, including the most liberal of them, before Mill. Milton's formulation was typical:

> *You, therefore, who wish to remain free, either be wise at the outset or recover your senses as soon as possible. If to be a slave is hard, and you do not wish it, learn to obey right reason, to master yourselves. Lastly, refrain from factions, hatreds, superstitions, injustices, lusts, and rapine against one another. Unless you do this with all your strength you cannot seem either to God or to men, or even to your recent liberators, fit to be entrusted with the liberty and guidance of the state and the power of commanding others, which you arrogate to yourselves so greedily. Then indeed, like a nation in wardship, you would rather be in need of some tutor, some brave and faithful guardian of your affairs.* ["A Second Defence of the English People" (1654), in Milton, *Complete Prose Works*, IV, 684.]

conclusions. That Milton, Locke, or the Founding Fathers fell short of Mill is taken as evidence of their shortsightedness. It was Mill's genius, this theory has it, to be bold where they had been timid, to complete what they had started. Or perhaps, a more sophisticated modern might think, it was not so much his genius that impelled Mill as the natural logic of ideas working itself out in theory and in practice.

IF TODAY we have so thoroughly imbibed the message of *On Liberty* that we think it the only natural, meaningful form of liberty, Mill's contemporaries had no such illusions. They knew his doctrine to be a bold and radical one. It was for this reason that they received it so ambivalently, with great respect but also with serious reservations. Almost every aspect of his argument came under scrutiny and criticism: the extent of the tyranny presently and potentially exercised by society, the degree of liberty and individuality required to counteract that tyranny, the distinction between self-regarding and other-regarding actions, the single principle justifying a limitation of liberty, and finally the examples or "applications" of that principle.

It is interesting that the most systematic and extensive critique of *On Liberty* was by an avowed utilitarian. James Fitzjames Stephen published his *Liberty, Equality, Fraternity* in 1872, only several months before Mill's death. Although Stephen took the occasion to criticize other of Mill's works as well—*Utilitarianism* and "The Subjection of Women"— the burden of his book, and certainly the part that attracted most attention, was the discussion of *On Liberty*. His basic objection to *On Liberty* was that it violated the elementary and, as Stephen saw it, the undeniable principle of utility: the idea that human behavior was governed by pleasure and pain, fear and hope, and that the function of the legislator, and of society as a whole, was to direct these motives toward socially desirable ends. So far, he argued, from prohibiting or even inhibiting the action of society, the principle of utility gave to society the right and duty to invoke whatever legal, social, and religious sanctions were available to it; these included the force of the law and of public opinion, the fear of damnation and the hope of salvation—all the instruments of compulsion, restraint, and guidance which might be pressed into service. To be sure, these sanctions should be used prudently and temperately; this too was part of the principle of utility. But it was no part of that principle to deny the legitimacy of sanctions or to abdicate the power of using them. Mill's doctrine, a form of moral laissez-fairism in which each individual was encouraged to do as he liked so long as he did not injure another, failed to distinguish between good and bad, let alone to give effect to that distinction. It also failed to appreciate the lesson of history, which was that the progress of civilization depended upon the expedient use of moral, religious, and legal coercion.

As virtue and happiness required the active support of society, so, Fitzjames Stephen reasoned, did wisdom and truth. Had Mill been content to argue that in that time and place the discussion of most controversial questions should be completely free and unrestrained, Stephen would have had no objection; the principle of utility might well have supported such a policy. But in making the freedom of discussion a prerequisite of truth, Mill was doing more than affirming the desirability of a particular social policy—he was making a metaphysical assertion about the nature of truth. And it was this assertion, that truth was necessarily the product of free discussion and necessarily antagonistic to authority, that Stephen found to be highly dubious. He was also skeptical of the claim that free discussion was necessary for the vitality of truth. As often as not, he argued, discussion had a debilitating and enervating effect, weakening rather than strengthening the consciousness of truth.

By the same token Fitzjames Stephen denied that liberty

of action was essential to the development of individuality, and he denied even more strenuously the assumption that individuality was necessarily meritorious. "Though goodness is various," he observed, "variety is not in itself good."[11] Mill had elevated liberty and individuality to the status of absolute ends instead of judging them pragmatically, expedientially, in terms of their utility on specific occasions. Liberty was no more good in and of itself than was fire; like fire it was "both good and bad according to time, place, and circumstances."[12] Stephen favored a considerable degree of liberty; but he did not favor it in an absolute form nor in the same form under all conditions. What disturbed him about Mill's doctrine was the possibility that it might leave society impotent in those situations where there was a genuine need for social action. He was also distressed by the thought that the abdication of social responsibility for beliefs and actions might be interpreted as a sanctioning of all beliefs and actions, a license to do that which society could not prohibit.

From the perspective of *On Liberty*, Fitzjames Stephen's book seems to be propounding something like a counter-doctrine to liberty—an invitation, perhaps, to the very "social tyranny" Mill had feared. Mill himself, who had always disliked Stephen as a person—he thought him insolent, domineering, and brutal[13]—had no more use for his book. He dismissed it with the comment that it would prove more damaging to Stephen than to himself and "more likely to repel than to attract people."[14]

It is unfortunate that we do not have Mill's reaction to an essay published about the same time by Leslie Stephen, Fitzjames's brother. Unlike Fitzjames, Leslie was a confirmed

11. James Fitzjames Stephen, *Liberty, Equality, Fraternity*, ed. R. J. White (Cambridge, Mass., 1967), p. 80.

12. *Ibid.*, p. 85.

13. *Later Letters*, IV, 1600 (JSM to E. E. Cliffe Leslie, May 8, 1869).

14. Bain, p. 111.

liberal and, indeed, a great admirer of Mill; as an under-
graduate at Cambridge in the fifties he had been one of a
circle that assembled regularly to read Mill's books and that
found in them, especially in the *Logic*, the gospel of the new
rationalism. Yet in 1872 he wrote an article on *On Liberty*
which, although far more respectful in tone than his
brother's book, was every bit as critical. His article deserves
more attention than his brother's book precisely because it
came from one who was otherwise well disposed to Mill
both politically and philosophically and who made no secret
of his distaste for his brother's politics and mode of thought.
(Many years later, repeating his criticisms of *On Liberty*
in his last great work on the utilitarians, he explicitly dissociated himself from his brother while admitting that Fitzjames had scored some telling points against Mill.[15])

Where Fitzjames Stephen's critique derived from a form
of utilitarianism that was almost Hobbesian in its view of
human nature and society, Leslie Stephen's criticisms were
more positivistic; if they sound familiar it is because many
of them might have been made by Mill himself—the "other"
Mill. Yet in spite of significant philosophical differences,
the brothers were remarkably in accord on specific points.
They agreed, for example, that variety in itself was not
necessarily a virtue; indeed, in his book Fitzjames Stephen
quoted his brother's article to that effect. "A nation," Leslie
Stephen had written, "in which everybody was sober would
be a happier, better, and more progressive, though a less
diversified, nation than one in which half the members were
sober and the other half habitual drunkards."[16] And with
greater reluctance than Fitzjames, Leslie Stephen admitted
that while a variety of opinions on some subjects and in
some conditions was desirable, variety was not an "ideal

15. Leslie Stephen, *The English Utilitarians* (London, 1900),
III, 244.
16. Leslie Stephen, "Social Macadamisation," *Fraser's Magazine*,
LXXXVI (1872), 150.

state of things" but rather a "preparatory stage" toward the achievement of a rational unity of opinion. What Mill was advocating, Stephen objected, was a "perpetual state of revolution and fermentation" amounting to the "apotheosis of anarchy." Such a state of anarchy might be necessary for the development of opinions but it was absurd to regard it as a final resting point. "The strongest justification of enquiry is precisely that it is the only safe road to ultimate unity."[17]

An undue emphasis on individuality, whether of thought or of action, was as misplaced, Leslie Stephen argued, as an excessive concern for variety. This kind of individuality was more conducive to eccentricity than to genuine originality. Nor did it necessarily promote the kind of energetic character that Mill hoped for. On the contrary, "a constant effort at believing what is not believable is precisely the habit most fatal to anything like vigour or originality." What did make for vigor and originality was the conviction that one's opinions were true and that they were important to the world; this conviction could make weak men into dogmatists but it also made strong men into heroes. Moreover, intellectual sympathy was as important as intellectual dissent in the formation of a strong opinion and character. "No human being can really believe anything very strongly which is entirely opposed to all the convictions of his fellow-creatures."[18]

Like other critics, Leslie Stephen was disturbed by the distinction which loomed so large in Mill's theory, that between the self-regarding and other-regarding spheres. He denied that the distinction could be sustained in moral affairs since all moral qualities could at any time affect others. What is more, the very abstinence from judgment could have an undesirable effect upon the character of the person who was deprived of the benefit of judgment. To be sure, the judgment of society might be stupid or ill-advised. But so might any particular act of legislation, and this was no reason to abstain from all legislation. Nor was it reasonable to claim that no one was competent to judge; by the same token it could be claimed that no one was competent to rule. Authority, if only the authority of society and public opinion, was as essential to the moral well-being of all people as to their political well-being. In the absence of good authority, people tended to idolize the mediocre and commonplace. What was wanted, he said, was not the denigration of all authority, which was the effect of Mill's doctrine, but a heightened respect for rational, legitimate authority.

> *The argument, in short, that all moral pressure ought to be destroyed because it may be misapplied implies the assumption that no spiritual authority can ever be set up because the old one turned out to rest on a rotten basis. As against this, we should hold that one main need of the day is to erect such an authority upon reason instead of upon arbitrary tradition. . . . Distant as the prospect may be, it is in that direction that we must look for the formation of firmer and healthier intellectual and moral conditions.*[19]

WRITING IN 1872, both Fitzjames and Leslie Stephen were able to take a more reflective and dispassionate view of *On Liberty* than the critics reviewing it upon its initial publication. Yet even the earlier reviews raised most of the same issues. Those reviews have been so amply summarized elsewhere that there is no need to dwell upon them here.[20]

19. *Ibid.*, p. 168.
20. A monograph by J. C. Rees, *Mill and His Early Critics* (Leicester, 1956), admirably summarizes the reviews, as well as exposing the misattribution to Mill of the essay, "On Social Freedom." For some of the recurrent themes of these reviews, see above, pp. 163–65.

Moreover, most of their criticisms had been anticipated by Mill himself in one or another of his own writings, so that a résumé of the reviews would read like a reprise of the "other" Mill. There is, however, one source of criticism that has not been sufficiently explored. This is what might be called the "unwritten reviews": essays and books which, without ever mentioning Mill or *On Liberty*, were directed pointedly against the doctrine of *On Liberty*. And some of these were by the most eminent Victorians.

John Henry Newman's *Apologia Pro Vita Sua* may be read in this sense. First published in 1864, it was, or seemed to be, directed to a very different order of affairs than that which concerned Mill. But an appendix to the second edition, published the following year, made it clear that Newman's quarrel with religious liberalism was only one aspect of his quarrel with liberalism in general and *a fortiori* with the kind of liberalism represented by *On Liberty*. The appendix enumerated the main propositions of the liberal heresy as Newman saw them. Some of these propositions might have been taken almost verbatim from *On Liberty*:

No one can believe what he does not understand.

No theological doctrine is any thing more than an opinion which happens to be held by bodies of men.

It is dishonest in a man to make an act of faith in what he has not had brought home to him by actual proof.

It is immoral in a man to believe more than he can spontaneously receive as being congenial to his moral and mental nature.

There is a right of Private Judgment: that is, there is no existing authority on earth competent to interfere with the liberty of individuals in reasoning and judging for themselves about the Bible and its contents, as they severally please.

*There are rights of conscience such, that every one
may lawfully advance a claim to profess and teach
what is false and wrong in matters, religious, social, and
moral, provided that to his private conscience it seems
absolutely true and right.*

There is no such thing as a national or state conscience.

*The civil power has no positive duty, in a normal state
of things, to maintain religious truth.*[21]

To Matthew Arnold, Mill was not quite the arch-heretic
he was to Newman. Compared with the other utilitarians
who were "doomed to sterility," Mill had enough perception of complicated truths to merit consideration as a writer
of "distinguished mark and influence"—although not
enough, Arnold hastened to add, to qualify him as a "great
writer."[22] Arnold's first reading of *On Liberty* had left
him rather well disposed to it; he recommended it to his
sister as "one of the few books that inculcate tolerance in
an unalarming and inoffensive way."[23] A later reading, however, must have given him cause for alarm and offense, for
much of his *Culture and Anarchy*, written several years
later, was directed, if not against *On Liberty* itself, at the
very least against the mode of thought represented by *On
Liberty*.

In *Culture and Anarchy* Arnold did not refer explicitly
to *On Liberty* (he mentioned Mill by name only once). But
the title of his second chapter, "Doing as One Likes,"
clearly echoed the principle advanced in *On Liberty*:

21. John Henry Newman, *Apologia Pro Vita Sua*, ed. A. D.
Culler (Riverside edn.; Boston, 1956), pp. 275–77.

22. Matthew Arnold, *Lectures and Essays in Criticism*, ed. R.
H. Super (Ann Arbor, 1962), p. 136. For a similarly qualified
view of Mill, see also Arnold's preface to the second edition of
Schools and Universities on the Continent, in *A French Eton*
(London, 1892), p. 156.

23. *Letters of Matthew Arnold*, ed. G. W. E. Russell (New
York, 1900), I, 111 (June 25, 1859).

"Liberty of Tastes and Pursuits, of forming the plan of our life to suit our own character; of doing as we like, subject to such consequences as may follow."[24] To Arnold, "doing as one likes" was an invitation to lawlessness and anarchy. It meant that anyone could claim the right to "march where he likes, enter where he likes, hoot as he likes, threaten as he likes, smash as he likes."[25] Nor was Arnold more tolerant of the principle that everyone could *say* as he liked. "The aspirations of culture," he warned, "are not satisfied, unless what men say, when they may say what they like, is worth saying—has good in it, and more good than bad."[26]

Like Newman, Arnold directed much of his criticism against religious liberalism. But some of that applied as well, perhaps even more pertinently, to secular liberalism. Elsewhere Arnold spoke of "Millism and Miallism" as the two variants of the modern heresy—"Miallism" (named after Edward Miall, the Congregational minister famous for his advocacy of Disestablishment) being as doctrinaire in its commitment to Dissent, to religious liberty and individuality, as "Millism" was to all forms of liberty and individuality.[27] In *Culture and Anarchy* Arnold recorded a dialogue with a Nonconformist manufacturer who boasted that until he had established an Independent chapel, his town had had no Dissenters, but now there were sharp contests between Church and Chapel. When Arnold said that this seemed a pity, the manufacturer responded: "A pity? Not at all! Only think of all the zeal and activity which the collision

24. Arnold, *Culture and Anarchy*, ed. J. Dover Wilson (Cambridge, Eng., 1957), p. 72; Mill, *On Liberty*, p. 75.

25. *Culture and Anarchy*, p. 76.

26. *Ibid.*, p. 50.

27. *A French Eton*, p. 156. In *Culture and Anarchy*, Arnold referred only to "Miallism" (pp. 31–33). See also preface to *St. Paul and Protestantism* (London, 1870), pp. xxxv ff.; "Friendship's Garland," in *Culture and Anarchy with Friendship's Garland and Some Literary Essays*, ed. R. H. Super (Ann Arbor, 1965), p. 46.

calls forth!" To which Arnold retorted: "Ah, my dear friend, only think of all the nonsense which you now hold quite firmly, which you would never have held if you had not been contradicting your adversary in it all these years!"[28] The riposte is as telling against Mill as against the Midland manufacturer. Mill's adversary theory of truth, his belief in the salutary effects of a "collision of opinions," his enthusiasm for intellectual and social dissent, were all condemned by the same logic that condemned the zealous Dissenter. Arnold's expression, the "Dissidence of Dissent,"[29] was meant to describe those who made a virtue of Dissent for the sake of dissent, but it applied no less to secular dissenters, to those who made a virtue of nonconformity in all areas of life—and thus to *On Liberty* preeminently, which celebrated not this or that form of dissent but the very principle of dissent.

There was much else in *On Liberty* that must have offended Arnold: the suspicion of tradition and authority, the limitations placed upon society and, even more, upon the state, the placing of the individual in an adversary relationship to both society and state. But above all it was Mill's principle of liberty that was antithetical to Arnold's idea of "culture." With some of Arnold's dicta about culture—that culture involved criticism, the free play of mind, a disinterested curiosity—Mill would have agreed. But Mill would have taken these as neutral concepts, the conditions of freedom which men could utilize as they liked, to lead them in whatever directions they liked. This was not at all the meaning Arnold attached to them. He invested them with positive purpose and substance. Criticism was serious, the play of mind free, curiosity disinterested, when and only when they were at the service of "right reason," "excellence," "sweetness and light," "total perfection." These qualities—not liberty and individuality but virtue and wis-

28. *Culture and Anarchy*, p. 21.
29. *Ibid.*, p. 56.

dom—were the proper ends of man. If anarchy was so fearful, it was not because it subverted this or that institution but because it subverted the culture that alone distinguished man from the animal and material world.

Other Victorians for other reasons rejected the principles and premises of *On Liberty*. Carlyle, for example, unlike Arnold, was not taken in by it for a moment: "In my life I never read a serious, ingenious, clear, logical Essay with more perfect and profound dissent from the basis it rests upon, and most of the conclusions it arrives at. Very strange to me indeed; a curious monition to me what a world we are in! As if it were a sin to control, or coerce into better methods, human swine in any way. . . . *Ach Gott in Himmel!*"[30]

But even had Carlyle not happened to express himself so graphically, his own work leaves no doubt of his "perfect and profound dissent" not from this or that aspect of *On Liberty* but from the whole of it. And so it was with many, perhaps most, of the eminent writers of the age. It would be a mistake to look for judgments of Mill only in the express reviews of his book or in the explicit comments of his contemporaries. The whole body of Victorian thought —the works of Ruskin and Morris, Kingsley and Maurice, Macaulay, Bagehot, Froude, Maine, Acton, and all the other greats and near-greats of the time—provides an implicit commentary on *On Liberty*, and, as often as not, an implicit judgment against it.

Indeed, some of the explicit comments about *On Liberty* cannot be taken at face value. Charles Kingsley is often quoted as having said that *On Liberty* made him a "clearer headed and braver minded man on the spot."[31] But that was in a letter to Mill thanking him for the gift of a book. To

30. *New Letters of Thomas Carlyle*, ed. Alexander Carlyle (London, 1904), II, 196 (May 4, 1859).

31. Quoted by Mill in *Later Letters*, II, 632 (JSM to Bain, Aug. 6, 1859).

his old friend F. D. Maurice, Kingsley confided that what he particularly liked about *On Liberty* was the discussion of the complementary nature of the Christian and pagan virtues, but that even this "truth" had been enunciated by Mill in a "one-sided way."[32] And he was evidently not so taken with the main principle of *On Liberty* as to renounce his socialism in favor of the individualism Mill had argued for.[33] Some years later he spoke of Mill in a manner that contrasted curiously with his earlier remark about clear-headedness and brave-mindedness: "When I look at his cold, clear-cut face, I think there is a whole hell beneath him, of which he knows nothing, and so there may be a whole heaven above him."[34]

Frederic Harrison's testimonial to the influence of *On Liberty* is also often cited, but, again, should be read with some reservations.

It is certain that the little book produced a profound impression on contemporary thought, and had an extraordinary success with the public. It has been read by hundreds of thousands, and, to some of the most vigorous and most conscientious spirits amongst us, it became a sort of gospel. . . . It was the code of many thoughtful writers and several influential politicians. It undoubtedly contributed to the practical programmes of Liberals and Radicals for the generation that saw its birth; and the statute book bears many traces of its influence over the sphere and duties of government.[35]

As a disciple of Comte, Harrison could not have failed to

---

32. *Charles Kingsley: His Letters and Memories of His Life,* ed. Mrs. Kingsley (London, 1888), p. 198 (undated).

33. While Kingsley was much less militant a socialist at this time than he had been in his youth, the decline of zeal had set in long before *On Liberty*.

34. *Charles Kingsley*, p. 295.

35. Frederic Harrison, *Tennyson, Ruskin, Mill and Other Literary Estimates* (London, 1899), pp. 292–93.

notice Mill's charge, in *On Liberty*, that Comte was seeking to create a "despotism of society over the individual." From Harrison's perspective, his countrymen may well have seemed under the domination of Mill. But from any other perspective, the "gospel" or "code" could not have been nearly so binding as he thought. If the "practical pro-grammes of Liberals and Radicals" or the evidence of the "statute book" testify to anything, it was to the greater lati-tude allowed to the government in matters of social welfare in the decades following the publication of *On Liberty*.[36]

It would seem, in fact, that Mill was, in his own time, both less a prophet and less a priest than one might think. Less a prophet, because the social tyranny he inveighed against, the inordinate pressures for conformity and the crushing burden of convention, did not come to pass; in moral and intellectual affairs, there was, as he admitted, greater liberty and individuality than before. And less a priest, because the actual policies he recommended, the mini-mal involvement of government in economic and social affairs, were not adopted; on the contrary, there was an expansion in these areas of both the legislative and the administrative functions of the state.

Yet there is a sense in which *On Liberty* did make, as Harrison said, a "profound impression" on a great many readers, although perhaps not especially on the more "thoughtful writers" and "influential politicians." Most of the other sources suggest that it was young people and lay readers, so to speak, rather than professional writers and established figures, who were most taken with it. Thomas Hardy recalled that students in the 1860s knew the book "almost by heart."[37] And John Morley, who had been a

36. Harrison may have been aware of this, for at one point he suggested that Mill's influence had "waned" after 1870, which considerably narrows the "generation" for whom *On Liberty* was a "sort of gospel." (*Ibid.*, p. 275.)

37. Hardy, letter to the Editor of *The Times* (London), May 21, 1906 (p. 6).

student at Oxford at that time, later described its impact: "I do not know whether then or at any other time so short a book ever instantly produced so wide and so important an effect on contemporary thought as did Mill's *On Liberty* in that day of intellectual and social fermentation."[38]

Part of that impact came from the sheer weight of Mill's reputation deriving from his other books. Well before *On Liberty*, his *Logic* and *Political Economy* had become the standard texts on those subjects, being read not only by students but by anyone with any intellectual pretensions. It was these books that Lord Balfour, the Conservative statesman and philosopher, had in mind when he said that when he was young, "Mill possessed an authority in the English universities . . . comparable to that wielded forty years earlier by Hegel in Germany and in the Middle Ages by Aristotle."[39] Leslie Stephen put it in much the same terms: "In our little circle the summary answer to all hesitating proselytes was 'read Mill.' . . . Hour after hour was given to discussing points raised by Mill as keenly as medieval commentators used to discuss the doctrines of Aristotle."[40]

The prestige of his name, therefore (as Mill himself anticipated), gave an initial momentum to *On Liberty* which immediately established it as a work of great importance. And the book itself was calculated to make the most of that advantage. Again Mill intimated something of this when he described it as a "philosophic text-book of a single truth." That single-mindedness gave it a concentrated power which

38. John Morley, *Recollections* (New York, 1917), I, 60.

39. A. J. Balfour, *Theism and Humanism* (London, 1915), p. 138.

40. Leslie Stephen, *Some Early Impressions* (London, 1924), p. 76. For similar estimates of Mill's influence as a philosopher, see Herbert Spencer, *An Autobiography*, II, 247; Henry Fawcett, "His Influence at the Universities," in *John Stuart Mill: His Life and Work* (Boston, 1873), pp. 74–75; John Morley, *Oracles on Man and Government* (London, 1923), pp. 4, 238; James Bryce, *Studies in Contemporary Biography* (London, 1903), p. 93; Henry Adams, *Cycle of Adams Letters* (Boston, 1920), II, 96 (Oct. 23, 1863).

a more complicated, qualified thesis would not have had. And the nature of that single truth added to its forcefulness. John Morley suggested that the moral appeal of *On Liberty* was so powerful as to make whatever flaws it might have had seem inconsequential.[41] One may go further and say that its moral appeal was all the more powerful precisely because of its flaws, its simplicism and reductivism. This would account for the fact that it made a "profound impression" on a great many people while receiving a very mixed response from the critics. The "one very simple principle" that alienated the sophisticated reader was precisely what seduced the ordinary reader. It was the boldness of the thesis that attracted attention and the substance of it that was emotionally and morally compelling. It is as if in defying reality and denying complexity, Mill was asserting the power of mind over matter, of will over all the petty, mundane, and ignoble circumstances governing our lives. And in making the individual the instrument of mind and will, pitting him against the forces of tradition, convention, and society, he gave him a heroic dimension the reader could not help but admire.

THE OTHER ANOMALY in this situation—that *On Liberty* should have made so strong an impression upon the reading public without significantly affecting public policy or even public behavior—may be accounted for by that peculiar phenomenon known as the "moral capital" of the Victorians. The Victorians, it has often been observed, lived off the capital of their ancestors in more than the literal sense. The metaphor has been used to explain the persistence of a strong moral consensus long after the decline of the religious faith that had originally sustained that morality. But it may also explain how people could be powerfully moved by Mill's

41. Morley, *Recollections*, I, 61–62.

doctrine while continuing to abide by old ways and beliefs. The fact is that even those who gave their intellectual assent to *On Liberty*, and who did so in the conviction that it was a radically new doctrine, did not advocate any radically new beliefs or policies, any novel opinions or "experiments in living." Even the most enthusiastic converts—John Morley, for example—seem to have tempered their new faith with a large admixture of the old. In their zeal for liberty they never quite gave up the Whiggish mode of liberalism that they (like Mill himself) had lived with for so long: a liberalism that prized liberty as one of several virtues, that had a healthy respect for social institutions and conventions, that was willing to use the resources of society and the state to further the public good, and that above all distrusted the application of simple formulas to complicated affairs.

What made it easier to assent to *On Liberty* was its stirring plea for freedom of speech, especially in religious matters. But for this, one did not need *On Liberty*; this victory had already been largely won. Where Mill went beyond the *Zeitgeist*—beyond the synthesis of utilitarianism, unitarianism, evangelicalism, and Whiggism that made up the prevailing mode of liberalism—was in extending the principle of freedom to the entire range of opinion and, more radically, to the entire range of action. It was the latter especially that was Mill's claim to novelty and boldness. But this novelty and boldness were mitigated by the familiarity of the principle in the more accustomed form of freedom of speech. The inclusion of liberty of speech and liberty of action within a single, simple principle was a brilliant (if perhaps unwitting) strategy. For it produced a doctrine that was every bit as "different" from the conventional one as Mill claimed, but that was also comfortably reassuring, the linking together of the two liberties inducing the reader to accept the newer liberty because he had already accepted the older one.

This radical extension of liberty, which gave the same status to individuality of behavior as to freedom of opinion, was possible only because most people were reasonably certain that individuality would not be abused, that men would continue to conduct themselves as they had always done. The moral capital amassed by generations of high-minded and well-behaved Englishmen gave them an illusion of security, as if morality were not only part of their cultural heritage but of their very blood. They forgot the barbarities of the recent past and the aberrations, as they thought them, of the "outcasts" lurking in "darkest England."[42] In the current state of English civilization, and with the prospects of continued progress before them, it seemed to them, as to Mill, that there was little risk in applying to behavior a freedom that had proved so innocuous in the realm of speech. They did not expect any great departures from customary modes of conduct; nor did they welcome the prospect of them. When Leslie Stephen had to face up to the fact that neither religion nor science could provide a basis for ethics, he reaffirmed his faith in morality: "I now believe in nothing, but I do not the less believe in morality. . . . I mean to live and die like a gentleman if possible."[43] And Frederic Harrison, who was unconventional enough in his religious and political opinions, was utterly conventional in his personal code of conduct. When his son asked him what a man should do if he fell in love and could not marry, he replied indignantly: "Do! Do what every gentleman does in such circumstances." And when his son persisted in want-

42. The famous tracts *The Bitter Cry of Outcast London* and *In Darkest England and the Way Out* (the first published anonymously and now attributed to William Preston and Andrew Mearns, the second by William Booth of the Salvation Army) date from a somewhat later period (1883 and 1890). But the expressions immortalized in those titles had been current earlier.

43. *Life and Letters of Leslie Stephen*, ed. F. W. Maitland (London, 1906), pp. 144-45.

ing to know why love was proper only in marriage, Harrison exploded: "A loose man is a foul man. He is anti-social. He is a beast. . . . It is not a subject that decent men do discuss."[44]

Harrison's son was typical of a later generation who found it easy to discuss subjects that "decent men" of his father's generation did not normally discuss. And Leslie Stephen's children became the leading lights of the Bloomsbury set, whose great pride it was that there was nothing they would not discuss—and very little, as has recently become evident, they would not do. If some of them, Lytton Strachey particularly, expressed contempt for Mill, it was partly because they identified him with all the other "eminent Victorians," partly because they found his utilitarianism mechanical and confining, a form of moral totalitarianism which presumed to tell men what to do for their own good and for the good of society. But that was the "other" Mill. To the Mill of *On Liberty* they could have had little objection; indeed, they, more than any previous generation, more than the "most vigorous and most conscientious spirits" of Harrison's time, could have taken *On Liberty* as their gospel and code.[45] They dared to do as they liked, and they did it with impunity. They flaunted their defiance of convention and contempt for bourgeois proprieties. They prided themselves on their absolute liberty and individuality. They declared themselves bound only to truth, beauty, and self— and by interpreting the first two subjectively, they reduced even truth and beauty to aspects of the self. When Virginia Woolf made her famous pronouncement, "On or about December 1910 human character changed," she had in mind the esthetic revolution ushered in by the London exhibition

44. Austin Harrison, *Frederic Harrison: Thoughts and Memories* (London, 1926), pp. 127–29.

45. Bertrand Russell had nothing but praise for *On Liberty*. See his "Lecture on a Master Mind: John Stuart Mill," *Proceedings of the British Academy*, XLI (1955).

of Post-Impressionist paintings.[46] But she could have been speaking of the moral revolution which the gospel of liberty had wrought among those happy few who were genuinely liberated from the Victorian ethic.

In Edwardian and Georgian England, the moral revolution was confined to a relatively small (although influential) group of "free spirits." It is only in our own time that that revolution is finally becoming democratized. The idea of moral liberation is no longer the preserve of an elite but is rapidly becoming the common ground of an entire generation. Having finally used up the moral capital of the Victorians, we find ourselves more and more thrown back upon the one idea which appears to be of unquestionable validity, the idea of liberty. It is the one principle that conservatives, liberals, and radicals alike profess. Whatever differences they have, whatever contradictory yearnings they may entertain (a longing for tradition in the case of conservatives, for community in the case of radicals), however much they may violate the principle in practice, it is today the only idea that commands general assent. And it commands assent in the form Mill gave it in *On Liberty*—not as one principle among many but as the supreme and ultimate principle, the final court of appeal.

It is a principle that, as Mill realized and as we are only now beginning to appreciate, has the largest cultural and social as well as political implications—indeed, cultural and social more than political. This too is as Mill intended it. Most of *On Liberty* was deliberately cast in terms of society and culture rather than politics. It was the pressure for conformity, the "social tyranny" and "despotism of custom," that Mill saw as the most insidious threat to liberty. In this respect *On Liberty* is an early specimen of a mode of

46. Samuel Hynes, *The Edwardian Turn of Mind* (Princeton, 1968), p. 325.

thought that has only recently become prominent, the tendency to think in terms of "cultural politics" rather than politics per se, to find political reality more accurately reflected in opinions, attitudes, perceptions, ways of thought and behavior, than in the more conventional arena of institutions, legislation, and electoral arrangements.

On Liberty is sometimes criticized for not addressing itself to important political problems. Indeed, it may seem odd that this work, dedicated to the principle of liberty, should be so conspicuously lacking in any discussion of political liberty: the right to participate in government, to vote, to be represented in Parliament, to serve as a Member of Parliament, to be assured of one's political rights, privileges, and liberties. But this criticism is beside the point. For Mill was not here concerned with this order of problem, with the individual as a member of the polity in this sense. He himself was fully aware of this. To his friends on the Continent, he explained that the liberty he was discussing was "moral and intellectual rather than political" and that it was, therefore, less relevant to those countries, notably those on the Continent, where political liberty was the more urgent problem.[47]

47. *Later Letters*, II, 539 (JSM to Theodor Gomperz, Oct. 5, 1857); *ibid.*, p. 550 (JSM to Pasquale Villari, Mar. 9, 1858). To Villari, Mill suggested that *On Liberty* was less relevant on the Continent because those countries were as superior to England in respect of moral and intellectual liberty as they were inferior to England in political liberty.

It is because Mill expressly excluded from *On Liberty* the subject of political liberty that one of his most important books, *Considerations on Representative Government*, published in 1861, and one of his most suggestive essays, "Thoughts on Parliamentary Reform," of 1859, do not figure in this study. But to the extent to which they do have a bearing upon *On Liberty*, they belong to the corpus of the "other" Mill. In both works Mill voiced the same criticism of modern democracy and society that he had in *On Liberty*: "The natural tendency of representative government, as of modern civilization, is towards collective mediocrity: and this tendency is increased by all reductions and extensions of the franchise." (*Representative Government*, pp. 265–66.) For this reason he opposed universal suffrage (although he favored some electoral reform) and pro-

If *On Liberty* is not about political liberty in this sense, neither is it about "civil liberties" in the current legal sense: the judicial protection of the rights of defendants. Mill never so much as alluded to this problem in *On Liberty*, and to the extent to which he dealt with it elsewhere, he did so in a spirit quite contrary to that of present-day civil-libertarians. Perhaps the most sustained argument ever made against the present conception of civil liberties was Bentham's *Rationale of Judicial Evidence*, the work edited by Mill himself in his youth. Whatever Mill's later differences with Bentham, he never quarreled with him on this subject. And Bentham's views were as heterodox in his own day as they are today. His intention was to simplify judicial procedure to the point where it would approximate the "natural system" of the "domestic tribunal"—the situation in which the father sits in judgment on his child or servant and "naturally," without the artificial impediments of rules and procedures, elicits the facts, passes judgment, and metes out punishment, all of this accomplished as promptly and expedi-

---

posed to correct the unfortunate tendencies of democracy by introducing a system of proportional representation and plural voting. Under such a system, every individual might have some voice and power in government but emphatically not an "equal voice" or an "equal claim to power." "It is the fact," Mill wrote in 1859, "that one person is *not* as good as another; and it is reversing all the rules of rational conduct, to attempt to raise a political fabric on a supposition which is at variance with fact." (*Essays on Politics and Culture*, p. 315.)

Yet in *On Liberty* he tried to do exactly what he counseled against in his political writings: to raise a social (not political) fabric on a supposition (the same supposition), "at variance with fact." Here, in respect to the society and culture, he did give to every individual an equal voice and an equal power. If the better person did come to prevail, it could only be by some process of natural selection. And that natural process could only function if everyone were equally free to voice his opinions and equally free to act upon them. Here there was no equivalent to proportional representation, no attempt to weight in advance each individual's voice or power. The society and culture were bidden to act on the assumption—however contrary to fact—that every person, every opinion, and every expression of individuality was "as good as another."

tiously as possible. In accord with this view of justice, Bentham proposed abolishing all "technical" rules of evidence, rules which then, as now, prohibited self-incrimination, protected privileged communications with lawyer, husband, or wife (the only privilege Bentham recognized was that of the priest), excluded hearsay, circumstantial evidence, and evidence obtained illegally or improperly, and otherwise limited what the judge might hear and the grounds on which he might pass judgment. With all of this Mill was in entire agreement, not only at the time he edited the *Rationale* but throughout his life.[48]

On these matters, then—political liberty as it is commonly understood and civil liberties in the current legal sense—*On Liberty* had nothing to say. Perhaps because it was not concerned with these subjects, Mill could afford to take a more absolutist position than he would otherwise have done. In political affairs he was much less sanguine about the capacity of every individual to participate fully and freely. Interested in promoting good government as well as representative government, he was quite prepared to weight the political process in favor of virtue and wisdom, so that while everyone had a share in representation, not everyone shared equally in it, still less participated equally in the actual operation of government. Similarly, in legal matters he was less solicitous of the rights and liberties of all individuals, his interest there being in the most expeditious execution of justice rather than in the greatest measure of liberty.

What *On Liberty* was primarily concerned with was the realm of culture and society. It is here that Mill made liberty and individuality preeminent. And it is here, in its emphasis on culture and society and in its particular cultural and social bias, that *On Liberty* has most in common with our own times—indeed, far more than it had with Mill's.

48. For a further discussion of Mill's views on "civil liberties," see the note appended to this chapter.

Note on Mill and "Civil Liberties"

IF BENTHAM'S CONCEPTION of a "natural" judicial system may come as a surprise to those who think of him as a progressive reformer and enlightened liberal, Mill's substantial agreement with Bentham on this subject may be even more surprising, especially in view of his considerable disagreements with him on other subjects.

In editing Bentham's *Rationale of Judicial Evidence* (published in 1827), Mill had added editorial notes which considerably sharpened Bentham's points. When Bentham's *Collected Works* was being prepared in 1837, Mill reviewed those notes and found nothing he wanted to delete (save for one note endorsing Bentham's objections to such terms as "law of nations, moral sense, common sense . . .").[49] He did, however, add a short preface to the *Rationale* apologizing for the tone of "confident dogmatism" of some of the notes.[50] But it was his presumptuousness he was apologizing for—he was all of nineteen when he started the editing—not the substance of his remarks, still less the substance of Bentham's work. In a letter to the editor of the *Collected Works*, Mill went out of his way to explain that he did not want it thought that he was "censuring" Bentham, that nothing was further from his intention.[51] Mill's expression of satisfaction with the *Rationale* at this time is all the more remarkable because this was at the very height of his anti-Benthamite period: he had already written one critical essay on Bentham (the Appendix to Bulwer Lytton's *England and the English*) and was about to start his major critique.

Toward the end of his life Mill again had occasion to refer to the *Rationale* and again he did so with entire approval. "I

49. Appendix to *Later Letters*, IV, 1981 (JSM to John Hill Burton, Dec. 9, 1837); see also *ibid.*, p. 1988 (to Burton, Oct. 25, 1838).

50. Bentham, *Collected Works*, VI, 201-3.

51. *Earlier Letters*, II, 368 (to Burton, Jan. 23, 1838).

agree with you," he wrote to one correspondent, "in going the complete length with Bentham as to the admissibility of evidence." He specifically cited the "practical mischief" that frequently resulted from the rule permitting a defendant not to testify. The only point, he added, on which Bentham had gone wrong was in allowing the judge to interrogate the defendant; in France, where judges commonly rose from the rank of public prosecutor, this practice had led to much abuse.[52]

On the issue of capital punishment Mill's position was similarly at variance with that of most civil-libertarians today—or, as he himself said, with "advanced liberal opinion" in his own day.[53] One of his rare interventions in Parliament was a speech opposing a motion to abolish capital punishment. He considered —and rejected—the familiar argument against capital punishment: the fallibility of judgment and the irreversibility of this extreme penalty. On the Continent, he admitted, the argument might have some validity, since there the system of justice was not weighted in favor of the innocent and did not afford much security against erroneous conviction. But in England the situation was quite the opposite: "Our rules of evidence are even too favourable to the prisoner; and juries and Judges carry out the maxim, 'It is better that ten guilty should escape than that one innocent person should suffer,' not only to the letter, but beyond the letter." If the judicial procedure was too lax, the penal system, he said, was even more so. Mill concluded his speech with a plea not only for the retention of capital punishment but for more severe punishments in general:

> *The mania which existed a short time ago for paring down all punishments seems to have reached its limits, and not before it was time. We were in danger of being left without any effectual punishment, except for small offences. What was formerly our chief secondary punishment— transportation—before it was abolished, had become almost a reward. Penal servitude, the substitute for it, was becom-*

52. *Later Letters*, IV, 1558 (JSM to T. E. Cliffe Leslie, Feb. 8, 1869); see also *ibid.*, III, 1524 (JSM to James Beal, Dec. 14, 1868).

53. *Autobiography*, p. 200.

ing, to the classes who were principally subject to it, almost nominal, so comfortable did we make our prisons, and so easy had it become to get quickly out of them. Flogging—a most objectionable punishment in ordinary cases, but a particularly appropriate one for crimes of brutality, especially crimes against women—we would not hear of, except, to be sure, in the case of garotters, for whose peculiar benefit we reestablished it in a hurry, immediately after a Member of Parliament had been garotted. With this exception, offences, even of an atrocious kind, against the person . . . not only were, but still are, visited with penalties so ludicrously inadequate, as to be almost an encouragement to the crime. I think, Sir, that in the case of most offences, except those against property, there is more need of strengthening our punishments than of weakening them: and that severer sentences, with an apportionment of them to the different kinds of offences which shall approve itself better than at present to the moral sentiments of the community, are the kind of reform of which our penal system now stands in need. I shall therefore vote against the Amendment.[54]

54. 3 Hansard 191: 1053–55 (Apr. 21, 1868).

SOME PARADOXES
AND ANOMALIES

LIONEL TRILLING HAS brilliantly delineated the "adversary culture" that dominates modern thinking: the belief that "a primary function of art and thought is to liberate
the individual from the tyranny of his culture . . . and to
permit him to stand beyond it in an autonomy of perception
and judgment."[1] *On Liberty* was animated by the same
spirit. Mill did not, to be sure, foresee all the implications
and consequences of the spread of this belief, least of all the
adoption by the mass culture itself of the products and
postures of the adversary culture. But the adversary stance
was as much part of *On Liberty* as it is of any manifesto
currently issuing from the *avant garde*. Liberty was urgently
required, for Mill as for many liberals today, because the
dominant culture—not this or that culture but any dominant
culture—is regarded as necessarily inhibiting and repressive.
The echoes of Mill's pleas for "experiments of living" and
"doing as we like" can be heard in the current praise of
"alternative life-styles" and "doing one's thing." His paean
to individuality recalls our own penchant for "autonomy"
and "authenticity." His distrust of society, custom, and

1. Lionel Trilling, *Beyond Culture* (New York, 1965), p. xiii.

public opinion are reflected in the current attack upon the "establishment" and the prevailing scorn for convention and conformity. His free individual was as effectively "alienated" from society as anyone today who casually invokes that word as a token of his independence and integrity.

If the adversary culture as it has recently developed—the "counterculture"—contains many contradictions and departs in many respects from the principles of liberty and individuality which it professes, this is what may be expected of any complicated social reality. But more important, its very contradictions and violations of principle may be instructive, if they should prove to be inherent in the principles themselves. It is evident, for example, that the celebrants of the counterculture are not always as solicitous of other people's liberties as of their own, that movements of "liberation" tend to emphasize group identity at the expense of individuality, that the counterculture itself spawns a host of new conventions and conformities, and that a new orthodoxy finally emerges, a "tradition of the new," as it has been aptly called, which takes pride in its *avant garde* status even as it enjoys all the perquisites of success.[2] Despite these anomalies, however, the counterculture continues to retain its adversary posture and to assert the values of individuality and liberty, as if the adversary posture itself were a sufficient warrant of those values. There is much, assuredly, in this counterculture that violates the spirit and intention of *On Liberty*. But in this important respect, in the implicit equation of individuality and liberty with the adversary posture, it is entirely in the tradition of *On Liberty*.

It was not only in relation to society and culture that Mill assumed an adversary stance. He did so also in relation to truth. And here too his doctrine has proved congenial to our own time—and, again, with consequences not entirely anti-

2. Harold Rosenberg, *The Tradition of the New* (New York, 1959).

cipated by him. By making truth so dependent upon error as to require not only the freest circulation of error but its deliberate cultivation, he reenforced the relativism of later generations. In the democratic marketplace of ideas, truth and error appear to be equal. Mill himself did not actually subscribe to this view. He did not mean to suggest that there was no such thing as truth or even that it was unknowable. He only meant to assert, as a practical proposition, that society could not presume to decide between truth and error. But it was the practical purport of his doctrine that has prevailed and that seems to lend credence to the current relativist temper.

Again, this is not a simple matter of distortion or even vulgarization. Mill's assumption that any authority is at best irrelevant and at worst harmful to the pursuit of truth, while error is necessary and beneficial, comes close to suggesting an inversion, a "transvaluation," of values. Indeed, relativism is the least radical consequence of his doctrine. One can imagine the emergence of some more perverse notions—the exaltation, perhaps, of error over truth, error being presumed to have a vitality, potency, and imaginative excitement lacking in the pedestrian truth. Nietzsche came close to this position when, in the interest of freedom itself, he disowned the tyranny of truth; his "free spirit" knew that "everything is permitted" only if "nothing is true." Mill would have been appalled by this proposition. But since he himself was dealing with truth as a social phenomenon, as it emerged in society, the social implications and consequences of his doctrine are as legitimate a matter of inquiry as its literal import and intent.

In the same way, Mill's view of morality has, unwittingly and yet almost inevitably, become assimilated into the current relativist view. Mill himself was not a moral relativist; he firmly believed that sobriety was inherently and absolutely superior to drunkenness, chastity to promiscuity, even altruism to self-interest. The affirmation of these virtues,

however, was not his purpose in *On Liberty*. His only purpose there was to establish the practical principle of neutrality—the principle that society could no more intervene in
matters of morality than in matters of truth. But in making
this practical point as strongly as he did, he could not help
weakening the status of morality and its hold upon the
individual. Philosophers can keep in mind the distinction
between social neutrality and moral relativity. But the ordinary person cannot be expected to appreciate these niceties.
He is likely to suppose that if morality is not the practical
concern of society, it is because morality itself is of little or
no concern either to society or to the individual. He may
also infer, from Mill's reflections on the difficulty of arriv-
ing at any truths, that moral truths in particular are of
dubious certainty, questionable validity, and therefore without legitimate authority.

Behind all of this—behind the adversary spirit and the
relativist temper—is the idea of liberty. It is this idea that is
Mill's most important bequest to us. And again we have
subtly altered his legacy. In adopting his idea of liberty, we
have done so as if it were the only natural, logical, and
meaningful idea of liberty. What Mill proposed as a bold
and new doctrine has come down to us as an obvious, axio-
matic truth. We assume that liberty must have the extension
that Mill gave to it, that it is significant only if it goes
beyond Milton's "neighbouring," indifferent opinions to
take in precisely the most radical and consequentially different ones, and that it is meaningful only if it includes liberty
of action on the same basis as liberty of speech. As a matter
of course, we give to liberty an internal as well as an external
dimension; to the extent to which the Calvinist ethic continues to function, we regard it as inhibiting and oppressive;
and the more efficacious it is, the more pernicious we find it.
We take it for granted that individuality and originality are
inherently good, authority and conformity potentially, if
not actually, bad. Where Mill had to argue strenuously for

the value of individuality, we invoke the idea of the "authentic," "autonomous" self, as if the very words are a warrant of merit, a necessary and sufficient assurance of virtue.[3]

To SPEAK OF Mill's "bequest" in this fashion, to draw parallels between *On Liberty* and current patterns of thought, or to suggest that the philosophical rationale of much of contemporary liberalism may be found in *On Liberty*, does not imply any mechanical notions of "cause" or "influence." Certainly it does not assume that *On Liberty* is read today with any care, if read at all, still less that it is applied with any forethought or deliberation. The transmission of ideas, as Acton suggested, does not follow so simple and direct a route. Nor is it only ideas that are involved in this process. There is also the complicated nature of modern society—industrialism, urbanism, democracy, technology—all of which have contributed, in different ways and for different reasons, to the impulse toward liberty and individuality, the animus against authority and conformity.

However complicated and circuitous the history of ideas, however many other circumstances impinge upon them, the ideas themselves, as Acton would have been the first to insist, are of considerable, sometimes of decisive moment. And the fact is that the idea of *On Liberty* did first emerge, clearly and unambiguously, in *On Liberty*. It was this work that formulated the idea, gave it logical coherence, and developed it systematically—and, perhaps more important, made it philosophically respectable. Mill himself was conscious of all this; it was what he meant when he described *On Liberty* as a "philosophic text-book of a single truth."[4]

3. For a subtle historical and critical account of the idea of authenticity, see Lionel Trilling, *Sincerity and Authenticity* (Cambridge, Mass., 1972).

4. *Autobiography*, p. 177.

He was probably the only person of his time, perhaps the only one in the past century, who could have elevated that single truth to the authoritative status of a "philosophic textbook." There were others—laissez-fairists and Social Darwinists, Transcendentalists in America, anarchists and nihilists in Russia, an occasional philosopher (Stirner most notably)—who asserted, in one fashion or another, the absolute liberty and sovereignty of the individual. But they lacked the philosophical disposition to sustain their theories and the personal distinction to give them weight. Mill alone, perhaps the most eminent of all the eminent Victorians, the "Purveyor-general of Thought" and "Saint of Rationalism," was capable of presenting that doctrine in the definitive form of a textbook.[5]

And textbooks, it is well known, do not have to be read to be influential. They only have to be there, to give credence and authority to ideas which most people accept unthinkingly. As Voltaire said of another seminal thinker: "Very few people read Newton, because it is necessary to be very learned to understand him; yet everybody talks about him"; and on another occasion: "We are all his disciples now."[6] *On Liberty* was, in fact, accessible to more people than was the *Principia*. But like all classics, it was more often bought than read, more often cited than studied. Its ideas entered the public domain as most influential ideas do, by a form of intellectual osmosis. Or perhaps it served as Mill hoped it would, as a "mental pemican" providing nourishment for later generations, for those thinkers who were capable of ingesting it in its pure form and who then regurgitated it for the benefit of the populace.

5. It was two Liberal prime ministers who bestowed these titles upon him: H. H. Asquith, *Some Aspects of the Victorian Age* (Oxford, 1918), p. 16; John Morley, *The Life of William Ewart Gladstone* (New York, 1903), II, 544.

6. Voltaire, *Lettres philosophiques* (Paris, 1964), II, 5 (letter 14); Peter Gay, *The Enlightenment: An Interpretation* (New York, 1969), II, 129 (quoting Voltaire, *Oeuvres*, VII, 335).

. . .

THE AFFINITY BETWEEN *On Liberty* and contemporary liberalism may be illustrated by a recent case in which *On Liberty* figured explicitly. The case is that of the legalization of homosexuality in England.

In 1954 the British Parliament appointed a committee to inquire into the laws relating to homosexuality and prostitution. Three years later the committee issued what has become known as the *Wolfenden Report*. The most controversial part of the report turned on the recommendation that "homosexual behavior between consenting adults in private should no longer be a criminal offence." The principle behind this recommendation was the importance of "individual freedom of choice and action in matters of private morality," the recognition of a "realm of private morality and immorality which is, in brief and crude terms, not the law's business." The report hastened to add that it did not intend to "condone or encourage private immorality"; it only wanted to make the individual responsible for his private morality or immorality. That the crucial word is "private" is implicit in the recommendation that the law continue to regard as criminal any "indecent act committed in a place where members of the public may be likely to see and be offended by it"; this would apply as much to heterosexual as to homosexual acts.[7] A similar principle was invoked in the case of prostitution. Prostitution was and would continue to be illegal only because it habitually impinged upon the public in such a way as to constitute a public nuisance. This is why it was the prostitute and not the customer who was punished. "It is not the duty of the law to concern itself with immorality as such. . . . It should confine itself to those activities which offend against public

7. *The Wolfenden Report: Report of the Committee on Homosexual Offences and Prostitution* (New York, 1963), pp. 48–49.

order and decency or expose the ordinary citizen to what is offensive or injurious."[8]

The *Wolfenden Report* was the subject of much discussion, not only because of its specific recommendations regarding homosexuality and prostitution (most of the proposals concerning prostitution were enacted almost immediately and those on homosexuality several years later), but because of its implications for the larger issues of liberty and law, the proper provinces of the individual and society. These implications were sharply brought out by two jurists who were eminently worthy of each other and of the occasion: Lord Devlin opposing the principles (although not all the recommendations) of the report and Professor H. L. A. Hart supporting both the principles and recommendations. It was Hart who pointed out how "strikingly similar" the principles of the report were to those of *On Liberty* and how similar too were Devlin's arguments to those voiced almost a century earlier by James Fitzjames Stephen in his critique of Mill.[9]

For Hart, as for the Wolfenden Committee, the distinction between public and private was crucial. Private immorality was not subject to law; public immorality, being an "affront to public decency," was subject to law:

> *Sexual intercourse between husband and wife is not immoral, but if it takes place in public it is an affront to public decency. Homosexual intercourse between consenting adults in private is immoral according to conventional morality, but not an affront to public decency, though it would be both if it took place in public.*[10]

In support of this distinction, Hart cited Mill's principle that

8. *Ibid.*, p. 143.
9. Hart, *Law, Liberty, and Morality*, pp. 14, 16.
10. *Ibid.*, p. 45.

coercion—the exercise of social and legal authority—was justified only to prevent harm to others. (He also might have quoted Mill on the difference between acts which were permissible so long as they injured only the agents involved and the same acts which, committed in public, became a "violation of good manners," an "offence against others," and hence punishable.[11]) Hart went on to admit that the distinction between public and private might sometimes be a "fine" one.[12] It might, for example, be argued that the knowledge of certain acts committed in private caused distress and therefore harm to those who regarded such acts as immoral. But this argument, he rejoined—again reminiscent of Mill[13]—would be invalid if liberty were given a high priority in the order of values. Harm would not then be so loosely interpreted as to include the distress occasioned by someone else's private acts. Public acts, however, were another matter and were commonly recognized as such. Indeed, the distinction between public and private, he pointed out, however fine in theory, was commonly accepted in practice and was reflected in most legal systems.

In 1963, when Hart wrote this essay, he did not feel the need to elaborate upon the distinction between public and private nor to defend it at any length. It was sufficiently well established in law and custom to pass without quarrel. In principle, to be sure, Hart did not accept either law or custom as sufficient reason for the validity or utility of any particular measure. But when that measure was justified on other grounds—in this case on the ground of liberty—the fact that it had the support of law and custom meant that it was not felt to be problematic and therefore did not require much defense. The unproblematic status of this distinction, however, was not to endure for long.

11. *On Liberty*, p. 153.
12. Hart, p. 47.
13. *On Liberty*, p. 138.

WITHIN ONLY a few years of the Wolfenden debate, indeed by the time its recommendations on homosexuality had been enacted, the argument had escalated far beyond the point where either the committee or Hart had left it. The idea of an "affront to public decency" has become almost as archaic as Mill's "violation of good manners." Most liberals now find it easier to agree with Mill in his indictment of a "moral police" than to credit the idea of an "offence against decency." Who is to determine, it is commonly asked, what is decent or indecent, mannerly or unmannerly, offensive or inoffensive? Who is to say what is properly private and what public or when private decencies become public indecencies? Are not these judgments at least as relative as all other opinions which pose as truth? And even if the truth could be established, is society any more justified in intervening in matters of morality and sexuality than in matters of religion and science? Is not the freedom of dissent as precious in the former cases as in the latter? And can the expression of moral and sexual dissent be confined any more easily to the privacy of one's home than can the expression of spiritual and intellectual dissent?

The escalation of the argument was entirely predictable— and entirely in keeping with the spirit of *On Liberty*. Mill's own attempts to distinguish between private and public, to disallow in public what he allowed in private, were at best unpersuasive, at worst equivocal. Having made the point that acts which were legal when performed privately might fall into the category of "offences against others" when performed in public, he went on to speak of "offences against decency" as coming within the same category—but upon these, he hastened to add, "it is unnecessary to dwell."[14] He was less reticent in other cases of private immoralities committed in public; but even here he did not commit himself

14. *Ibid.*, p. 153.

to the intervention of society. Much as he would have liked to put the procurer or keeper of a gambling house out of business, he could not bring himself to do so without imperiling his basic principle: "Over himself, over his own body and mind, the individual is sovereign," or its corollary, "Whatever it is permitted to do, it must be permitted to advise to do."[15]

The distinctions Mill found it difficult to establish in theory are now, a century later, almost impossible to sustain in practice. And those he thought too securely established to dwell upon are now subjected to tortuous analysis. What he took for granted has become problematic, and what he thought problematic has been outrightly denied. Even more extraordinary is the rapidity with which society has gone from one stage to the next. Within a single decade, the freedom to read pornography in the privacy of one's home has become, in practice if not in law, the freedom to circulate it through the mails and to buy and sell it in bookstores. The freedom to act it out has been extended—like Mill's example of gambling[16]—from the private home, to clubs by private subscription, to public movie houses and theaters. Pornographic representations in the form of photographic stills have given way to moving pictures and then to live shows. The exhibition of normal heterosexual intercourse (the temptation to put normal in quotes is almost irresistible— testimony to the pervasive relativism of our culture) has been succeeded, almost as a matter of course, by homosexual intercourse, and thence by every permutation and combination of sexual coupling. Not all these extensions of liberty have received the formal sanction of the law, but they have all been tacitly condoned at one time or another by official authorities and vigorously defended by prominent liberals and reputable liberal organizations. Some dozen years ago eminent critics were called upon to testify to the "redeeming literary or social merit" of books which, were it not for

15. *Ibid.*, pp. 73, 154. See above, pp. 14, 114–15.   16. *Ibid.*, p. 155.

such merit, would have been held to be unpublishable. To-day many of these same critics repudiate this criterion as inherently illiberal and insist upon nothing more or less than the simple claim of freedom regardless of merit.

Not all liberals are happy with these developments. A. P. Herbert, the English playwright and Member of Parliament, fought long and hard for the act of 1968 which abolished censorship on the stage. Only two years after the passage of the act, he publicly deplored the fact that the movement which he had intended as a "worthy struggle for reasonable liberty for honest writers" had ended as the "right to represent copulation, veraciously, on the public stage."[17] Similarly, in this country the civil-liberties lawyer Morris Ernst has recently been moved to protest that he had only meant to ensure the publication of *Ulysses*, not the public perform-ance of sodomy.[18] But theirs are the familiar plaints of revolutionaries unable to keep pace with their own revolu-tion. What they cannot deny is that it is their own revo-lution that has left them behind. Even in retrospect they cannot point to anything in their principles that would have put an effective limit to that revolution. They were too busy agitating for "liberty for writers" to spell out in any detail or with any conviction the qualifications of "reason-able" liberty for "honest" writers. Indeed, to have insisted upon these qualifications, to have devised legal or institu-tional means by which to enforce them, would have seemed to them a legitimization of the censorship they were deter-mined to abolish.

In view of these experiences, one may properly ask whether *On Liberty* itself provided any effective limits, whether there was anything in Mill's doctrine to prevent this escalation of demands. Looking back upon the essay, one finds a great emphasis on the positive potentialities of liberty and very little regard for its negative potentialities. When

17. *The Times* (London), August 26, 1970 (p. 9).
18. *The New York Times*, January 5, 1970 (p. 32).

Mill exalted liberty and individuality, it was in the expectation that they would have infinitely beneficial results; but there was nothing in his doctrine to prevent them from having the most mischievous effects. He looked to liberty as a means of achieving the highest reaches of the human spirit; he did not take seriously enough the possibility that men would also be free to explore the depths of depravity. He saw individuality as a welcome release of energy and ingenuity, as if individuals cannot be as energetic and ingenious in pursuing ignoble ends as noble ones. Where most modern and all ancient philosophers had dwelt upon the need to check the human passions and had devised elaborate means to do so, the only check Mill provided for was the prevention of harm to others. Where they had sought to promote the good, he sought only to promote liberty, explicitly enjoining society from intervening for purposes of doing good either to the individual or to society as a whole. There was no room in his doctrine for the classical concept of moderation; the aspiration of liberty was to be as absolute, not as moderate, as possible. Nor was there room for other ends which might temper the passion for liberty—virtue, justice, obedience to natural or divine law. Other ends might coexist with liberty, even be furthered by liberty, but they could not be permitted to limit or interfere with liberty.

It is the exclusive as well as the absolute nature of his doctrine, its "simple principle" and "single truth," that has been an invitation to excess. It is this that has made it difficult to justify and sustain distinctions, to discriminate among particular liberties, to weigh the good and evil attending this or that liberty in this or that circumstance, to tolerate the lesser evil of a diminished liberty in order to prevent a greater evil or promote a greater good, to recognize the claims of other values without denigrating the value of liberty itself.

Trotsky used to argue that if one said A, one would be obliged to say B, C, and on to Z, the first commitment to revolution implying a total commitment and, conversely, the first symptom of regression leading inexorably to counter-revolution. The same spirit of totality and inexorability pervades Mill's doctrine, starting with liberty of thought in the "most comprehensive sense"—"absolute freedom of opinion and sentiment on all subjects"—going on to the liberty of expression as "practically inseparable" from the liberty of opinion, and concluding with liberty of action which, save for the one qualification about harm to others, was similarly comprehensive and absolute.[19] To stop short of any of these propositions, Mill implied, was to jeopardize the whole. Each presupposed and required the other. And each was necessary in its totality.

It is the same logic that governs much liberal thinking today. Action, sometimes even action harmful to others, may be granted immunity by assimilating it to speech, interpreting it "symbolically," as a form of speech with gestures. And freedom of speech without a commensurate freedom of action is regarded as meaningless, a "merely formal" freedom without content and substance. The Kantian formula, "Argue but obey," which was intended to assure the most essential quality of man, the freedom to use his reason, and to promote the essential purpose of society, the reconciliation of law and liberty, is now looked upon with profound suspicion. What had originally been devised as a liberal strategy to enlarge liberty is now thought of as a conservative strategy to diminish liberty.

The denial of distinctions, the all-or-nothing mentality, is one of the most prominent features of current liberalism. Any limitation of liberty is regarded as an invitation to tyranny. Instead of being acutely aware, in this period of rapid social change, of the possible gradations and variations of liberty within a liberal system, most liberals identify the

19. *On Liberty*, p. 75.

latest acquisition or extension of liberty with the very essence of liberty. Each extension suggests, as its logical and necessary sequel, another extension, as if the earlier liberty would be incomplete or insecure without the later. And any intimation that the later addition might be ill advised is taken as an assault upon the whole, as if to reject Z were to deny everything down to A. Thus the recent Supreme Court decision permitting local communities to prohibit pornography lacking in "redeeming social value"—restoring, in effect, a criterion that had been in use until recently —has been represented as an attack upon our entire body of liberties. The censorship of "blue movies," we are told, is only a prelude to the censorship of everything else—*Ulysses* and Shakespeare are commonly cited as the next victims— as if the fate of pornography is indissolubly bound together with that of all art and literature, as if we have not, in our own lifetimes, actually lived through periods, and without experiencing them as oppressive or illiberal, when *Ulysses* was permitted but hard pornography was not.

It is ironic that liberals who hotly reject the "domino theory" in foreign affairs implicitly hold to some such theory in the realm of civil liberties, the denial of any particular liberty presumably setting in motion a process that will result in the toppling of all liberties. And liberals for whom the "fabric of society" metaphor is normally a code word for conservatism tend to think of all liberties as so firmly woven together in a seamless fabric that no one liberty may be separated from the rest without unraveling the whole. Thus many a liberty—of pornography or obscenity, for example—is defended not for its own sake but for the sake of liberty as a whole, as if liberalism were as monolithic a structure as communism was once thought to be.

YET CONTEMPORARY LIBERALISM is anything but monolithic. Indeed, what is most conspicuous about it is the disjunction between the "civil" and "social" realms, between what is sometimes called "negative" and "positive" liberty.[20] The same liberals who insist upon the largest measure of individual liberty in one area—the freedom to see, read, say, and act as they please, to be free of moral restraints and social conventions—also tend to insist upon the largest measure of social and government controls in other areas—to provide for economic security, racial equality, social justice, environmental protection, and the like. That the latter involve a considerable diminution of individual liberty is not denied by liberals; nor does this mitigate their zeal. The disjunction is in fact so deeply ingrained in the modern liberal sensibility that to remark upon it, to see it as a problem, is taken as the sign of a conservative disposition.[21]

Again, the example of Mill is instructive. For just as the expansionist impulse—the tendency to enlarge and extend liberty as if by a logical compulsion—was evident in *On Liberty*, so was the disjunctive impulse. In both cases, to be sure, Mill stopped short of the extremes to which we have gone. In respect to government intervention, he was especially cautious. We have seen how strenuously (if inconsistently) he sought to limit the consequences of the idea that "trade is a social act."[22] Yet there were instances where

20. See Isaiah Berlin, "Two Concepts of Liberty," in *Four Essays on Liberty* (Oxford, 1969). "Positive liberty" is sometimes associated with the "new liberalism" of T. H. Green and, later, L. T. Hobhouse.

21. It is for this reason that most liberals think of Milton Friedman and Friedrich Hayek as conservatives ("nineteenth-century liberalism" being presumed to be the equivalent of "twentieth-century conservatism"), while Friedman and Hayek regard themselves as the real liberals and deny the title to those who exhibit this disjunction. There is no doubt that the position of Friedman and Hayek is the more consistent one. But neither is there any doubt that current usage favors those who allow for a considerable measure of government intervention in economic and "social" affairs. In some other context, this problem of nomenclature might be semantic. But here, where the issue is precisely the evolution of the idea of liberty, the current usage must be respected as a reflection of the social reality.

22. See above, pp. 110 ff.

he recognized the need for government intervention. And the fact that these instances could not be subsumed under the qualification of harm to others—or if they could, so could a great many other instances as well—suggests that the principle of liberty was not the entirely satisfactory, entirely sufficient guide to social relations he tried to make of it. Under the pressure of particular social needs that he felt to be urgent (education, the control of population, the safety of workers), he had to by-pass that principle.

In view of Mill's general commitment to the doctrine of laissez-faire, these particular instances may appear to be exceptions to the rule, exceptions which do not impair the rule itself. Yet the instances are too important, too central to the problem of the individual and society, to be passed off so lightly. If the principle of liberty cannot incorporate within itself social needs of such urgency, another principle will have to be invoked for this purpose. Mill himself specifically rejected the alternative principle which he identified as the theory of "social rights."[23] But since he provided nothing but liberty to put in its place, he left the door open to something very like such a theory.

Later generations, lacking Mill's commitment to laissez-faire, have not limited government intervention to a few specified cases. As liberated from classical political economy as from classical political philosophy, most liberals today are conspicuously uninhibited in their demands for government controls. And since they have no positive conception of society or the state to guide or restrain them, they are at the mercy of any *ad hoc* proposal, any momentary enthusiasm, that may come their way. Having extended the principle of liberty as far as it will go in one direction, when that principle is found wanting they abandon it entirely and pursue the opposite principle to its outer extremes.

In this sense, the disjunction in contemporary liberalism is only superficially in contradiction with the principle of

23. *On Liberty*, p. 146. See above, p. 101.

liberty. At a deeper level it bears witness to the profound hold which that principle has upon the modern imagination. Having made an absolute of liberty and having established the individual as sovereign, the liberal has no integrated view of the individual in society which can moderate either his passion for liberty or his desire for regulation and control. When liberty proves inadequate, government rushes in. And since the only function assigned to government by the principle of liberty is the negative one of protection against injury, when government is obliged to assume a positive role, neither its proper powers nor its proper limits have been defined. The paradox is inevitable: government tends to become unlimited when liberty itself is thought to be unlimited.

This paradox brings others in its wake. While contemporary liberalism has enormously enhanced the roles of society, government, and the state, it has provided them with no principles of legitimacy. Indeed, its theoretical commitment to liberty has undermined those principles which traditionally performed the function of legitimization. Thus, even as the government becomes more importunate, the law, which is the legitimizing instrument of government, has become enfeebled almost, it sometimes seems, to the point of impotence. Society makes larger demands upon the individual, but public opinion, the voice of society, is derided. The state has developed a formidable apparatus of power; but it has lost the presumption of respect and the assurance of obedience.

The anomalies are almost endless. It is curious, for instance, that liberals who have no faith in the free marketplace as a medium for the efficient production and distribution of material goods should rely more than ever on the free marketplace for the production and distribution of spiritual goods—ideas, morals, manners, art, and artifacts. They favor government regulation to ensure the safety of cars and the nutritional content of bread, the probity of stockbrokers and the competence of doctors. Where their material, physical, and financial interests are concerned, they try to protect themselves against risk, loss, and harm. But they take no similar precautions in their spiritual and moral affairs. Here they brook no government or social interference; here the individual is assumed to be totally competent and totally free. It once took a philistine like the notorious Mayor Jimmy Walker of New York to jeer at the idea that anyone could be corrupted by a book. Today that is the common tenet of faith among most liberals. But while most liberals deny the corrupting or depraving effect of a bad book, they have no doubt of the corrupting and depraving effects —spiritually as well as physically—of slums and bad housing.

The double standard as it now operates is relatively recent, certainly post-Mill. The older Whig tradition had no compunctions about the intervention of society and government whether in the sphere of economics or of morals. The legitimacy and propriety of intervention in any particular case were determined by considerations of tradition, law, circumstance, and expediency. At a later period a distinction was made between the two spheres, but then the tendency was to be laissez-fairist in the "business part" of life, as Mill called it, rather than in the moral part; the latter was deemed to be too important to be left to the unguided impulses of individual passions and interests. It remained for *On Liberty* to reverse this order. There, for the first time, not only the state but still more society were enjoined from intervening in intellectual, moral, and cultural affairs. There trade alone was given the status, in principle, of a "social act." This was an extraordinary assertion for Mill to have made, not only because it was in striking contrast to his earlier position but also because it assumed that only the exchange of material goods involved people in a social relationship and that all other forms of intercourse—the communication of ideas and attitudes, of manners and morals—did not.

This reversal on Mill's part was not intended to imply a

reversal of priorities or values. He did not mean to suggest, in *On Liberty*, that spiritual goods were any less important than material goods. But this may have been the unwitting implication of his work. By making morality and culture unproblematic—unproblematic, that is, so far as society and the state were concerned—he helped move the center of attention, and thus the sense of importance and value, to that area which was problematic, where society and the state were obliged to intervene. He himself would never have said that no one was ever corrupted by a book. But by refusing to society any role in the prevention or punishment of such corruption, while granting to society the right to prevent or punish the adulteration of food, he encouraged men to reorder their priorities and redefine their values.

It was to be a long time before the full import of *On Liberty*, the reordering of social priorities and the redefinition of moral and cultural values, was to be felt. The moral and intellectual capital of the Victorians lasted longer than might have been expected. In some quarters, and in the privacy of men's lives, much of it remains even today. But in public life it has been almost entirely dissipated. Here we are left with the heritage of *On Liberty*. What public philosophy we have is that which Mill bequeathed to us.

OTHER PHILOSOPHIES have attempted to challenge the preeminence of liberalism—Marxism, Freudianism, more recently Existentialism. The first two have been the most serious contenders, each positing a deterministic system which is antithetical to anything approaching an absolutist conception of liberty or individuality. For a time, especially in the 1930s, it seemed that one or both of these had succeeded in making liberalism appear archaic, the vestige of an obsolete bourgeois society clinging to the illusion that the individual was the master of his fate and the free agent of his will. Since then, however, both doctrines have evolved in a manner that suggests that they themselves have succumbed to the seductions of the doctrine of liberty. In the currently fashionable mode of Marxism, that of the "early" Marx, the emphasis has shifted from class to "generic man," from a deterministic theory in which the decisive realities are the material and historical conditions of society to a philosophy which is presumed to be humanistic and even individualistic, from revolution in the classical Marxist sense to liberation in Marcuse's sense.[24] And psychoanalysis has undergone something of the same transformation, the revisionist theories having the effect of undermining the deterministic structure of classical Freudianism. In varying ways and to varying degrees, the new modes of psychoanalytic thought

24. Whether this interpretation of the "early" or "young" Marx is correct, or whether this Marx—the Marx of *The German Ideology* and *Economic and Philosophic Manuscripts*—can be reconciled with the classical Marx—the Marx of *The Communist Manifesto, Capital*, etc.—is not here at issue. What is significant is the prevalence of this interpretation and, if not the identification of the two Marxes, at the very least the displacement of the later Marx by the earlier one. By the standards of a rigorous, old-fashioned Marxism, the young Marx as he is commonly represented today would be condemned as an "infantile leftist," a romantic idealist.

Marcuse's philosophy is an ingenious attempt to combine the two Marxes—and to combine them as well with a psychoanalytic theory which departs considerably from orthodox Freudianism. His ambivalent relationship to the "New Left" illustrates some of the conflicting strains in his thought. On the one hand, he praised the student rebels for the qualities that, as he saw it, inspired their rebelliousness: their individualism, spontaneity, nonconformity, hostility to all authority, refusal to be "coopted" into the "system." . . . On the other hand, he warned them that these very qualities prevented them from achieving the kind of "revolutionary discipline" necessary for a properly organized revolutionary movement and a viable socialist state. What Marcuse would have liked, in effect, was to harness the counterculture to the socialist revolution, to combine the "new individualism" of the New Left with the class consciousness and party organization of the Old Left. This is what he meant when he besought the New Left to maintain an "objective ambivalence" between "personal and political rebellion, private liberation and social revolution." (Herbert Marcuse, *Counterrevolution and Revolt* [Boston, 1972], pp. 47 ff.)

have sought to liberate the id from the restraints of the ego and the ego from the restraints of the superego. They have held out the promise of a civilization without "discontents" and a social order that may be nothing less than utopian; they have visions of a sexuality of unlimited freedom and variety and of a human character that is almost infinitely malleable.[25]

25. In a more moderate form this was the intent of the early revisionists such as Karen Horney and Erich Fromm. The more radical implications of this mode of thought are evident in the recent work of Norman O. Brown (in the idea, for example, of "polymorphous perversity") and, somewhat less systematically, in the writings of Robert Lifton (especially in his concept of "protean man"). (Norman Brown, *Life Against Death* [New York, 1959] and *Love's Body* [New York, 1966]; Robert J. Lifton, *History and Human Survival* [New York, 1970].)

The schools of ego psychology and existential psychology have contributed no such striking phrases to the vocabulary of psychoanalysis, but they represent much the same tendencies. The first has redefined the ego so as to make it an expansive, permissive instrument rather than, as for Freud, a restricting, inhibiting one: "The ego's strength is not measured by the earlier psychoanalytic standard of what in a personality is denied or cut off, but rather by all the extremes that an individual's ego is able to unify." (Paul Roazen, *Freud: Political and Social Thought* [New York, 1968], p. 234.) And the second (*Daseinanalyse*, as it is often called) insists as strenuously as existentialism itself upon the individual, his freedom to choose, to make of himself what he will. Where the Freudian limits the individual's psychic freedom by making his future a product of his past, the existentialist inverts this relationship: "What an individual seeks *to become* determines what he remembers of his *has been*. In this sense, the future determines the past." (Hendrik M. Ruitenbeek, ed., *Psychoanalysis and Existential Philosophy* [New York, 1962], p. xvii.) Thus, not only is the individual liberated from the Freudian determinism; he is liberated even from the ordinary common-sense determinism in which the past is given, fixed, an unalterable fact of life.

It is interesting to compare the existentialist's treatment of determinism with Mill's discussion of "necessity" in the *Logic*. The doctrine of necessity, Mill said, "weighed on my existence like an incubus" (*Autobiography*, p. 118), until he finally managed to solve it in the *Logic*. The solution lay in the idea that a man's character was not only formed *for* him—by education, circumstances, his physical and mental structure—but also formed *by* him—by will, volition, choice: "We are exactly as capable of making our own character, *if we will*, as others are of making it for us." (*Logic*, p. 550.)

It would be interesting to trace these movements of thought, to watch the original orthodoxy revised and relaxed until the individual is liberated, in the case of Marxism, from the confines of class, history, and material life, and in the case of Freudianism, from the determinants of body, psyche, and society. But that would be the subject of another study. Here one can only point to the common denominator in both movements, the sense in which the newer schools of thought seek to restore to the individual the very qualities Mill had made so much of: liberty, individuality, spontaneity, creativity, variety, vigor, and energy. And one can find the same significance in the current modishness of existentialism, where the "autonomy" and "authenticity" of the individual are posited in their most extreme forms, where the only principle of morality is deemed to be the freely willed action, and where immorality is nothing other than "inauthenticity," the "bad faith" that comes from the violation of free will.[26]

IT WOULD ALSO BE interesting, but again part of another study, to try to account for the resilience and endurance of liber-

---

26. One can carry further the analogy between Mill's argument and that of the existentialist. The idea of eccentricity, for example, functioned for Mill in much the same way as the *acte gratuit* does for the existentialist. And Mill's assertion of the need for freedom of choice, in which it is the act of choice rather than the substance of the choice that is decisive, has been echoed by all existentialists. "The human faculties of perception, judgment, discriminative feeling, mental activity, and even moral preference, are exercised only in making a choice. He who does anything because it is the custom makes no choice." The quotation is from *On Liberty* (p. 116), but it could as well have appeared in *Being and Nothingness*. To be sure, the existentialist has gone further than Mill in appreciating, as Mill did not, the tragic implications of freedom, the "dreadful burden" imposed by it. But since the existentialist has made that freedom the essential condition of man's humanity, he can no more relieve man of that burden than Mill could.

alism, which survived all the efforts to kill it and all the announcements of its death. Indeed, it was in response to these provocations that liberalism acquired a new vitality and urgency. After the experiences of the 1930s and 1940s, many radicals (the "Old Left," as they are now called), who had once been thoroughly contemptuous of "bourgeois" liberty, found that there was much to be said in favor of such liberty. Reacting against the Communist and Nazi dictatorships—and perhaps also, in some instances, against their own complicity in the Communist ideology and movement—they rediscovered the virtues of liberty. And their reaction was often commensurate with the evils they were combating. Against the total denial of liberty, they insisted upon an absolute measure of liberty.

In the aftermath of absolute despotism, it was natural to seek refuge in absolute liberty. And the traumatic effects of Nazism and Stalinism have remained with us since. Even those liberals who are temperamentally and philosophically averse to doctrinaire modes of thought, who do not ordinarily take kindly to "one very simple principle," who are more comfortable with pluralist values than with absolute principles, are inclined to make an exception of liberty. Liberty, it is generally assumed, is secure only if it is accepted as an absolute. Anything less is thought to leave it exposed and vulnerable. Confronted with the total subversion of all liberties, we readily agree to a doctrine that makes an absolute of liberty. Against the threats of one or another variety of totalitarianism, we think it necessary to have a principle as total and unyielding, as absolute and imperious, as the enemy with which it must do battle.

There is a beguiling plausibility in this way of thinking. It seems to resemble the famous Talmudic prescript for a "fence around the Torah"—the observance of a law beyond its literal requirement to make certain that the literal requirement itself is never violated. The wisdom of this dictum is abundantly borne out by experience. But there is a crucial difference between the ancient precept and the modern one. The Talmudic fence is of modest dimensions, extending only to a small and well-defined area surrounding the particular edict; it cannot extend too far lest it impinge upon another edict as sacred as the first. The doctrine of liberty, by contrast, is of infinite extension. It claims dominion over the entire range of social relations. It knows only one limit, harm to others, and that interpreted narrowly. For the rest it is absolute and sovereign.

Ultimately, by its very absoluteness, the doctrine tends to discredit itself—to discredit not only liberty in general but any particular liberty. By claiming jurisdiction over areas where it has no natural authority, it calls into question the validity of the general principle. At the same time, by making all particular liberties dependent on the general principle, by invalidating all those other principles—history, tradition, prescription, law, interest, nature, utility, prudence—which once served to validate particular liberties, it undermines each particular liberty together with its particular rationale. Liberty may thus find itself without credibility or authority in the very area where it is most urgently needed. So far from making all liberty absolutely secure, the absolutist doctrine may have the perverse effect of depriving the most essential liberties—liberty of speech, most notably—of even that relative security they would enjoy under more modest auspices.

This is not an idle play of ideas, an apocalyptic image of what might conceivably happen if the logic of an idea is permitted to run amuck. It is in fact what has actually happened at critical moments in recent history. When a great many intellectuals, after the Russian Revolution, decided that "negative" liberty did not satisfy the "positive" needs of society, that indeed negative liberty might interfere with the realization of what they took to be more urgent social needs, they lost respect for liberty as such. Since it was not the absolute value it had been made out to be, they took it to be of no value at all. If it did not do what they thought needed doing, they were prepared to discard it altogether. And since liberty was supported by no other structure of values—since history, tradition, custom, prudence had been discredited by the doctrine of liberty itself —there was nothing to restrain their zeal in the pursuit of their new cause. Having discovered that the social revolution could not accommodate itself to absolute liberty, revolutionaries felt free to abolish liberty as ruthlessly as they had abolished the old regime. It was not only absolute liberty that fell victim to their good intentions; free speech itself was sacrificed with hardly a regret. Historians were later to discover with astonishment that Bolshevism was, in this respect, actually regressive compared with Tsarism. If only out of blundering, corruption, and sheer inefficiency, Tsarism had permitted a larger latitude to individuals, even larger opportunities for organized opposition, than Bolshevism.

As a result of these experiences—the Stalinist and Fascist terrors and their own earlier seduction by communism— many liberals are apt to misread the lessons of history. They are inclined to think that only absolute liberty can forestall absolute despotism, that the only corrective to the absolute sovereignty of the state is the absolute sovereignty of the individual. But this is to replace one fallacy with another. By limiting the alternatives to the two extremes, liberals may be inviting precisely the disaster they seek to avoid. In overstating the case for liberty, they may unwittingly do a disservice to the cause they so strenuously seek to promote. That absolute liberty cannot, in fact, sustain itself is suggested by the disjunction in contemporary liberalism, the increasing claims of liberty and individuality in one area and the increasing demands for social and government control in another. But this disjunction is inherently untenable and unstable. It invites excess in the one direction as in the other. It makes for a kind of schizophrenia in public life which can prove as fatal to the body politic as to the individual.

It also makes for a kind of sophistry which is equally fatal to liberty. From the perspective of absolute liberty, distinctions of degree tend to be obliterated. A greater amount of liberty may be felt to be as much a grievance, because it falls short of the absolute, as a lesser amount. A more liberal society is thought to be only slightly less onerous than an illiberal society. Where all authority is regarded as a threat to the individual, legitimate authority is reduced to the level of illegitimate authority. Indeed, those social and political systems which profess to be liberal, which are in fact liberal as compared with other systems, are most vulnerable since it is their own principles they seem to violate. The closer approximation to the ideal creates greater expectations and, therefore, greater frustration and resentment when these expectations are not realized. Dictatorships disappoint less because they promise less.

This too is no fanciful play of ideas. It is the logic that informs the recurrent pronouncements that the "so-called" democracies are no better than dictatorships, that a flawed party system is as bad as a one-party system, that a lack of racial equality is equivalent to genocide, that toleration is as repressive as intolerance because it implies that society decides what is to be tolerated, that any pressure for social conformity is as much a violation of the self as the most egregious act of a tyrant.

Liberals have learned, at fearful cost, the lesson that absolute power corrupts absolutely. They have yet to learn that absolute liberty may also corrupt absolutely.[27] It is a lesson

27. The echo of Acton is suggestive. Acton himself was caught up in the same dilemma: on the one hand a yearning for a liberty that would be absolute, a single moral principle admitting of no exception or qualification; on the other an appreciation of the plural, partial, prudential liberties that were part of the Whig heritage. It was because the absolutist view finally dominated his thought—what Max Weber described as the "ethic of ultimate ends" in distinction to the "ethic of responsibility"—that Acton turned so bitterly against Burke and the Whig tradition. (See Himmelfarb, *Lord Acton* [London, 1952], pp. 209 ff.)

that has to be learned not only for the sake of justice, virtue, community, and whatever other qualities we value in human society, but also for the sake of liberty itself. A polity that cannot credit the legitimate and positive functions of society, government, and the state will inevitably make way for one that is prepared to give *carte blanche* to society, government, and the state. A people that cannot respect the principles of prudence and moderation is bound to behave so imprudently and immoderately as to violate every other principle, including the principle of liberty.

It is by some kind of poetic justice that we may find redemption in the very thinker who, more than any other single person, inspired the modern fallacy. There is no better corrective to the Mill of *On Liberty* than the "other" Mill. The philosophers of antiquity were assuredly wiser and more profound than either Mill. They had inquired more carefully and deeply into the nature of passion, reason, virtue, and justice; they had been more probing and systematic in their analysis of men's souls and their polities. But they do not speak with ease and assurance to men who are, for good or bad, peculiarly, unalterably "modern." It is here that the other Mill, operating within a tradition that is undeniably modern and at the same time reminiscent of and respectful toward the old, has most to say to us. When Bagehot praised Mill for his capacity for "intellectual combination," his ability to synthesize a wide variety of ideas, it was this Mill he had in mind. The virtue of the *Logic* and the *Political Economy*, he said—notably omitting any mention of *On Liberty*—was the way they brought together what was normally kept apart: "an incessant reminiscence of the past and an equally incessant foresight of the future."[28]

28. Walter Bagehot, "The Late Mr. Mill," *The Economist*, May 7, 1873, reprinted in *The Collected Works of Walter Bagehot*, ed. Norman St. John-Stevas (Cambridge, Mass., 1968), III, 555–56.

The tradition of the other Mill has other luminaries: Montesquieu, Burke, the Founding Fathers, Tocqueville, Halévy. It is curious that only one of them is English, but significant that the others drew heavily on the English experience. For it is the English tradition that is peculiarly represented here, a tradition that can more easily be defined in terms of English history than of English thought. That the other Mill did not write a systematic "Principles of Social Philosophy" equivalent to his *Principles of Political Economy* is perhaps unfortunate. Or perhaps it is of the nature of that social philosophy to resist systematization, to find expression more naturally in essays inspired by particular circumstances and problems. For it is precisely the historical, circumstantial dimensions of Mill's thought that give it its special character.

Yet Mill's thinking was not so historical, so circumstantial, as to be without philosophical principles. Unlike some of the other great essayists of his time, Mill had an essentially philosophical mind. The elucidation of general principles was never far from the forefront of his consciousness. If he did not himself write a treatise on social philosophy, it would not be hard to deduce, from the body of his writings, the principles that would have gone into such a treatise. And these principles add up to a very different kind of philosophy from that represented by *On Liberty*.

It was this other Mill who, in notable contrast to *On Liberty*, argued that "government exists for all purposes whatever that are for man's good: and the highest and most important of these purposes is the improvement of man himself as a moral and intelligent being";[29] that "men do not come into the world to fulfill one single end, and there is no single end which if fulfilled even in the most complete manner would make them happy";[30] that every man should be encouraged to "*use* his own judgement," but that to

29. Mill, *Earlier Letters*, I, 36 (JSM to d'Eichthal, Oct. 8, 1829).
30. *Ibid*.

337

encourage him to *"trust* solely to his own judgement, and receive or reject opinions according to his own views of the evidence" was to make him a "mere slave to the authority of the person next to him";[31] that an essential ingredient of civilization was an education in discipline to inculcate in each person the habit of "subordinating his personal impulses and aims, to what were considered the ends of society";[32] that civilized society also presupposed the existence of some "fundamental principles" which men agreed in "holding sacred" and which they placed *"above* discussion";[33] that morality depended upon the cultivation of the "social feelings" and "collective" interest of mankind transcending the individual's selfish feelings and interests, and that this moral end could best be promoted by "laws and social arrangements," "education and opinion";[34] that the sign of an "advancing civilization" was the fact that man was "riveted" more and more to his "social state" and removed more and more from a state of "savage independence" or "miserable individuality";[35] that the moral defect of Fourierism was its reliance entirely on the "spontaneous actions of the passions" and on the notion that "nobody is ever to be made to do anything but act just as they like."[36]

This is assuredly not the Mill of *On Liberty*. But it is a Mill who more truly deserves the title of "liberal." For it is his liberality of mind and temper that can prevent us from being seduced and ultimately tyrannized by any "one very simple principle," even so honorific a principle as liberty.

31. "The Spirit of the Age," *Essays on Politics and Culture*, p. 15.
32. "Coleridge," *ibid.*, p. 136.
33. *Ibid.*, p. 138.
34. "Utilitarianism," *Essays on Ethics, Religion and Society*, pp. 231, 218.
35. *Ibid.*, pp. 231, 216.
36. *Later Letters*, I, 22 (JSM to Harriet Taylor, Mar. 31, 1849). For the context of these quotations, see above, chaps. I–V.

BIBLIOGRAPHY

THE BIBLIOGRAPHY includes only those works cited in the footnotes. More comprehensive bibliographies may be found in Michael St. John Packe, *The Life of John Stuart Mill* (London, 1954); *Mill: A Collection of Critical Essays*, ed. J. B. Schneewind (Notre Dame, 1969); and in the issues of *The Mill News Letter* published by the University of Toronto Press. Mill himself compiled a list of his own writings which serves as the basis of the *Bibliography of the Published Writings of John Stuart Mill*, ed. N. MacMinn, J. R. Hainds, and J. M. McCrimmon (Evanston, Ill., 1944). An admirable edition of Mill's *Collected Works* is currently being issued by the University of Toronto Press. *On Liberty* has not yet been issued in this edition and I have used the familiar Everyman one. The reviews of *On Liberty* and other contemporary journal articles are not included in this bibliography, but references to them may be found in the footnotes.

Mill's *Autobiography* presents a special bibliographical problem. The differences among the several editions have been well described by Jack Stillinger, "The Text of John Stuart Mill's *Autobiography*," *Bulletin of the John Rylands Library*, XLIII (1960). In this study I have generally cited the Columbia University Press edition which corresponds most closely to the final version that Mill himself intended for publication. I have, however, used the Early Draft of the autobiography to elucidate the state of Mill's mind at the time of its initial composition and early revision.

Acton, John E. E. *Letters of Lord Acton to Mary Gladstone.* Ed. Herbert Paul. 1st edn., New York, 1905.

Adams, Henry. *Cycle of Adams Letters.* Boston, 1920.

The Amberley Papers. Ed. Bertrand and Patricia Russell. London, 1937.

Arnold, Matthew. *Culture and Anarchy.* Ed. J. Dover Wilson. Cambridge, 1957.

————. *A French Eton.* London, 1892.

————. *Lectures and Essays in Criticism.* Ed. R. H. Super. Ann Arbor, 1962.

————. *Letters of Matthew Arnold.* Ed. G. W. E. Russell. New York, 1900.

————. *Schools and Universities on the Continent.* London, 1868.

Asquith, H. H. *Some Aspects of the Victorian Age.* Oxford, 1918.

Bagehot, Walter. *The Collected Works of Walter Bagehot.* Ed. Norman St. John-Stevas. Cambridge, Mass., 1968.

Bain, Alexander. *John Stuart Mill.* London, 1882.

Balfour, A. J. *Theism and Humanism.* London, 1915.

Bentham, Jeremy. *Collected Works.* Ed. John Bowring. London, 1843.

————. *An Introduction to the Principles of Morals and Legislation.* Dolphin edn., New York, 1961.

————. *Plan of Parliamentary Reform.* London, 1817.

Berlin, Isaiah. *Four Essays on Liberty.* Oxford, 1969.

Brown, Norman O. *Life Against Death.* New York, 1959.

————. *Love's Body.* New York, 1966.

Bryce, James. *Studies in Contemporary Biography.* London, 1903.

Burn, W. L. *The Age of Equipoise: A Study of the Mid-Victorian Generation.* London, 1964.

Carlyle, Thomas. *New Letters of Thomas Carlyle.* Ed. Alexander Carlyle. London, 1904.

Devlin, Patrick. *The Enforcement of Morals.* Oxford, 1968.

Freud, Sigmund. *Letters of Sigmund Freud.* Ed. Ernst Freud. New York, 1960.

Froude, J. A. *Thomas Carlyle: A History of the First Forty Years of His Life.* London, 1882.

————. *Thomas Carlyle: A History of His Life in London, 1834-1881.* London, 1884.

Gaskell, E. C. *The Life of Charlotte Brontë.* New York, 1857.

Gay, Peter. *The Enlightenment: An Interpretation.* Vol. II: *A Science of Freedom.* New York, 1969.

Gibbon, Edward. *Autobiography.* Ed. Lord Sheffield. World's Classics edn., London, 1950.

Gomperz, Theodor. *Briefe und Aufzeichnungen.* Ed. Heinrich Gomperz. Vienna, 1936.

Harrison, Austin. *Frederic Harrison: Thoughts and Memories.* London, 1926.

Harrison, Frederic. *Tennyson, Ruskin, Mill and Other Literary Estimates.* London, 1899.

Hart, H. L. A. *Law, Liberty, and Morality.* New York, 1963.

Hayek, F. A. (ed.). *John Stuart Mill and Harriet Taylor: Their Friendship and Subsequent Marriage.* Chicago, 1951.

Himmelfarb, Gertrude. *Victorian Minds.* New York, 1968.

Holmes-Laski Letters. Ed. M. D. Howe. Cambridge, Mass., 1953.

Holyoake, George. *Sixty Years of an Agitator's Life.* London, 1892.

Houghton, Walter E. *The Victorian Frame of Mind, 1830–1870.* New Haven, 1957.

Humboldt, Wilhelm von. *The Limits of State Action.* Ed. J. W. Burrow. Cambridge, 1969.

Hynes, Samuel. *The Edwardian Turn of Mind.* Princeton, 1968.

Jefferson, Thomas. *Writings of Thomas Jefferson.* Ed. H. A. Washington. New York, 1861.

Kant, Immanuel. *The Philosophy of Kant.* Ed. Carl J. Friedrich. Modern Library edn., New York, 1949.

Kingsley, Charles. *Charles Kingsley: His Letters and Memories of his Life.* Ed. Mrs. Kingsley. London, 1888.

Lifton, Robert J. *History and Human Survival.* New York, 1970.

Locke, John. *A Letter Concerning Toleration.* Ed. Patrick Romanell. New York, 1955.

————. *Two Treatises on Government.* Ed. Peter Laslett. Cambridge, 1967.

Macaulay, T. B. *The Works of Lord Macaulay.* Ed. Lady Trevelyan. London, 1875.

Marcus, Steven. *The Other Victorians: A Study of Sexuality and Pornography in Mid-Nineteenth Century England.* New York, 1964.

Marcuse, Herbert. *Counterrevolution and Revolt.* Boston, 1972.

Marmontel, Jean François. *Memoirs.* Trans. Brigit Patmore. London, 1930.

Mayhew, Henry. *London Labour and the London Poor.* London, 1861.

Mill, James. *An Essay on Government.* Library of Liberal Arts edn., New York, 1955.

————. *Essays on Government, Jurisprudence, Liberty of the Press, and Law of Nations.* New York, 1967.

Mill, John Stuart. *The Autobiography of John Stuart Mill.* Ed. John Jacob Coss. Columbia University edn., New York, 1924.

————. *Dissertations and Discussions.* Vols. I–II, London, 1859; vol. III, London, 1867; vol. IV, London, 1875.

————. *The Earlier Letters of John Stuart Mill,* 1812–1848. Ed. Francis E. Mineka. Vols. XII–XIII of *Collected Works.* Toronto, 1963.

————. *The Early Draft of John Stuart Mill's Autobiography.* Ed. Jack Stillinger. Urbana, Ill., 1961.

————. *Essays on Economics and Society.* Ed. Lord Robbins and J. M. Robson. Vols. IV–V of *Collected Works.* Toronto, 1967.

————. *Essays on Ethics, Religion and Society.* Ed. J. M. Robson. Vol. X of *Collected Works.* Toronto, 1969.

————. *Essays on Politics and Culture.* Ed. Gertrude Himmelfarb. New York, 1962, Anchor edn., 1963.

————. *The Later Letters of John Stuart Mill, 1849–1873.* Ed. Francis E. Mineka and Dwight N. Lindley. Vols. XIV–XVII of *Collected Works.* Toronto, 1972.

————. *The Letters of John Stuart Mill.* Ed. Hugh S. R. Elliot. London, 1910.

————. *On Liberty,* in *Utilitarianism, Liberty, and Representative Government.* Everyman edn., London, 1940.

————. *Principles of Political Economy.* Ed. V. W. Bladen and J. M. Robson. Vols. II–III of *Collected Works.* Toronto, 1965.

————. *Representative Government,* in *Utilitarianism, Liberty, and Representative Government.* Everyman edn., London, 1940.

————. "Speech on Perfectibility," in *John Stuart Mill's Autobiography.* Ed. Harold J. Laski. World's Classics ed., London, 1958.

————. "The Subjection of Women," in *On Liberty, Representative Government, The Subjection of Women.* Ed. Millicent Garrett Fawcett. World's Classics edn., London, 1969.

————. *A System of Logic.* London, 1949.

————. *Three Essays on Religion.* London, 1874.

————. *Utilitarianism,* in *Essays on Ethics, Religion and*

Society. Ed. J. M. Robson. Vol. X of *Collected Works.* Toronto, 1969.

Mill, John Stuart, and Mill, Harriet Taylor. *Essays on Sex Equality.* Ed. Alice S. Rossi. Chicago, 1970.

Milton, John. *Complete Prose Works of John Milton.* Ed. Don M. Wolfe. New Haven, 1959–66.

Montesquieu, Charles de Secondat, Baron de. *The Spirit of the Laws.* Trans. Thomas Nugent. New York, 1949.

Morley, John. *The Life of William Ewart Gladstone.* New York, 1903.

————. *Nineteenth-Century Essays.* Ed. Peter Stansky. Chicago, 1970.

————. *Oracles on Man and Government.* London, 1923.

————. *Recollections.* New York, 1917.

Newman, John Henry. *Apologia Pro Vita Sua.* Ed. A. D. Culler. Riverside edn., Boston, 1956.

Norton, Charles Eliot. *Letters of Charles Eliot Norton.* Ed. Sara Norton. Boston, 1913.

Paine, Thomas. *Common Sense and the Crisis.* New York, 1960.

————. *The Rights of Man.* Penguin edn., London, 1969.

Parliamentary Debates. Hansard, 3rd series.

Rawls, John. *A Theory of Justice.* Cambridge, Mass., 1971.

Rees, J. C. *Mill and His Early Critics.* Leicester, 1956.

Report from His Majesty's Commissioners for Inquiring into the Administration and Practical Operation of the Poor Laws. London, 1834.

Rieff, Philip. *Freud: The Mind of the Moralist.* New York, 1959.

Roazen, Paul. *Freud: Political and Social Thought.* New York, 1968.

Rosenberg, Harold. *The Tradition of the New.* New York, 1959.

Ruitenbeek, Hendrik M. (ed.). *Psychoanalysis and Existential Philosophy.* New York, 1962.

Russell, Bertrand. "Lecture on a Master Mind: John Stuart Mill," *Proceedings of the British Academy*, XLI (1955).

Sidgwick, Henry. *Miscellaneous Essays and Addresses*. London, 1904.

Spencer, Herbert. *An Autobiography*. London, 1904.

———. *Life and Letters of Herbert Spencer*. London, 1908.

———. *Social Statics*. New York, 1965.

Spinoza, Benedict de. *The Political Works*. Trans. A. G. Wernham. Oxford, 1958.

Stephen, James Fitzjames. *Liberty, Equality, Fraternity*. Ed. R. J. White. Cambridge, 1967.

Stephen, Leslie. *The English Utilitarians*. London, 1900.

———. *Life and Letters of Leslie Stephen*. Ed. F. W. Maitland. London, 1906.

———. *Some Early Impressions*. London, 1924.

Sterling, John. *Essays and Tales*. Ed. Julius Hare. London, 1848.

Tillotson, Kathleen. *Novels of the Eighteen-Forties*. Oxford, 1954.

Trevelyan, G. O. *Life and Letters of Lord Macaulay*. London, 1876.

Trilling, Lionel. *Beyond Culture*. New York, 1965.

———. *Sincerity and Authenticity*. Cambridge, Mass., 1972.

Voltaire. *Lettres philosophiques*. Paris, 1964.

Wilson, David A. *Life of Thomas Carlyle*. London, 1924.

The Wolfenden Report: Report of the Committee on Homosexual Offences and Prostitution. New York, 1963.

INDEX

Index

A Note About the Author

Gertrude Himmelfarb has been professor of history at the City University of New York since 1965. She was a Fellow of the American Academy of Arts and Sciences and has received fellowships from the Guggenheim Foundation, the Rockefeller Foundation, the National Endowment for the Humanities, and the American Council of Learned Societies. Her previous books include *Lord Acton: A Study in Conscience and Politics* (1952), *Darwin and the Darwinian Revolution* (1959), and *Victorian Minds* (1968), which was nominated for a National Book Award. Miss Himmelfarb has also edited books on Acton, Malthus, and Mill.

A Note on the Type

This book was set on the Linotype in Janson, a recutting made direct from type cast from matrices long thought to have been made by the Dutchman Anton Janson, who was a practicing type founder in Leipzig during the years 1668–87. However, it has been conclusively demonstrated that these types are actually the work of Nicholas Kis (1650–1702), a Hungarian, who most probably learned his trade from the master Dutch type founder Kirk Voskens. The type is an excellent example of the influential and sturdy Dutch types that prevailed in England up to the time William Caslon developed his own incomparable designs from these Dutch faces.

Composed by Cherry Hill Composition.
Printed and bound by The Book Press,
Brattleboro, Vermont.

Typography and binding design based on a design
by Warren Chappell.